Critical Management Studies

edited by
Mats Alvesson
and
Hugh Willmott

SAGE Publications
London • Newbury Park • New Delhi

Editorial arrangement and Chapter 1 © Mats Alvesson and
Hugh Willmott, 1992
Chapter 2 © Stanley Deetz, 1992
Chapter 3 © John Forester, 1992
Chapter 4 © Gibson Burrell, 1992
Chapter 5 © John Mingers, 1992
Chapter 6 © Michael Power and Richard Laughlin, 1992
Chapter 7 © Glenn Morgan, 1992
Chapter 8 © Kalle Lyytinen, 1992
Chapter 9 © Brian D. Steffy and Andrew J. Grimes, 1992
Chapter 10 © Walter R. Nord and John M. Jermier, 1992

First published 1992. Reprinted 1999

SAGE Publications Ltd
6 Bonhill Street
London EC2A 4PU

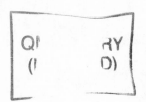

SAGE Publications Inc
2455 Teller Road
Newbury Park, California 91320

SAGE Publications India Pvt Ltd
32, M-Block Market
Greater Kailash – I
New Delhi 110 048

British Library Cataloguing in Publication data

Critical Management Studies
 I. Alvesson, Mats   II. Willmott, Hugh
 650

 ISBN 0–8039–8454–5
 ISBN 0–8039–8455–3 (pbk)

Library of Congress catalog card number 92–050448

Typeset by Type Study, Scarborough
Printed in Great Britain by
Selwood Printing Ltd., Burgess Hill, West Sussex

Contents

Notes on Contributors

Mats Alvesson is Professor of Business Administration at the University of Gothenburg, Sweden. His recent books include *Corporate Culture and Organizational Symbolism* (with P. O. Berg, 1992) and *Cultural Perspectives on Organizations* (in press). His research interests include critical theory, gender, power, management of professional service organizations, organizational culture and symbolism, and the philosophy of science.

Gibson Burrell is Professor of Organizational Behaviour at the University of Warwick. With colleagues, he is currently attempting to develop a postgraduate course which will be a complete inversion of an MBA. Critical Theory will form one of the bases of this ABM programme.

Stanley Deetz is Professor of Communication at Rutgers University, New Brunswick, New Jersey. He is the author of several books, including *Democracy in an Age of Corporate Colonization* (1992) and *Managing Interpersonal Communication* (1986). In addition he has published numerous essays on participatory decision-making, human relations and communication in corporate organizations. He is currently editor of the *Communication Yearbook* series.

John Forester is Professor of City and Regional Planning at Cornell University. His recent publications include *Planning in the Face of Power* (1989) and *Making Equity Planning Work* (with Norman Krumholz, 1990). He is interested in the ethics and politics of planning and public management, including issues of practical judgement, the character of public deliberations, power and professional rhetoric.

Andy Grimes is Professor of Management and Organization at the University of Kentucky, having previously held appointments at the Universities of Wisconsin and Stanford. His research has centred around radical views of organizations, with particular reference to the operation of power and control. A recent research focus has been the structure and technology of alternative organizations. He has published in the major management journals such as *Administrative Science Quarterly*, *Academy of Management Journal*, *Human Relations* and *Academy of Management Review*.

John M. Jermier is Professor of Organizational Behavior in the Department of Organization Science and Management, University of South Florida. Much of his work has focused on the development of a critical science of organizations with a particular interest in research philosophy and methodology. He serves as Senior Consulting Editor of *Leadership Quarterly* and on the editorial review boards of *Administrative Science Quarterly* and *Organization Science*. He is currently writing, with Walter Nord, a book on critical organization science.

Richard Laughlin is Professor of Accounting at Sheffield University Management School. He has published in a wide range of journals, books and conference proceedings, many of which are related to the use of Critical Theory in understanding and changing the design and context of organizational accounting and accountability systems. His current research is into the organizational effects of recently imposed financial and accountability changes on the public sector in the United Kingdom.

Kalle Lyytinen is Professor of Information Systems at the University of Jyväskylä. His research interests include social theory-based research into information systems, system design methods and design methodologies, management of information systems, research strategies and their selection, and information system failures. He has published extensively on information systems design and their failures in several leading journals, and serves on the editorial boards of *Journal of Information Systems*, *European Journal of Information Systems*, and *Accounting, Management and Information Technology*.

John Mingers is Lecturer in Operational Research and Systems at Warwick Business School, University of Warwick. His research interests include autopoiesis and its applications, the use of systems methodologies in problem situations, the development of the Critical Systems approach, and the use of OR and decision support methods in voluntary and community organizations. He has published over 30 papers in these areas.

Glenn Morgan is Lecturer in the Manchester Business School. He is the author of *Organizations in Society* (1990) and his research interests are in the application of critical management theory to the financial services industry.

Walter R. Nord is currently Professor at the University of South Florida. He has published widely in scholarly journals and has edited or authored a number of books, the most recent of which include *Implementing Routine and Radical Innovations* (with S. Tucker), *Meanings of Occupational Work* (with A. Brief) and *Organizational Reality: Reports from the Firing Line* (with P. Frost and V. Mitchell). He is currently co-editor of *Employee Responsibilities and Rights Journal* and has been a recent past book review editor for the *Academy of Management Review*.

Michael Power is Lecturer in Accounting and Finance at the London School of Economics. His current research interests include the relationship between accounting and the law, brand accounting and the problem of intangibles, risk-based approaches to audit, critical approaches to environmentalism in accounting and related management disciplines. He is currently an Associate Scholar of the European Institute for Advanced Studies in Management, Brussels.

Brian Steffy is Professor in Human Resources Management and Organization Theory at Franklin and Marshall College, Lancaster, Pennsylvania. He has published numerous empirical studies on job stress, the causes of medical malpractice, productivity measurement, fairness in employee selection and intraorganizational mobility. His current work focuses on the impact of theory on practice, specifically the ways that existing work-related theories limit our definition and subsequent understanding of the 'self' at work.

Hugh Willmott is Senior Lecturer in the Manchester School of Management. He has been responsible for organizing the series of Labour Process Conferences and is an editor of the *Organization and Employment Studies Series*. He has edited six books which include *Job Redesign*, *Managing the Labour Process* and *Labour Process Theory*. Hugh Willmott has also published numerous articles in a wide range of leading management, accounting, finance and social science journals. He is currently working on a number of projects whose common theme is the critical examination of the changing organization and management of work in modern society.

1

Critical Theory and Management Studies: An Introduction

Mats Alvesson and Hugh Willmott

The disciplines of management are generally understood to be devoted to the (scientific) improvement of managerial practice and the functioning of organizations. It is assumed that questions directly and indirectly connected to efficiency and effectiveness are central; and that knowledge of management is of greatest relevance (only) to managers. In the literature on management, managers are routinely presented as carriers of rationality and initiative (for example in many versions of strategic management and corporate culture), while other actors appear as objects of managerial action. Management is considered to be a socially valuable technical function, normally acting in the general interest of workers, employers, customers and citizens alike. In contrast, this collection contributes to a rapidly expanding body of knowledge that questions the wisdom of taking the neutrality or virtue of management as self-evident or unproblematical. From the standpoint of Critical Theory (CT), which provides the primary inspiration for this volume, management is too potent in its effects upon the lives of employees, consumers and citizens to be guided by a narrow, instrumental form of rationality. (For introductions and overviews to CT, see Connerton, 1980; Held, 1980; Jay, 1973; White, 1988.)

This book contributes to a growing literature that is responsive to management as a social phenomenon meriting serious critical examination (e.g. Bendix, 1956; Child, 1969; Anthony, 1977, 1986; MacIntyre, 1981; Storey, 1983; Knights and Willmott, 1986; Jackall, 1988; Reed, 1989; Engeldorp Gastelaars et al., 1990). However, with the possible exception of the last of these, their respective analyses of management are not directly informed by the tradition of Critical Theory which is central for this volume. Rather, they draw inspiration from Weber, from moral philosophy or from Marx's analysis of the labour process, though the relevance of Critical Theory for the study of management is acknowledged, in passing, by some of them. The relationship between these schools is explored in Alvesson and Willmott (forthcoming).

Interestingly, Horkheimer (who was to become the influential director of the Institute of Social Research, the institutional base for the Frankfurt School of Critical Theory) identified white-collar employees, amongst which may be included many managers and supervisors, as the social group that merited most urgent critical examination (Horkheimer, 1989). He also set out the distinctive emancipatory commitment of Critical Theory, contrasting it with the scholarly, bourgeois orientation of the (positivist) scientist who assumes a seemingly objective, instrumental relationship to the object of study and contrives to reserve the exercise of value judgements for conduct in other spheres (e.g. politics). Rejecting this bourgeois division of science and politics, Horkheimer (1976: 220, 224) contended that

> The scholarly specialist 'as' scientist regards social reality and its products as extrinsic to him and 'as' citizen exercises his interest in them through political articles, membership in political parties or social science organizations, and participation in elections. . . . Critical thinking, on the contrary, is motivated today by the effort really to transcend the tension and to abolish the opposition between the individual's purposefulness, spontaneity, and rationality, and those work-process relationships on which society is built. Critical thought has a concept of man as in conflict with himself until this opposition is removed. [Critical] theory never aims simply at an increase in knowledge as such. Its goal is man's [sic] emancipation from slavery.

The contributors to this volume share Horkheimer's concern. This collection arises from a two-day meeting, convened in Spring 1990, at which drafts were discussed by the contributors and a handful of other participants. Two kinds of contribution were invited. First there are those that focus specifically upon the relevance of Critical Theory for analysing the specialist disciplines of management. Included in this group are the chapters on accounting (Power and Laughlin), information systems (Lyytinen), marketing (Morgan), operational research (Mingers) and personnel/human resource management (Steffy and Grimes). Although not fully comprehensive, these contributions together provide a wide coverage of the management specialisms and yield considerable insight into how Critical Theory has relevance for their analysis and development.

The second group of papers ranges more widely over the terrains of management and organization to explore how its theory and practice may be advanced by the emancipatory impulse of Critical Theory. Forester suggests how Habermas's theory of communication may be applied to undertake empirical studies of organizational work; Burrell highlights the subversive potential of pleasure, and counterposes this to management's use of pleasure as a resource for control;

Deetz also explores the way in which employees become disciplined within organizations and relates this to the suppression of democratic values within corporations; finally, the chapter by Nord and Jermier contemplates the relevance of Critical Theory for the development of more enlightened management practice.

In each of the chapters, Critical Theory provides a point of reference for advancing critical studies of management. True to the tradition of Critical Theory, which has always encouraged creative borrowing from diverse empirical and philosophical disciplines (Horkheimer, 1989), a number of the contributors simultaneously engage with other schools of critical analysis where these resonate most strongly with their concerns. For example, in his discussion of operational research, Mingers suggests that a Foucauldian analysis of power relations may offer important insights into its non-zero sum organization – a view that is also evident in Morgan's examination of marketing and Deetz's discussion of the disciplinary power of corporations. So, although the emancipatory intent of Critical Theory provides a common thread upon which to string this collection, its contributors are more attracted to its emancipatory spirit than to the authoritative letter of any particular Critical Theorist.

Broadening the Agenda of Management Studies

Working within different specialist fields of management, the interest of the contributors in Critical Theory flows from a disillusionment with traditional forms of management theory and practice. For them, management is simply too important an activity and field of inquiry to be left to the mainstream thinking of management departments and business schools. Established management discourse and practice tends to incorporate and 'swallow up' larger and larger domains of social and personal life, such as culture, conflict and even pleasure, as Burrell (Chapter 4 in this volume) suggests. As the presumed centre of an increasingly large number of distinct activities and processes, management expands and its claims are correspondingly magnified. As this occurs, it becomes increasingly vital to subject it to critical examination.

When saying this, we are not denying that mainstream texts and practices are often 'well intentioned' in their concern to eliminate inept and self-serving practices. We do, however, regard much of their contents as tunnel-visioned and dangerous – practically as well as intellectually, ecologically as well as culturally. As a counterweight to technical (or technocratic) images and ideals of management – in

which a narrow focus on the improvement of means/ends relationships is predominant – there is a strong case for advancing sociological, historical, philosophical and critical studies of management.
Coming to regard mainstream theory and practice as limited and
oppressive, contributors to this collection have been attracted by the
capacity of Critical Theory both to account for the ideological use of
science as an objective authority, and to renew its emancipatory
potential (Habermas, 1971, 1974). Echoing and amplifying Horkheimer's early formulation of Critical Theory, the concern to
recognize and renew the emancipatory impulse of science has been
most lucidly and forcefully expressed by Habermas (1971, 1974):

> Science as a productive force can work in a salutary way when it is suffused
> by science as an emancipatory force, to the same extent as it becomes
> disastrous as soon as it seeks to subject the domain of praxis, which is
> outside the sphere of technical disposition, to its *exclusive* control. The
> demythification which does not break the mythic spell but merely seeks to
> evade it will only bring forth new witch doctors. (Habermas, 1974: 281)

The contributions to this volume share Habermas's commitment to
break the mythic spell of conventional management theory and
practice to which people in organizations, managers included, are
routinely subjected. Instead of assuming the neutrality of management theory and the impartiality of management practice, each
contribution challenges the myth of objectivity and argues for a very
different, critical conception of management in which research is
self-consciously motivated by an effort to discredit, and ideally
eliminate, forms of management and organization that have institutionalized the opposition between the purposefulness of individuals and the seeming givenness and narrow instrumentality of
work-process relationships.

The task of critically examining management perspectives becomes more urgent in the context of the rapid expansion of academic
departments, faculty positions and students, academic and popular
writings within the field. This is not least because of the increasing
social, political and ecological significance of decisions made by
managers within modern corporations, as Deetz (1992: 2) has
argued:

> The modern corporation has emerged as the central form of working
> relations and as the dominant institution in society. In achieving
> dominance, the commercial corporation has eclipsed the state, family,
> residential community, and moral community. This shadowing has
> hidden or suppressed important historical conflicts among competing
> institutional demands. Corporate practices pervade modern life by
> providing personal identity, structuring time and experience, influencing

education and knowledge production, and directing entertainment and news production.

To the extent that management has a 'productive' role to play in organizational work – and it would be unwise (and certainly inconsistent with Critical Theory) to assume or exaggerate its vital importance (Carter and Jackson, 1987; Pfeffer and Salancik, 1978) – it is not restricted to facilitating the innovation, production and distribution of valuable social goods. Companies and management also 'produce' people – workers, customers, as well as citizens in other capacities. That is to say, they shape and promote needs, wishes, beliefs and identities. Advertisements and other forms of consumer marketing create, maintain and reinforce gender stereotypes, problematize identities and make self-esteem precarious. That they foster a materialistic and egoistic lifestyle is a well-known and comparatively obvious aspect of corporate activity (Lasch, 1978; Pollay, 1986). But companies – and thus their leading actors – also bear some responsibility for unemployment, for pollution and ecological disasters, for psychic and social problems associated with the (often low) quality of work and for the exploitation of workers. Companies and top managers selectively promote or even block innovations (Egri and Frost, 1989). Moreover, as Deetz (1992, Chapter 2 in this volume) stresses, they also act as a powerful force that undermines democratic accountability in modern Western society. The technocracy of management overrules the democracy of citizens.

To restrict management studies to the presumed neutral development of knowledge for the realization of corporate goals is narrow-minded and politically partial. But, at the same time, the effects of corporate activity cannot plausibly be equated with the decisions and actions of management. The grandiose role ascribed to their heroes by many management writers must be rejected. On the other hand, the role and nature of managers cannot be reduced to following market and other external imperatives. While social systems cannot be understood as operating free of agents, the dominant social group in corporations presents an important (and neglected) focus for critical investigation (Willmott, 1984, 1987). We develop this point below.

Prising Management Open

Closely associated with the notion of critical studies of management is the ideal of representing other interests and perspectives than those immediately associated with a managerial position (the manager managing people and activities). There are a number of groups that have a legitimate interest in being represented in the illumination and development of management functions, processes and discourses. Management is not the sole preserve of (predominantly male) managers: subordinates, customers and citizens in general have a legitimate interest in management. For example, the significance of gender relations has been seriously neglected in management and organization studies. Only very recently have feminist voices been heard, but even then they are often restricted to issues of access to existing professional/managerial career tracks (Marshall, 1984). Rarely do they address broader issues or engage in deeper critiques of management theory and practice (for exceptions, see e.g. Alvesson and Billing, 1992; Ferguson, 1984; Hearn and Parkin, 1987). A careful scrutiny of managerial discourse and practice in terms of voices that not only speak loudly, but also quietly or cannot – yet – be heard is an important task for critical management studies.

The existence of a diversity of groups and interests in the practice and discourse of management can be illuminated by contrasting management as a technical function with management as a socio-political phenomenon. When considering management as a technical function, we can point to a number of activities that at the present time, and for the foreseeable future, will be undertaken. These include the physical and intellectual labour of production and distribution, including the planning and co-ordinating of activities. Precisely what is produced and how it is manufactured or delivered will doubtless change. But engagement in productive activity necessarily involves the performance of a variety of tasks and processes that can be examined as technical functions. However, their particular organization – which includes the issue of who is to occupy positions of authority within the division of labour and who is to derive greatest advantage (symbolic as well as material) from this *social* division – is inescapably a matter of politics that cannot be determined neutrally by an impartial appeal to the requirements of an impersonal, technical logic. Or, rather, when such appeals are made, they are heard by CT as involving more or less conscious efforts to defend or advance sectional interests in the name of a universal interest.[1]

From this perspective, there are recurrent struggles over the question of whose purposes, or interests, work (production) is to serve – the owner, the manager, the producer, the consumer? Equally, there are struggles over how work is to be organized – autocratically, bureaucratically, democratically? These struggles may not take the form of widespread collective actions that challenge the status quo. But they exist nonetheless in the efforts of owners to exert tighter control upon corporate management; in the efforts of employees, including managers (except possibly at the very highest level), to circumvent hierarchical control; and in the efforts of (e.g.

green) consumers (citizens) to influence the specification and manufacture of products.

Studies of management that take little or no account of such struggles are intellectually shallow and politically naive. To correct these deficiencies, it must be recognized that the technical function of management could be organized and controlled in ways that do not systematically privilege the ends of those who currently own and manage modern organizations. In principle, the ideal of democracy could be extended from the political (parliamentary) to the economic sphere by facilitating much greater participation in decision-making and making those who undertake the management functions more widely accountable for their actions.

As we noted earlier, those who currently occupy management positions are not mere functionaries. They cannot be adequately studied as ciphers who simply serve the predetermined needs of some higher entity (e.g. capital or the state) or who just act selfishly in accordance with their own personal interests. Caught between contradictory demands and pressures, they experience ethical problems, they run the risk of dismissal, they are 'victims' as well as perpetrators of discourses and practices that unnecessarily constrain their ways of thinking and acting. Managerial ideologies – notably a belief in their prerogative to manage – tie them to ideals and identities that, paradoxically, limit their options as they simultaneously appear to secure for them a position of relative power and influence. As Nord and Jermier (Chapter 10 in this volume) suggest, critical social science is of direct relevance to managers in interpreting such experience, and it is therefore not entirely surprising that many managers are receptive, as individuals, to its concerns.

At the same time, it is important to recognize that subordinates are frequently more critical of what they regard as the technical incompetence of their supervisors than of the *social* division of labour out of which hierarchies and elites are produced. Managers are not alone in believing in managerial ideologies or advocating the expansion and refinement of technocracy. An important role for critical social science is to relate what is perceived to be a manifestation of individual, technical incompetence to a system that institutionalizes the non-accountability of managers to their subordinates. The central problem of management resides in the social relations of production which *systematically* foster and sustain very limited and often distorted forms of communication between those occupying positions within the horizontal and vertical divisions of labour. For example, exercises designed and controlled by managers to improve levels of 'involvement' and 'participation' amongst employees will invariably be limited in their effectiveness so long as employees are excluded from the design and operation of these programmes – an exclusion that stems as much from the desire of managers and owners to retain control as from the suspicion or indifference of employees towards such programmes. Employees undoubtedly have an interest in 'better' management, but this cannot be sensibly equated with the (reformist) preservation of the existing structure of social relations in which managers are virtually unaccountable to those whom they manage.

A non-technocratic agenda for management studies requires that its functions and processes be examined in a critical light – that is, a light which considers not only means–ends relationships, but also ends and institutionalized conditions of management discourse and practice. Issues of power and ideology are to be taken seriously – a move that pays attention to various interest groups and perspectives that are under-represented or silenced in mainstream writings and in corporate talk and decision-making. For these groups, there exist issues and ideals other than the effective utilization of resources in order to attain certain (economic) ends – for example, workplace democracy, quality of work, gender equality (absence of gender domination), environmental protection, informed and independent consumption, and so on. In sum, critical management studies have an agenda for research, teaching and (indirectly) organizational practice that understands management as a political, cultural and ideological phenomenon, and that gives a voice to managers not only as managers but as persons, and also to other social groups (subordinates, customers, clients, men and women, citizens in other capacities) whose lives are more or less directly affected by the activities and ideologies of management.

Critical Theory as a Counterpoint to Mainstream Management Studies

There are, of course, a number of theoretical perspectives that can be applied to accomplish a broadening of the agenda for management studies. Pluralistic theory and interpretive analysis have each expanded our understanding by taking interest differences, and the subjectivities of management and organization, into account. However, as Mingers (Chapter 5 in this volume) notes, these orientations do not investigate deep-seated aspects of interest divergence or the structural aspects of power relations. They focus on what is articulated by actors, not what is prevented from being articulated or how particular possibilities for interest articulation are produced – for example through the production of identities and experiences that select and structure the issue and interests that can be raised (Deetz,

1992). Perspectives concerned with such issues include neo-Marxism, feminism, poststructuralism (e.g. Foucault, 1980, 1982) and radical Weberianism (focusing on the modern organization as an iron cage). In the present volume, however, the primary focus is upon Critical Theory, in the sense of the Frankfurt School and its followers (primarily Habermas) as well as authors clearly sympathetic to this stream (such as Bernstein, 1976; Fay, 1987; Lukes, 1978).

Critical Theory, it is suggested, provides *a* (not the!) *critical-constructive* intellectual counterpoint to mainstream management studies. For CT has the strength of being sufficiently broad to serve as a source of critical reflection on a large number of central issues in management studies: epistemological issues, notions of rationality and progress, technocracy and social engineering, autonomy and control, communicative action, power and ideology. In comparison, Marxist, Foucauldian and feminist perspectives are more specialized and restricted. In the case of Foucault's work, a comparatively limited field of vision and the absence of a clear 'positive' message – in the sense of suggestions for radically progressive management and organizational practice – limit its appeal as an inspiration for developing critical management studies. And in comparison to orthodox Marxism, CT has been more alert to the development of advanced capitalistic society, including the growth of administration and technocracy. Arguably, most if not all social phenomena involve a gender aspect, but it would be reductionistic to capture most aspects of management, production and consumption basically in feminist terms, although we recognize that critical feminism provides an invaluable complement to, as well as critique of, Critical Theory (Fraser, 1987).

We here refrain from any further commentary upon the relationship, critiques and debates between CT and other forms of critical analysis (see Alvesson and Willmott, forthcoming, for an overview). We would argue, however, that in the present context of developing management studies there is less point in stressing theoretical rigour and orthodoxy than in welcoming a broad inspiration from a variety of theories and ideas that share 'enough' affinities to advance or enrich critical studies of management (see Mingers, Chapter 5, and Nord and Jermier, Chapter 10, in this volume). What, then is this broad inspiration?

By proceeding from an assumption of the *possibilities* of a more autonomous individual, who, in the tradition of Enlightenment, in principle can master his or her own destiny in joint operation with peers, CT acts as an intellectual counterforce to the ego administration of modern, advanced industrial society. As employees in large bureaucracies and consumers of mass goods, people are affected by corporations, schools, government and mass media to develop personalities, beliefs, tastes and preferences to fit into the demands of mass production and mass consumption and express standardized forms of individuality. CT challenges the domination of this instrumental rationality, which tends to reduce human beings to parts of a well-oiled societal machine (Steffy and Grimes, Chapter 9 in this volume).

CT also directs attention to how science and technology have broadened their influence in society and reduced the scope for debates about political and ethical issues. Politics tends to be reduced to administration, and social engineering appears as the solution to all societal problems (Habermas, 1971). Knowledge based on science and placed in the hands of an army of engineers, administrators, managers, psychologists and computer specialists is viewed as the best or even the only possible way of effective problem-solving. Images and ideals of 'professional management' which emphasize the skilled employment of neutral and objective techniques – from accounting and personnel appraisal to conflict management – are examples of this technocratic understanding of knowledge and social affairs. Against this, CT insists on the political nature of what is seemingly neutral or technological and highlights the dangers of technocracy for human autonomy and responsibility.

Two approaches to attaining the CT ideal of emancipation can be identified. The first is based on the idea of the consciousness of the autonomous critic, who, by (partially) escaping the ideologies and false consciousness of a particular society, illuminates these features and calls for a more enlightened form of practice. In this process, the task of CT is not only to point at deficiencies in a particular society, including its dominant thought patterns, but to identify as yet unrealized potentials that are locked, as it were, within existing institutions and stocks of knowledge. CT has thus critiqued authoritarian family patterns, authoritarian states (Nazism, communism), science, technology, mass media, the capitalistic economy, consumption, the Enlightenment, various social theories and philosophies of science (Fromm, 1941, 1976; Habermas, 1971; Horkheimer and Adorno, 1947; Marcuse, 1964).

The second approach to emancipation, proposed by Habermas and dominating the agenda of CT during the last decade, is founded in a philosophy of language. Here, a procedure-based idea of critique is suggested. In free dialogue, citizens can investigate ideas, beliefs and statements utilizing opportunities that are understood to be inherent in language (in a society of free speech). It is suggested that in speech acts, validity claims of all statements can be investigated by raising and then rejecting or validating various claims according to

(a) their comprehensibility, (b) their accuracy, (c) their honesty and (d) their normative appropriateness (that is, correspondence with accepted cultural values) (see Forester and Lyytinen, Chapters 3 and 8 in this volume.) According to this formulation, CT"s task is to assess the practical structure of hegemonic discourse and so then to counteract systematic communicative distortions of jargon, misrepresentation, deceit, and illegitimacy (distortions of comprehensibility, accuracy, honesty, and normative appropriateness, respectively) (Forester, 1989; Habermas, 1979, 1984).

Overall, CT offers a point of departure that is radically different from that of conventional management theory. It argues that forms of rationality – whether expressed, for example, in formal decision-making models or in corporate culture management – proposed by mainstream management studies inhibit deeper reflection on means–ends relationships, the current social order and predominant goals. CT, in contrast, seeks to encourage a questioning of taken-for-granted assumptions about contemporary social reality and the models for the satisfaction of human needs and wants that are so widely assumed in advanced capitalist society. For example the sense of identity, self-esteem and 'human nature' is intimately tied to the purchase, possession and consumption of goods. At the same time it is very doubtful whether this leads to more than a transitory experience of satisfaction or security (Fromm, 1976; Lasch, 1978; Wachtel, 1983), an observation that has far-reaching consequences for the evaluation of the overall rationality of the purpose of contemporary forms of management theory and practice in affluent society.

A Research Agenda for Critical Studies in and of Management

Based on CT as a primary source of inspiration, yet open to other orientations that complement and/or stand in a position of 'fruitful tension' to CT, a number of foci for a critical understanding of management (application of CT) can be identified: resisting technicistic and objectivistic views; drawing attention to asymmetrical power relations and discursive closures associated with taken-for-granted assumptions and ideologies; exploring the partiality of shared and conflictual interests; and paying careful attention to the centrality of language and communication. We briefly examine these below.

Developing a Non-objective View of Management
Techniques and Organizational Processes

In opposition to traditional social science and management studies, CT proceeds from a 'non-objectivist' understanding of ontology and epistemology (Burrell and Morgan, 1979). Social reality then appears as much more arbitrary and precarious than is indicated by common sense, management theory and management techniques. The presumptions that knowledge products and techniques can mirror reality, and thus turn it into an object for efficient action, are questioned. Instead of suggesting that knowledge more or less exactly mirrors corporate economic reality, accounting, for example, is understood to be inescapably implicated in creating that reality (see Power and Laughlin, Chapter 6 in this volume). Instead of reflecting people's diverse needs and wants, marketing produces (people as) consumers as it divides them into market segments, thus producing social stereotypical categories (such as gender and youth) (see Morgan, Chapter 7 in this volume). Needless to say, management's role in the social construction of social and economic reality is not omnipotent, and to some extent it must adapt its techniques and actions to a produced sociohistorical reality that also exists before a particular management starts its operations. But any claim, however qualified, that management is essentially a matter of grasping and manipulating elements of objective reality (such as structures or cultures) through efficiency-enhancing techniques appears as a grave mystification that is practically as well as intellectually deficient.

Exposing Asymmetrical Power Relations
According to CT, the practices and discourses that comprise organizations are never politically neutral. Sedimented with asymmetrical relations of power, they reproduce structures in which there is differential access to valued material and symbolic goods. Top management is routinely privileged in decision-making and agenda-setting and in defining and shaping human needs and social reality. An objective of CT is to challenge the centrality and necessity of the dominant role of elites in defining reality and impeding emancipatory change.

By questioning the rationality of elite structures, CT seeks to reduce the disadvantages of groups other than those of the managerial elite in determining the practices and discourses that comprise organizational realities. As is clear from the writings of Foucault and other poststructuralists, power neutralization is, at best, a very tricky project, and at worst, a matter of self-deception. This is because CT, in common with all kinds of knowledge, exerts a disciplining effect upon subjectivity. In the development of methodologies for change, the issue of power must be taken seriously and handled in a 'constructive' way, something which scholars proceeding from a CT perspective on management so far have done only to a limited extent (see for example, Mingers and Lyytinen, Chapters 5 and 8 in this volume).

Counteracting Discursive Closure
Related to the problems of objectivism and power is the commitment to critically explore taken-for-granted assumptions and ideologies that freeze the contemporary social order. What seems to be natural then becomes the target of 'de-naturalization': that is, the questioning and opening up of what has become seen as given, unproblematic and natural. This can also be formulated as a counteracting of discursive closure. Whereas earlier versions of CT tended to operate with the notion of false consciousness, the implicit idea of a 'true' consciousness is rejected, and typically ideology as a concept 'is best seen as drawing attention to arbitrary representational practices rather than a false or class consciousness', as Deetz (Chapter 2 in this volume) notes. Expert cultures, such as those of management specialisms, are 'socially structured silences' that 'exhaust the space of possible discourse' (Power and Laughlin, Chapter 6 in this volume). CT's role is thus one of encouraging 'noise' to break these silences – to trigger critical comments and inspire dialogue.

Revealing the Partiality of Shared Interests
Another vital focus for critical management studies concerns the dynamic partiality of consensus and shared interests. This understanding is positioned between traditional consensus (including weaker forms of pluralism theory) and more pronounced conflict assumptions (such as in Marxism and other types of radical theory). In opposition to traditional Marxist understandings, CT does not assume the primacy of a fundamental contradiction between capital and worker interests, nor is (higher-level) management lumped together with capital. Nonetheless CT does draw attention to contradictions in society and organizations, and to latent social conflicts. These are related by recognizing the political nature of techniques and seemingly objective descriptions. For example, the colonization of the lifeworld (cultural meaning patterns) by the system's formalized media (Power and Laughlin, Chapter 6 in this volume) or the formulation of complex, ever-changing interrelated messes as isolated and tractable problems to be dealt with by techniques for optimization (Mingers, Chapter 5 in this volume) are critically examined; and in this way conflict is reviewed as a potentially constructive, liberating force.

Especially in Habermas's (1984) idea of communicative rationality it is suggested that conflictual matters can quite often be brought into the open and resolved through dialogue in which participants explore each other's validity claims and let the force of the better argument decide. As many commentators have pointed out, this model for handling social conflicts has clear limitations (e.g. Bubner, 1982; Thompson, 1982) and it must be appreciated that arriving at arguments and opinions that all concerned recognize as the best possible ones (i.e. most truthful, most normatively appropriate) is a rarely fulfilled ideal. Nevertheless, the prospect in principle of this outcome, encouraged by the possibilities in language and the opening of an arena for free debates created by societal modernization (e.g. the discrediting of religious dogmas and authoritarian states), makes appropriate a focus on the partiality of shared interest as well as conflicts. CT's change model – which certainly requires development (Laughlin, 1991) – incorporates encouragement of conflictual awareness as well as dialogue-based reductions of these conflicts.

Appreciating the Centrality of Language and Communicative Action

An interest in communication is to some extent inherent in all the areas mentioned above, but such an interest can also be a central focus of investigation.

> Critical theory, as we draw on it here, assesses social and political-economic structures as systematic patterns of practical communicative interaction. . . . The critical, ethical content of the theory focuses attention on the systematic and unnecessarily distorted nature of communicative interactions, on the promises, appeals, reports, and justifications that so shape the lives of citizens of our societies. (Forester, 1989: 139)

It is argued that communication is central to all structures and actions – however instrumental or self-evident they may appear. Establishment of facts, appeals to norms of legitimacy, inner dispositions expressed by a speaker and the framing of attention are involved in all statements (Forester, Chapter 3 in this volume). The task of CT is to examine their organization to discern forces that distort the process of communication.

An interest not only in communicative action – which involves speakers as well as listeners, as Forester emphasizes – but also in language as a holder of 'historically developed dimensions of interests', which operates behind the backs of the participants, connected to its quality as a system of distinction, resonates with the emancipatory concerns of CT. This latter perspective understands language not as representational – able to refer to external objects through containing a fixed meaning or at least making clarified meanings possible – but as inherently ambiguous and constitutive. Language viewed in this way means, as Deetz (Chapter 2 in this volume) stresses, that it is not how people use language to accomplish goals as much as how language constitutes the identity of groups and their relations that is of greatest significance.

These two views on communication and language represent somewhat different approaches to critical analysis with different practical implications. From one standpoint, language represents possibilities for clarifying meanings and reducing ambiguity and contradictions in language use. From the second standpoint, informed by poststructuralism, critical theory strives to open up representations in a way that may have emancipatory consequences, although not of the (potentially) relatively clear character indicated by the first, Habermasian position to which most of the contributors to this volume are more strongly drawn.

Irrespective of one's position on the nature and possibilities of language the two standpoints agree on the importance of challenging dominant ways of representing social reality. Management and management techniques, as Power and Laughlin (chapter 6 in this volume) suggest, can be conceptualized as forces pushing to the 'delinguistification' of a domain, presented as beyond disputes of meaning and ambiguity.

Contributions of CT

Having sketched some core elements of a broad research agenda for CT-inspired management theory, we now indicate some of its more specific contributions.

Critique of Technicist and Other Self-constraining Understandings

Large parts of management studies, partly in North America, are guided by neo-positivistic and technicist understandings of social science and the development of knowledge. As Steffy and Grimes (Chapter 9 in this volume) argue, this leads to narrow and fragmented forms of explanation which, in their words, 'may become a normative force that displaces the purposeful discourse among subjective selves'. CT offers a broader reflective space in which diverse kinds of knowledge and method are confronted as the larger context of science and technology is taken into account. The relevance of Habermas's (1971, 1972) ideas on knowledge-constitutive interests and the role of science and technology as ideology is most fully illustrated by the contributions of Mingers and Steffy and Grimes.

Critique of Power and Ideology

When striving to take issues of power and ideology into account, management studies normally focus on the observable, explicit and superficial aspects of power and ideology – for example departures from formal lines of authority. In contrast, CT directs attention to the deeper and more pervasive aspects of control. CT contends that dimensions of power and ideology are of greatest significance in domains where they are not easily recognized as such. In particular, it suggests that language and communicative action produce and reproduce the world-taken-for-granted, thereby giving priority to certain (unrecognized) interests and presenting social reality as natural and given (see especially Deetz, Chapter 2 in this volume).

Counterpictures: Utopian Ideals
Another contribution of CT is to encourage unashamedly utopian thinking in management, through offering concepts and ideas that challenge current management practice. By providing counterpoints to established practice, fixed thinking is relativized and loosened up. A denaturalization and unfreezing of the way phenomena are understood is a crucial element in emancipation. A latent utopian element is a part of all critical thinking, but providing explicit counterpictures directly stimulates interest and can arouse a process of critical self-reflection. One example, treated by Burrell in this volume, is the domain of the erotic in organizational life.

Critically Informed Managerial and Administrative Practice
In its most philosophical form CT is notoriously theoretical. However, Forester (1985, 1989), in particular, has persuasively argued that Habermas's work, in particular, can inspire and guide alternative forms of administrative practice:

> critical theory gives us a new way of understanding action, or what a planner does, as attention-shaping (communicative action), rather than more narrowly as a means to a particular end (instrumental action). . . . we can understand structures of action, e.g. the organizational and political contexts of planning practice, as structures of selective attention, and so systematically distorted communication. (Forester, 1985: 203)

The ideals of CT in counteracting communicative distortions may then directly be taken into account in public administration. Profit motives and the more contradictory relations between participants in private corporations may compound the difficulties that constrain its application. Even so, Forester's case for a Critical Theory version of planning – 'pragmatics with vision' (1985: 221) – indicates that CT has much relevance for everyday organizational action. Another example is how an expert in issues of personnel management can depart from a technocratic position to the one in which some responsibility is taken for facilitating an 'ideal speech' situation as an alternative basis for rationally justifying knowledge in relationship to its consistency with statistical indicators on law-like causal patterns (Steffy and Grimes, Chapter 9 in this volume). Another example is work on critical methodologies for change (for example by Ulrich), in which the authority of experts is challenged by encouraging the testing of judgements and statements (reviewed and discussed by Mingers, Chapter 5 in this volume).

A Managerial Turn in Critical Theory?

Habermas's recent efforts to ground CT in the presuppositions of language rather than the structure of consciousness have been described as a 'linguistic turn'. Can the contributors to this volume be characterized as proponents of a 'managerial turn'?

At the most fundamental, metatheoretical level, the answer must be in the negative. The concern of critical students of management is not to change the basis or direction of critical theorizing but, rather, to apply it to the mundane but important world of management. In this respect, they may be seen to exemplify the intent of Critical Theory: to combine the respective strengths of philosophical and empirical modes of investigation. The empirical focus is upon the theory and practice of management in the organization and development of modern (e.g. advanced capitalist) societies. The philosophical focus ensures that the taken-for-granted world of management is examined critically, with the intent that the opposition between science and politics – individuals as neutral observers/managers and as engaged citizens – is debunked and overcome.

So, rather than a 'turn', the concern of this volume is to recall the commitment of Critical Theory in a way that issues both an appeal and a challenge to Critical Theorists (who have largely disregarded the empirical realm of management) and to management academics and practitioners (who have taken little notice of the tradition of CT). From the former is sought an application of their deep appreciation of the philosophical foundation of CT to inform and enrich the theory and practice of the mundane, empirical world of management. From the latter is sought a reformulation of management theory and practice that is informed by an engagement with the arguments of Critical Theory.

In making this appeal, it is to be stressed that, whether CT analysis is developed by those with an empirical or a philosophical background, its plausibility will depend upon its salience within the context of management studies (Alvesson and Willmott, 1992). There is a tendency in CT, and also in its applications within management studies, to concentrate upon management and corporations as a matter of power and ideology as if this realm of social relations is reproduced independently of the instrumental activities that transform nature and deliver goods and services. While this instrumental side cannot be reduced to something purely economic or technical, it is inadequately understood if reduced to ideological and cultural phenomena. The latter emphasis is crucial, but it omits consideration of vital aspects of management practice. Management is not only about the disciplining of labour (including managerial labour) but also about the production and distribution of socially useful goods and services – such as word processors, which few academics would be willing to exchange for the typewriter, let alone the quill.

'Sociologism' must be resisted in critical management studies. If CT is to engage in a successful, although 'modest', managerial turn, idealized and abstract models of the good society or ideal communicative action must be confronted and complemented with understandings that are fully attentive to the material and technical organization of modern society. Those who are versed in the problem-solving specialisms of management, such as Information Systems, Operational Research and even Human Resource Management, can give CT a much-needed kick in the direction of studying everyday corporate life. Conversely, the relevance of CT, such as Habermas's complex theory of communication, could no doubt be better appreciated if those most familiar with its complex features were to apply it to the study of management. The present volume is intended as a stimulus to such work.

Note

1 Typically, managers are obliged to justify their existence by demonstrating their value to the organization as a whole. Yet the demonstration of their value in the language of universal benefit barely conceals their sectional interests – as functional specialists or as an elite within organizations – in developing or sustaining arrangements that, they anticipate, will secure their (institutionalized) position of comparative privilege. A key skill in the management game is to pursue sectional interests – of management as a whole or (functional and product) divisions within management – whilst appearing to be fully committed to the organization as a whole – for example, by mediating between, or synergizing, the claims or contributions of diverse social groups (Pfeffer, 1981).

References

Alvesson, M. and Billing, Y. D. (1992) 'Gender and organization: toward a differentiated understanding', *Organization Studies*, 13(1): 73–103.

Alvesson, M. and Willmott, H. (1992) 'On the idea of emancipation in management and organization studies', *Academy of Management Review*, 17(3).

Alvesson, M. and Willmott, H. (forthcoming) *Making Sense of Management. A Critical Analysis*. London: Sage.

Anthony, P. (1977) *The Ideology of Work*. London: Tavistock.

Anthony, P. (1986) *The Foundations of Management*. London: Tavistock.

Bendix, R. (1956) *Work and Authority in Industry*. New York: Wiley.

Bernstein, R. J. (1976) *The Restructuring of Social and Political Theory*. Oxford: Blackwell.

Bubner, R. (1982) 'Habermas' concept of critical theory', in J. B. Thompson and D. Held (eds), *Habermas. Critical Debates*. London: Macmillan.

Burrell, G. and Morgan, G. (1979) *Sociological Paradigms and Organizational Analysis*. London: Heinemann.

Carter, P. and Jackson, N. (1987) 'Management, myth and metatheory – from scarcity to postscarcity', *International Studies of Management and Organization*, 17(3): 64–89.

Child, J. (1969) *British Management Thought*. London: Allen & Unwin.

Connerton, P. (1980) *The Tragedy of Enlightenment*. Cambridge: Cambridge University Press.

Deetz, S. (1992) *Democracy in an Age of Corporate Colonization: Developments in Communication and the Politics of Everyday Life*. Albany: State University of New York Press.

Egri, C. and Frost, P. J. (1989) 'Threats to innovation; roadblocks to implementation: the politics of the productive process', in M. Jackson, M. P. Keys and S. Cropper (eds), *Operational Research and the Social Sciences*. New York: Plenum.

Engeldorp Gastelaars, Ph. v, Magela, S. and Preuss, O. (1990) (eds) *Critical Theory and the Science of Management*. Rotterdam: University Press.

Fay, B. (1987) *Critical Social Science*. Cambridge: Polity Press.

Ferguson, K. (1984) *The Feminist Case against Bureaucracy*. Philadelphia: Temple University Press.

Forester, J. (1985) 'Critical theory and planning practice', in J. Forester (ed.), *Critical Theory and Public Life*. Cambridge MA: MIT Press.

Forester, J. (1989) *Planning in the Face of Power*. Berkeley, CA: University of California Press.

Foucault, M. (1980) *Power/Knowledge*. New York: Pantheon.

Foucault, M. (1982) 'The subject and power', *Critical Inquiry*, 8: 777–95.

Fraser, N. (1987) 'What's critical about critical theory? The case of Habermas and gender', in S. Benhabib and D. Cornell (eds), *Feminism as Critique*. Cambridge: Polity Press.

Fromm, E. (1941) *Escape from Freedom*. New York: Holt, Rinehart & Winston.

Fromm, E. (1976) *To Have or to Be?* New York: Harper & Brothers.

Habermas, J. (1971) *Toward a Rational Society*. London: Heinemann.

Habermas, J. (1972) *Knowledge and Human Interests*. London: Heinemann.

Habermas, J. (1974) *Theory and Practice*. London: Heinemann.

Habermas, J. (1979) *Communication and the Evolution of Society*. Boston: Beacon Press.

Habermas, J. (1984) *The Theory of Communicative Action, Vol. I: Reason and the Rationalization of Society*. Cambridge: Polity Press.

Hearn, J. and Parkin, W. (1987) *'Sex' at 'Work'. The Power and Paradox of Organisation Sexuality*. Brighton: Wheatsheaf Books.

20   *Critical Management Studies*

Held, D. (1980) *Introduction to Critical Theory*. London: Hutchinson.
Horkheimer, M. (1976) 'Traditional and critical theory' (1937) in P. Connerton (ed.), *Critical Sociology*. Harmondsworth: Penguin.
Horkheimer, M. (1989) 'The state of contemporary social philosophy and the tasks of the Institute for Social Research', in S. E. Bronner and D. M. Kellner (eds), *Critical Theory and Society*. London: Routledge.
Horkheimer, M. and Adorno, T. (1947) *The Dialectics of Enlightenment*. London: Verso.
Jackall, R. (1988) *Moral Mazes: The World of Corporate Managers*. Oxford: Oxford University Press.
Jay, M. (1973) *The Dialectical Imagination*. Boston: Little Brown.
Knights, D. and Willmott, H. C. (eds) (1986) *Managing the Labour Process*. Aldershot: Gower.
Lasch, C. (1978) *The Culture of Narcissism*. New York: Norton.
Laughlin, R. (1991) 'Environmental disturbances and organizational transitions and transformations: some alternative models', *Organization Studies*, 12: 209–32.
Lukes, S. (1978) 'Power and authority', in T. Bottomore and R. Nisbet (eds) *A History of Sociological Analysis*. London: Heinemann.
MacIntyre, A. (1981) *After Virtue*, London: Duckworth.
Marcuse, H. (1964) *One-dimensional Man*. Boston: Beacon Press.
Marshall, J. (1984) *Women Managers. Travellers in a Male World*. Chichester: Wiley.
Pfeffer, J. (1981) 'Management as symbolic action: the creation and maintenance of organizational paradigms', in L. L. Cummings and B. M. Staw (eds), *Research in Organizational Behavior*, Vol. 3. Greenwich, CT: JAI Press.
Pfeffer, J. and Salancik, G. R. (1978) *The External Control of Organizations. A Resource Dependence Perspective*. New York: Harper & Row.
Pollay, R. W. (1986) 'The distorted mirror: reflections on the unintended consequences of advertising', *Journal of Marketing*, 50 (April): 18–36.
Reed, M. (1989) *The Sociology of Management*. Hemel Hempstead: Harvester Wheatsheaf.
Storey, J. (1983) *Managerial Prerogative and the Question of Control*. London: Routledge & Kegan Paul.
Thompson, J. B. (1982) 'Universal pragmatics', in J. B. Thompson and D. Held (eds), *Habermas. Critical Debates*. London: Macmillan.
Wachtel, P. (1983) *The Poverty of Affluence. A Psychological Portrait of the American Way of Life*. New York: Free Press.
White, S. (1988) *The Recent Work of Jürgen Habermas*. Cambridge: Cambridge University Press.
Willmott, H. (1984) 'Images and ideals of managerial work', *Journal of Management Studies*, 21: 349–68.
Willmott, H. (1987) 'Studying managerial work: a critique and a proposal', *Journal of Management Studies*, 24: 248–70.

2

Disciplinary Power in the Modern Corporation

Stanley Deetz

Corporate organization conceived as political systems is a common and productive image for organizational analysis (Morgan, 1986). Conceptions developed from this root image have been useful in describing key processes of power and conflict and are likely to become more important as the social impact of large corporate units is more fully understood. Conceptualizing organizations as political systems draws attention to the ways large corporations serve as primary sites where different values, forms of knowledge and groups' interests are articulated and embodied in decisions, structures and practices. As political institutions, corporations are seen as providing meaning and personal identity to their various stakeholders as well as goods, services and income. But the political conception is more than an evocative metaphor.

Corporate organizations serve as a polity. In modern societies they make most public decisions on the use of resources, the development of technologies, the products available and the working relations among people. In many countries the corporate sector makes more public decisions than its governmental counterparts. Unfortunately, the common uncritical acceptance of corporations as naturally existing commercial entities, and concern with managerially conceived issues of efficiency and effectiveness, have led most analyses to be uninterested in the relation of organizational processes to the democratic interest in public participation (Burrell, 1988). Even political conceptions of corporations are often reduced to concern with personal interests and internal strategies. The corporation is overlooked as an important site of *public* decision-making. Understanding corporations as political entities in relation to a democratic society calls for studies that investigate the significance of the exercise of power and control within corporations rather than studies that are concerned with the operation and enhancement of managerial control.

Several authors have recently used concepts from Critical Theory to support studies of social arrangements and practices which foster wider and more open participation in the collective determination of the future (see Alvesson, 1987a for a review). Much of this work has focused on power, ideology and symbolic/cultural practices (Clegg, 1989; Mumby, 1988; Alvesson, 1987b). In order for these works to provide descriptions of more appropriate corporate practices, processes of communication and the issues of a modern democratic politics require greater elucidation. Central to such a project is an understanding of the relations among power, discursive practices and conflict suppression as they relate to the production of individual identity and corporate knowledge.

Understanding these relations requires a conception of political processes of everyday life. While the idea was hardly new and not always articulated clearly, during the 1960s significant segments of the general society, as well as scholars, began to develop a concern with these subtle political processes. Educational institutions, the workplace, the family and media were examined with regard to how they represented different group and individual interests in their decisions, and even more basically how they shaped the very meanings available for public thought and expression. In contrast to the traditional concern with the freedom of public expression and state political processes, the very concept of what was the 'public' became contestable (e.g. Donzelot, 1979). From such a conception, the political battles of the last twenty-five years, at least in the Western world, can be seen as waged over the content of the subjective world, and not just its expression, though such conflicts often remain obscured and misrecognized. Certain feminist groups popularized the sense of the issues in their slogan 'the personal is political'. Or as Baudrillard (1975) more completely argued, the issues cannot be attributed to economic distribution and speaking opportunities within the existing mode of representing interests; the fight must be against the monopoly of the 'code' itself. With such a view, concern shifts to examining alternative codes; and analysis often demonstrates that 'free' and autonomous expression suppresses alternative representations, and thus hides the monopoly of existing codes. The primary force of domination can no longer be seen as economic exploitation with false consciousness providing its excuse but can be conceptualized as the arbitrary, power-laden manner of 'world', 'self' and 'other' constitution. With such a conceptual shift, analysis focuses on systems that develop each subject's active role in producing and reproducing domination. Democratic communication in these terms must be about the formation of knowledge, experience and identity, not merely their expression. The development of the conceptual shift to a politics of meaning and identity construction is, however, often limited by linguistic and social forces, including the borrowing of most conceptions of power, domination, freedom and democracy from political theories concerned with the relation of the individual to the modern state. This can be seen in 'negotiated order' theories, for example. In most of these conceptions the free agent, knowledge and decision-making are based on eighteenth-century conceptions of the individual and reason, views which both help sustain managerial domination in corporations and hamper the development of alternatives (see Laclau and Mouffe, 1985: 115ff.).

Modern Critical Theory's emancipatory project must claim some conception of reason and individual agency yet not be insensitive to issues raised by the politics of everyday life. The political analysis of organizations ultimately must be grounded in a conception of open participatory democracy, but this must be informed by new concepts of the personal and of communication processes. The most common conceptions of the human character and the communication process are imaginary: that is, they are constructed as real within particular social/historical systems of domination. If we understand this imaginary nature we can displace the constructed-as-presumed-free subject as centre and origin of meaning and better understand how the subject is produced. And if discourse itself is understood as power-laden rather than neutral and transparent, we can better reveal the sites of power deployment and concealment. Studies like those of Alvesson (1987b) and Mumby (1988) have worked out new conceptions of power in organizations but can be seen as advancing a conception which Abercrombie et al. (1980) well criticized as the 'dominant ideology thesis'. The presumption appears to be that ideology is produced by some dominant agents who are somehow outside of it, that it is produced by identifiable material forces, and that it becomes fixed as a material sign located in some linguistic configuration or institution. Clegg (1989) has shown in his recent work how the limitations of these analyses can be corrected by using Foucault's (1977, 1980) conception of 'disciplinary' power. Power can be considered creative rather than limiting, it is inseparable from knowledge rather than directing it, and its productive force comes from below as well as above. An analysis using the conception of discipline allows a more sensitive description of the deployment and workings of power than ideology critique alone. The concern here will be with the workings of power in the formation of competing interests and representations, rather than with the possibility of false interests or distorted expression. This will include a reconception of power in regard to cultural formations, an analysis of possible hidden antagonisms in discourse and the manner of the suppression of conflict among them, and a description of the role of organizational analysis in the recovery of antagonism and member agency.

Corporations are the Site of Public Political Decisions

Concern with the representation of interests in corporations has provided useful initial conceptions for examining the politics of corporate practices. Critical Theory's concern with interest representation is an essential step toward a more basic conception made possible by recent works. From a Critical Theory perspective, organizational processes and products fulfil certain human needs. These needs have been described as the interests or 'stake' that various parties (managers, workers, consumers, suppliers and the wider society) have in the organization. Beyond these work-related distinctions, interest differences can often be demonstrated in groups divided by gender, ethnic and racial considerations.

Organizational structures, communication and decision systems, technologies and work design influence the representation and fulfilment of different human interests (Young, 1989). While people produce organizations, all people are not equal in their ability to produce or reproduce organizations that fulfil their interests. From a Critical Theory perspective, organizations thus can never be considered politically neutral. In contemporary practice, managerial groups are clearly privileged in decision-making and most concepts of it. Other groups can be seen as exercising only occasional and usually reactive influences and are often represented as simply economic commodities or 'costs'. The advantages given to management are based on neither rational nor open consensual value foundations nor are they simply acquired through management's own (though often latent) strategic attempts. They are produced historically, and actively reproduced, through discursive practices in corporations themselves (Deetz and Mumby, 1990). The managerial advantages and prerogative can be seen as taking place through economic-based structures *and* systems of discursive monopoly. In modern corporations such an advantage is not so much conceptualized as a right or legitimate but is unproblematically reproduced in routines and discourses. As such this privilege is treated as natural and neutral. The presumed neutrality makes understanding the political nature of organizations more difficult. Order, efficiency and effectiveness as values aid the reproduction of advantages already vested in an organizational form. Concepts of organizational effectiveness tend to hide possible discussion of whose goals should be sought and how much each goal should count (Cameron and Whetten, 1983).

Critical Theorists have shown that workers and the general society have interests in work that are only partially and indirectly shared by management and owners. These include the quality of the work experience and work environment, mental health and safety, the skill and intellectual development of the worker, the carry-over of thinking patterns and modes of action to social and political life, and the production of personal and social identity (Alvesson, 1987a). Organizational life could be an explicit site of political struggle as different groups try to realize their own interests but the conflicts there are often routinized, evoke standard mechanisms for resolution, and reproduce presumed natural tensions (e.g. between workers and management). The essential politics thus becomes invisible. Even more basically, the work site could be considered a polysemic environment where the production of the individual or group interests could itself be seen as an end product (or temporary resting place) in a basic conflictual process defining personal and group identity and the development and articulation of interests. Such potential conflicts are even more completely suppressed in the normalization of conception, identity formation and non-decisional practice than is shown by Critical Theory's ideology critique. The production of the conflicts that exist, and the lack of other equally plausible ones, does not signify false consciousness so much as a type of discursive closure, a central conception for this analysis. The possible development of alternative interests and the subsequent tension between them is often suppressed in organizational practices and discourse through representational marginalization, reduction of alternative interests to economic costs, socialization of members, and the shift of responsibility to the individual.

Known power differences often lead to inequitable interest representation, but power differences are sometimes quite subtle. Different stakeholders are not always in a position to analyse their own interests owing to the lack of adequate undistorted information or insight into fundamental processes. Both stockholders and workers can be disadvantaged by particular accounting practices and the withholding of information. Further, the presence of ideology in the external social world or at the workplace, perpetuated through legitimation and socialization processes, can indicate the inability of certain or even all groups to carefully understand or assess the implicit values carried in their everyday practices, linguistic forms and perceptual experiences. And even more basically, even if they could be assessed, the individual assessing the ideology is a product of a social situation. As Lukes argued, the interior itself is contestable: 'Man's wants themselves may be a product of a system which works against their interests, and in such cases, relates the latter to what they would want and prefer, were they able to make the choice' (1974: 34). Under such conditions what might be accepted as legitimate power differences are best represented as a system of domination, since the empirical manifestation is that of free consent yet structures are reproduced that work against competitive practices and fulfilment of the variety of interests. With such a view, what are taken as legitimate consensual processes are more often evidence of domination and suppressed conflict than of free choice and agreement. Ideological critique alone is not sufficient to account for the full nature of this domination. The presence of ideology and failure to understand self-interest fails to account for how compliance and consent may be a result of clear member understanding of the material conditions for their success. As Przeworski (1980) has argued, the desire to live well provides a pressure towards active participation in the corporate system. In many workers' minds, corporations have delivered the goods and workers have received a necessary and even desired standard of living for their participation. Who is to speak better than they of the quality of the tradeoffs that they have made? The same interpretation could be made of Burawoy's (1979) description of the 'making out' game. In his analysis the organization of 'making-the-rate' provides predictability, security and favourable relations even though the worker is co-opted. The worker is not living an illusion or failing to accomplish interests. The more deeply these systems are probed, the more clear it is that the individual is making a 'rational decision'. But in making rational, aware decisions, a structure of advantage is perpetuated, one of self *and* corporate advantage. The identities and decisions structured here, however, are not politically neutral or simply advantageous. They participate in the construction of a future in which there is a larger stake. The decisions lack an open democratic character not because the calculus or calculations are distorted, but because the human character and needs are specified in advance rather than responsive to the situational complexities. The lack of conflict in these self-referential systems precludes the discussion and open determination of the future (see Mingers, 1989). A non-contentious decision has already been made (see Deetz, 1992).

The concern expressed here is not just managerial domination, but the corporate development of the obedient, normalized mind and body, which is held up against equally legitimate but unrealized alternatives. The interest is in describing the ways by which managers and workers both become obedient in their own structurally prescribed manner (Burrell, 1988: 227). While managers and sometimes owners gain in these structures, the force which drives them is not simply or directly those gains. Rather it is a set of practices and routines which constitute identities and experiences and in doing so provide unproblematic asymmetries, privileged knowledge, and expertise located in some and not others, and in doing so instantiate inclusions and exclusions in decisional processes (Knights and Willmott, 1985). The path I will begin here, and believe must be extended in research, is to reclaim conflicting experiences through describing the practices and routines by which alternatives are disregarded or rendered invisible. The understanding of the processes by which value conflict becomes suppressed and certain forms of reasoning and interests become privileged requires an investigation into the politics of meaning, language and personal identity.

The Discursive Politics of Knowledge and Identity

The most significant product of any corporation is its members. The very notions of free contract, social relations and agency as well as personal identity as a manager, secretary or worker are corporate productions and reproductions. Laclau and Mouffe summarized the three positions central to the corporate individual: 'the view of the subject as an agent both rational and transparent to itself; the supposed unity and homogeneity of the ensemble of its positions; and the conception of the subject as origin and basis of social relations' (1985: 115). The first is necessary for the illusion of freedom which allows the subject to be conceptualized as freely subordinating him/herself in the social contract of the corporation and having choices based on self-interests there. The second sets out the hope of a well-integrated society where the work relations fit without conflict into other institutions and coexist with the democratic processes and the basis for consensual decision-making and mutual understanding. And finally, the individual is conceptualized as the fundamental site of meaning production and chooser of relations with others; hence the personal itself is protected from the examination necessary if it were seen as an arbitrary historical social production resulting from certain social arrangements. Each of these conceptions is misleading and reproductive of forms of domination. Alternative conceptions, however, are difficult to come by.

The politics of identity and identity representation is the deepest and most suppressed struggle in the workplace and, hence, the 'site' where domination and responsive agency are most difficult to unravel. Conceptions which place experience within individuals, present language as a neutral transparent representation, and treat communication as if it were simply a transmission process make it difficult to describe these processes carefully. The position here differs greatly from this. As recent social theory has shown, conceptualizing the individual as the original site of meaning and decisional choices is misleading. Rather, each individual exists with produced identities placed in an already meaningful world. Both the subject and the presumed objective world arise out of a set of discursive and non-discursive practices which constitute the subject and produce a world of distinguished objects (Knights and Wilmott, 1989). Central to understanding the workplace is an understanding of these practices. Prior to any analysis focusing on managers, workers or women and their various interests and reasoning processes is a concern with how these classifications come to exist at all. This leads further to questions regarding how they are reproduced as meaningful, how they are utilized in producing certain types of conflict and their resolutions, and how they preclude other interests and conflicts within and among the various groupings. With identities come interests and relations with other identities, but the first identities are not fixed but are themselves arbitrary social productions. Social groupings and their interests, types of rationality, and the concept of profit are social productions. Each is produced as distinguished from something else. The questions posed for Critical Theory are thus not how these things exist, have power, or explain organizational behaviour, but rather how they come to exist, coexist and interrelate in the production and reproduction of corporate organizations and work in the process of potential inner and outer colonization.

Several questions arise that are of concern. Which personal/relational identities are produced in the modern corporation? How are these identities specified with particular forms of interests and types of knowledge? How are these identities discursively and non-discursively inscribed, interrelated and reproduced? How do such identities become naturalized and reified so as to be taken for granted and suppress the conflict with potential competing identities? I will begin with a summary of what is known about these issues by initially exploring the linguistic constitution of identities through systems of distinctions and then move to consider the deployment of specific discursive practices.

Language as a System of Distinction
The most common misleading conception of language is that it represents an absent, to be recalled, object. Instead, language is primarily constitutive rather than representational. The character of the object and expression arise together. As a system, language holds forth the historically developed dimensions of interests – the attributes of concern or the lines along which things of the world will be distinguished. Language holds the possible ways we will engage in the world and produce objects with particular characteristics. Thus when we consider language from a political point of view within organizations, the interest is not primarily in how different groups

use language to accomplish goals, the rationality in language usage, nor how the profit motive influences language use. The concern is with the dimensions utilized to produce classifications and thus produce groups and their relations. And further, we must understand how representational conceptions of language themselves aid in making classification and identity production appear neutral and based in natural divisions rather than articulating choices with distinct political effect.

Saussure (1974) is most often given credit for the insight that language is primarily a system of distinctions rather than representational. This was accomplished in two arguments. First, signifiers (words or signs) and the signifieds (the potential constituted object to be referenced) are separate and arbitrarily related. This severed any assumption of natural, ahistorical or universal connections between specific words and constituted objects. Any particular language or set of distinctions is a social historical product, developed in social relations and subject to change. And secondly, the meaning of signs is neither intrinsic nor derived from the signified but derived from their difference from other signs in the language chain. Each word can reference only on the basis of its relation and contrasts with other words, a contrast which is reproduced in objects. For example, a term such as 'worker' has meaning only as it distinguishes from 'manager', 'unemployed' or 'lazy' within a particular socially produced linguistic chain. The word makes thematic a perspective against a hidden background of what it is not, which is simultaneously articulated. This part of Saussure's work is useful to the analysis here, though like others (Giddens, 1979; Derrida, 1976), I will reject Saussure's notion that the meanings of signs are fixed as conventions of a speech community. Every sign system contains the possibility of conflicting meanings; the fixing of signs against the plurality of meaning becomes the significant issue here.

Because it is a system of distinction, every linguistic system puts into place certain kinds of social relations and values – that is, certain things that are worthy of being distinguished from other things – and puts into play the attributes that will be utilized to make that distinction. For example, whenever we distinguish between men and women, in using a description that notes gender we claim that distinction along the line of gender is important and valuable to this society and that particular attributes can be used to make that distinction. Both the choice of distinction based on gender and the choice of attributes is arbitrary. It is chosen in choosing the signifying system. The word 'man' or 'woman' does not simply represent something real out there. It puts into play a way of paying attention to the 'out there'. The employment is not neutral. The distinction performs a production of identity for the subject as a woman or man and for the persons as objects with certain rights and characteristics. As the chain of signifiers fans out, the female can be upheld as a mother in a kinship system, a wife in a marital relation, and so forth. In each case, each individual so constituted is both advantaged and disadvantaged in the way that institutional arrangements specify opportunities and constraints. But the distinction remains arbitrary. The signifiers are arbitrary in the sense that, at the next moment, distinction on the basis of gender can be overlooked, rendered irrelevant, or difficult – in the sense that the system of relations between signifiers could be different.

To many it appears self-evident that men and women are different and that therefore the distinction is important. But such 'self-evidence' guides attention away from the political consequences of making the distinction and the choice of sites where it is deployed. The distinction enters into the play of power in the organization in important and conflicting ways. On the one hand, many would wish that the gender distinction would become irrelevant in the place of work so that the identity of people constituted as women, as well as pay and routine treatment practices, would be based on other dimensions of distinction and other constituted identities. Yet rendering gender invisible would exclude the possibility of women organizing and working towards distinct group interests which arise in a gendered society. Thus the distinction socially separates women, marginalizes female experience and provides a unitary identity which denies personal complexity and internal identity conflict. Yet it also provides a ground for resistance and retains a place for conflict of a different sort. The same type of analysis can be applied to each identity produced in the corporation. The double effect of representational practices is a key issue in any emancipatory project in corporations. First we must understand the ideological nature of distinction and then move on to develop the complexities of alternative practices within the discursive system.

Gender distinction is only one of many critical distinctions in the workplace, e.g. worker/manager, data/not data, private/public information, rational/irrational and expert/non-expert. Understanding the importance of the gender issue reminds us of the multitude of classificatory activities that have political implications and that are protected by seeming to be self-evident and empirical. Further, each of these becomes interwoven in a complex of signifiers, e.g. gender becomes tied to forms of understanding and knowledge, private and public becomes critical to various forms of expertise and proprietary information. Occupational classification is only one of many signifying practices that have significance for gender politics, e.g. stories, jokes, and dress codes each implement distinction and an associated chain of signifiers. Far less has been done about these things than about gender and occupational classification. If people could work back through the systems of distinctions they implement, they would often find a gap between what they reflectively think and feel and what they unwittingly express. The point is not to determine what they 'really' or freely think. But recalling the arbitrariness of such constructions is a step in understanding the plurality of equally plausible subject articulations momentarily out of the reach of proclaimed 'naturalness and self-evidence'. It is this self-evidence and presumed transparency of language that must be given up to understand power and the politics of experience. It is this that ideological criticism has accomplished well. This can easily be seen in the work on the linguistic production of subject identity.

The Linguistic Production of Subject Identity
Althusser (1971) has given the most commanding treatment of the relation of language to the production of the human subject. In Althusser's analysis language is the most general ideological mediation. Building on Saussure, language to Althusser is not a system of signs that represent. Rather, language appears as discourse, a material practice which systematically forms that of which it speaks. Language as an ideological practice mediates between individuals and the conditions of their existence. This mediation is not between preformed individuals and objective conditions but it is the means by which the individual becomes a subject, a process called *interpell-ation*. Quoting Althusser: 'I shall then suggest that ideology "acts" or "functions" in such a way that it "recruits" subjects among individuals (it recruits them all), or "transforms" the individual into subjects (it transforms them all) by that very precise operation which I have called *interpellation* or hailing' (1971: 162–3). The specific relationship between subject in a particular world and the individual is *imaginary*. That is, the 'subject' is always an image or a constructed self rather than an individual in a full set of relations to the world. A 'real' form of domination or control is unnecessary to the extent that the individual takes the imaginary construction as if it is real. Or as Weedon has suggested,

> The crucial point . . . is that in taking on a subject position, the individual assumes that she is the author of the ideology or discourse which she is speaking. She speaks or thinks as if she were in control of meaning. She 'imagines' that she is the type of subject which humanism proposes – rational, unified, the source rather than the effect of language. It is the imaginary quality of the individual's identification with a subject position which gives it so much psychological and emotional force. (1987: 31)

It is of little surprise that the individual makes the mistake since the processes through which this misrecognition takes place are subtle and complex. Pêcheux (1982), following Althusser (1971), argued that ideology 'interpellates individuals into subjects' through many complex, 'forgotten' interdiscourses whereby each subject has a signified, self-evident reality which is 'perceived-accepted-submitted to'. As Thompson (1984: 236) has presented Pêcheux's analysis: the hidden-forgotten discursive formation

> creates the illusion that the subject precedes discourse and lies at the origin of meaning. Far from this being the case, it is the subject which is 'produced' or 'called forth' by the discursive sequence; or more precisely, the subject is 'always already produced' by that which is 'preconstructed' in the sequence.

But discursive sequences are never singular and closed. The issue of concern, however, is not that an illusion or image is produced but, rather, the politics of preferring one type of image over others, precluding the conflict and dialogue among them, and structuring self-referential relationships that have no outside.

The consideration of alternative meanings and alternative subjectivities poses a threat to the individual's claimed identity, thus the individual rejects the possibility of freedom. The individual will often protect the constructions as natural and as one's own even though they are not, and reject alternatives as mere constructions that are unnatural and, ironically, politically motivated (see Knights and Willmott, 1985, 1989). The first political act is forgotten as attention is paid to the second. As such, the individual is not simply identifying with those in power; that power is the subject. The subject as mediated through language is always ideologically produced. There is no place out of the formation to claim an independent subject. The individual experiences a particular world, one which is the product of socially inscribed values and distinctions like the subject itself. Only on the basis of this does the individual claim personal beliefs or values or come to share them with others. A particular ideology is a particular way of being in the world, a social sharing prior to any individual taking it on as his/her own.

Let me sum up here by suggesting that systems of thought, expression and communication media contain embedded values that constitute a particular experience through the making of distinction and relations through perception. The very ordinariness of common sense hides implicit valuational structure of perceptual experience. Each discourse and attendant technology constitutes ways of knowing the world, privileges certain notions of what is real, and posits personal identities. Both mediated and non-mediated discourses posit a subject, have an epistemology, and structure value choices. The development of technical knowledge and conceptions of expertise do not simply advantage those who have them, but their presumed existence enables the qualification and disqualification of members' ways of knowing and are thus a major element in conflict suppression and the production of identity and experience. But language and expression alone do not exhaust the production of the subject's identity.

Institutions as Discursive Practices

Everyday life is filled with institutional artefacts, routines and standard practices. Each implements values and establishes a subject's point of view. Institutional practices are concretized (sometimes literally) in the construction of buildings, the laying of sidewalks, the writing of legal codes, the placement of postings and signs, the development and implementation of technologies, and the development of stories, jokes and vocabularies. Cultural researchers have long noted the presence of such features. Unfortunately, they are often treated as expressive of the individual or culture, and their role in the constitution of the subject and world is lost. Institutional forms are textual, they are human creations which, like language, position a subject and direct the construction of particular experiences with particular conflicts and opportunities for alternative perceptions.

For example, the change of banking facilities from an imposing, secure singular site to home-like, dispersed branches and finally automatic teller machines can be seen as expressive of changing images and needs, but more fundamentally produces and continually reproduces a different 'subject' with different social relations and a different object: 'money'. Such a reading recognizes that this happens against the backdrop of other possible relations and absences and possible subjects. The old 'subject' in the new configuration becomes absent and is difficult to produce even if the person wanted to. The modern person is produced as consumer, even of money. It is not simply the case that attitudes towards savings have changed; rather the institution, the very subject and routine of saving, is different. Interest rates, legal requirements and tax laws, for example, are among many institutional practices that both make possible these changes and are changed by them.

But the banking and monetary system itself is produced in a particular way of relating other social changes and practices and it alone does not produce the modern person even in relation to money. The person is a home owner, a product consumer, a parent, and so forth. The relation between institutional arrangements produces a complex subject, a subject which is at once dispersed among many and competing institutions and unified as a common produced identity across interrelatable institutions. The desire for, or expectation of, autonomy in certain institutions can create dependency in others. For example, to the extent that freedom and the pursuit of happiness are institutionally inscribed as a leisure activity, dependency and control become acceptable and even necessary characteristics of the place of work as a means of fulfilling the promise of leisure. The worker may demand greater work, presumably for his or her own interest. Not only across institutions: the modern workplace itself evidences such dispersion and provides a set of practices which unify, and thus suppress, the potential conflicts. The very complexity frequently hides the onesidedness of the matrix and stops exploration of possible identities that would be constituted in different institutional arrangements. The task of working out these relationships at any particular corporate site or for the more general corporate experience is great. And as the complexity increases the descriptive and critical adequacy of economic and ideological explanations becomes increasingly limited.

The subject is subject to a range of discourses, some of which conflict. Meaning is not a singularity claimed by an individual text, or even an intersection of texts. It is pluralistic and 'deferred' in the sense that there can be no final determination. Unitary meaning is temporary and only held in place by force before it drifts away in a never-ending web of other texts. Only on the basis of the appearance of plurality could ideology be identified at all or could the subject be claimed as an agent. There is never one linguistic expression in one institutional arrangement, but many. And further, our interest does not end with the construction of the subject but extends to the realities in which subjects find themselves.

The notion of the psychological subject as an autonomous originator of meaning which phenomenology first showed to be an abstraction is now more precisely replaced by competing points of view arising in many simultaneous texts. People thus are not filled with independently existing thoughts, feelings, beliefs and plans that are brought to expression. As they move about the world, reading books, watching television or doing work, they take on the subjects of these texts as their own (Giddens, 1984: 184). The self is not independent of texts but always finds itself in them. The unity of the reflected subject carries with it possibilities and problems and most importantly conceals its own social/cultural origin and an illusion of a certain presence and freedom: an illusion suggested at the outset as essential to domination in corporate functioning. The power given to the self to define its own meaning is an unwarranted privilege, conceals the process of construction, and leaves the subject unaware of multiple systems of control. Once texts are freed from the privilege of the subject or rational meaning, a new set of analyses of the organization of texts becomes possible.

Control of Identity Production
If the subject and the subject's world are an arbitrary production carefully (intentionally but without simple origin) integrated to appear necessary and unproblematic, we must account for their accomplishment, the complexity of the formation, and the political gains and losses in particular formations. Such an analysis, of course, parallels Gramsci's (1971) conception of hegemony. Gramsci argued that the willing assent of the mass was engineered through the production of the normality of everyday life beliefs and practices. Rather than visible control by elites, 'organic intellectuals' (e.g. teachers, writers, experts) produce a variety of cultural forms that express and shape values, actions and meanings, and reproduce hidden forms of domination. The site of hegemony is the myriad of everyday institutional activities and experiences that culminate in 'common sense', thus hiding the choices made and 'mystifying' the interests of dominant groups. Dominant group definitions of reality, norms and standards appear as normal rather than political and contestable. Bourdieu (1977) has extended this in his discussion of the role of 'symbolic elites' in defining the preferred representational systems in a society. And to some extent, this part of Gramsci's work is recalled in a new way when Foucault (1977) identifies psychiatrists, doctors and wardens as controllers of discourse. Their definitions of deviance and normality can be seen as expressions of power that often arbitrarily support certain ways of life as normal and others as pathological.

In a partial and overly simplistic conception, corporate managers, technical experts and consultants armed with their own social, economic and managerial science become the 'organic intellectuals' of our present formation. Their power, however, is not so simple. The modern corporate power is not a monolithic extension of class politics, but more like a web of arbitrary asymmetrical relations with specific means of decision and control. While certain groups benefit from these arrangements, they are in no simple way designed for these gains. The force of these arrangements is primarily in producing order, forgetfulness and dependency. Ideology critique is frequently limited by the assumption of hidden real interests or the possibility of new power-free rationality. Ideology as a concept is best seen as drawing attention to arbitrary representational practices rather than a false or class consciousness. Our opening to the future is better seen in the perpetual critique of each consensus and claim to rationality, but not for the sake of better reasoning and new consensus. The recovery of lost conflict and the retention of ongoing decision-making against presumption and closure can be developed as the central critical goal. This is best seen in reconsidering the nature of power. Understanding the deployment of power and the manner of its advantaging will require a number of reconceptions.

Power and Discursive Formations

The major problem ideological criticism faces rests in its conception of power. In many Critical Theory works, especially in Habermas, power differences per se are equated with domination and are held to be in opposition to reason. The Critical Theory ideal of a new public forum wherein competing claims and interests can be expressed and resolved requires a unitary rational subject, which has been shown as an illusion and itself part of a domination system. And further, the negative notion of power does not allow for the formation of perhaps arbitrary and distorted power blocs which may be essential to the development of alternative practices in actual power-laden contexts. The issue of power must be reconsidered within the Critical Theory project. The trick is to understand the power-laden nature of all human association and yet to retain some place and hope for democratic decision-making so that all is not reduced to arbitrary power advantages.

In Western societies few issues have commanded the discursive attention of the twin issues of freedom and the exercise of power. Foucault (1980), perhaps better than anyone else, has demonstrated that it is frequently because of these discussions rather than an inattention to power that we have failed to understand its presence and manners of deployment. So too in corporate organizations the attention to inter-group conflict, coalitions, regulations and rights has often led us further from understanding power and domination. As indicated, most conceptions and analyses of power in organizations have been derived from political scientists. Each of these conceptions was primarily designed to discuss power in relation to the influence different people or groups have in political processes or the rights of individuals in opposition to possible state domination. This I believe to be true in the Critical Theory tradition. Discussions of leadership, coalition formation, special interests and authority in corporations are often only distinguished from similar 'public' process by scale and the special applicable rights. Similarly, discussions of loyalty and collective priorities closely parallel conceptions developed for the relation to the state. Foucault has shown how each of these conceptions is tied to sovereign rights as expanded in 'juridico' discourse. Since power is conceived as restrictive of individual freedom, the question 'by what right or necessity is the rule made' serves as a fundamental issue for the exercise of power.

Disciplinary Power

Following Foucault (1980), disciplinary power rather than sovereign power is of utmost significance. The state or central administration still has much power but it is limited if only because, in its negative form, it is always felt as oppressive. This is merely the public extension of the same rational grounding for Critical Theory. Power is restriction and oppression. In corporations a kind of sovereign power exists and can be described as parallel in character to that of the state. But attention to these is misleading and often conceals the actual procedures of power and the operant sites of its deployment. Most significantly, in modern corporations control and influence are dispersed into norms and standard practices as products of moral, medical, sexual and psychological regulation – disciplinary power (see Burrell, 1988). This is a conception of power Habermas (1984, 1987) attempted to account for in his 'constitutive steering media' but he appears unable to sustain his critique of the power formations without appealing to a 'lifeworld' which is still laden with power, only of a different form. Foucault's conception of disciplinary power allows a more complete description of the enabling as well as constraining constitutive capacity identified as power.

Disciplinary power resides in every perception, every judgement, every act. In its positive sense it enables, and negatively it excludes and marginalizes. Participatory democracy is itself a power-laden discipline, one which encourages certain practices (e.g. concept formation) and works against others (e.g. perceptual repetition and private interests). Rather than analysing power in the organization as if it were a sovereign state, the conception of power has to be reformed to account for this more massive and invisible structure of control. Administration has to be seen in relation to order and discipline if its power is to be understood. I believe that we gain in this conception over Edwards's (1979) discussion of the emergence of 'bureaucratic' control. It is not just the rule and routine which become internalized, but a complex set of practices which provide common sense, self-evident experience and personal identity. The question is not simply how to account for the presence of management defined as control rather than co-ordination, but also how control operates in 'organic' as well as 'bureaucratic' structured organizations.

Disciplinary power for Foucault is omnipresent as it is manifest and produced in each moment. Power is thus not dispersed in modern society to citizens who argue and vote, but spreads out through lines of conformity, commonsense observations, and determinations of propriety. Disciplinary power is evidenced in the production of a normalized body and response which is produced, reproduced and supported by arrangements of the material world which result in co-ordination and consent, not only regarding how the world is but how it should be. The focus on order with accompanying surveillance and education shifts control away from the explicit exercise of power through force and coercion and places it in the routine practices of everyday life. As Smart described his conception:

> Hegemony contributes to or constitutes a form of social cohesion not through force or coercion, nor necessarily through consent, but most effectively by way of practices, techniques, and methods which infiltrate minds and bodies, cultural practices which cultivate behaviours and beliefs, tastes, desires, and needs as seemingly naturally occurring qualities and properties embodied in the psychic and physical reality (or 'truth') of the subject. (1986: 160)

What is of interest then is not so much the powerlessness of the state, which presumably represents the will of the people, but the organization of these innumerable sites of power through other institutions and the complicity of the state in these hidden power relations.

Foucault (1977) defined the modern penal systems as the most extreme and purest exemplar of disciplinary power. The order, routine, rehabilitation, and always surveillance, provide a vivid example of *formal* order. Giddens (1984) has objected that the model does not map well on even the more formal organizations since individuals go home and relate to many competing institutions. I am inclined to go half-way with him. The model does not map well but because the modern corporation is the better exemplar of the full extent of disciplinary power. It goes home with its members, proposes electronic and self-surveillance, and colonizes competing institutions. The modern corporate form of work organization has become a new centre providing a modern co-ordination and relief of tension from competing institutional practices that the state arose to replace (suppress) in its time (Deetz, 1992). Not only does the work experience structure a type of identity, but such identities are extended through corporate-sponsored media images in news, entertainment and advertising.

Disciplinary power has been present in corporations from their outset. Perhaps the clearest case is the development of the assembly line. The assembly line transformed an explicit authority relation between the worker and supervisor into a partially hidden one.

Rather than the supervisor having to tell the worker how hard or fast to work and dealing with the question, 'by what right', the movement in the line already accomplished it. In the process the functional relation changed. This can be seen in Edwards's (1979) conception of the assembly line in terms of 'technical control'. The assembly line extended and enabled a particular worker capacity. Instead of being restrictive of the worker it facilitated an accomplishment. The assembly line, like the new organization, was a new tool extending collective bodies' capacity to produce. But it was also a new kind of tool. Rather than being subjugated to the body's rule, it subjugated the body into an extension of itself – a docile, useful body. Like any technology, it 'subjects' the individual in a particular way (Deetz, 1990). While there was still no doubt that authority and explicit power kept the worker at the line and that it was the company's decision to implement work in this way, the relation to the supervisor could also change. Through training, the worker could keep up with the line with less effort, so the supervisor could be on the side of the worker in the worker's complicity with the systems that controlled him or her. The management interest in suppressing and routinizing conflict could be realized, often with the full involvement of the worker. While new forms of resistance are made possible, they are also made less likely by the complicity and new form of surveillance. Piece-rate payments on up through the various worker participation programmes merely extend this basic model (Burawoy, 1979). Systems such as these do not lend themselves well to ideological criticism. They are not filled with false needs or hidden values. Rather it is the truth and naturalness of the domination, the *free* acceptance, that makes it so powerful.

In the modern context, disciplinary power exists largely in the new 'social technologies of control'. These include experts and specialists of various sorts who operate to create '*norm*alized' knowledge, operating procedures and methods of inquiry, and to suppress competitive practices. These are the accountants with standard (hardly known or contestable) accounting practices, efficiency experts and personnel officers. Like Gramsci's (1971) organic intellectuals, the outcome of their activities is a hegemonic social cohesion lacking the conflicts and differences that characterize an open world context. But unlike Gramsci's conception, the effect is neither simply coherent nor primarily accomplished through values and ideological consent. Foucault's conception of hegemony is a free-floating set of conflicts and incompatibilities which yet maintain asymmetrical relations. Power relations arise out of aims, objectives and strategies but there is no simple choice-making group or guidance to the network of power. In Foucault's words, the rationality of power is characterized by tactics that are often quite explicit at the restricted level where they are inscribed . . . tactics which, becoming connected to one another, attracting and propagating one another, but finding their base of support and their condition elsewhere, end by forming comprehensive systems: the logic is perfectly clear, the aims decipherable, and yet it is often the case that no one is there to have invented them, and few who can be said to have formulated them. (1980: 95)

For example, no management group can control the actions, let alone the thoughts, of other groups. The presence of fear (warranted or not), assumptions of knowledge differences, principles of least effort, wanting rewards and so forth must be provided by the controlled groups. However, these are not usually knowingly controlled and such things are not formed outside of specific power relations which are often supported by other institutions. But rarely is explicit power displayed by management. The explicit and unilateral display of authority more often denotes the breakdown of power relations rather than the presence of them. It is the last resort of normal power relations.

Another key aspect of Foucault's conception of disciplinary power is the presence of new forms of surveillance. While the worker was always watched, disciplinary control allowed a new form of surveillance: self-surveillance. Self-surveillance uses norms backed by 'experts' for areas heretofore in the 'amateur' realm. Foucault (1977) developed Bentham's 'panoptic' prison design as the root vision of this new self-surveillance. In Bentham's design a single guardhouse stood with a view into each cell, but the prisoner could never tell when he was being watched. The surveillance, hence, could be more complete than from a number of guards walking the cell block; the prisoner imagined being watched constantly. Certainly this is a feeling enforced in the modern organization, particularly at the managerial levels. Whether or not it is true, the employee can never tell who might use what against him or her or when a statement will come back to one's own demise. And the wider the group participating in decision-making, the fewer people are safe confidants. Worker participation programmes, for example, can move the work group from interest solidarity to member self-surveillance. No cohort in resistance exists when everyone/anyone can be a member of the 'management team'. The implicit lawyer at the side censors discussion today as well as the fear of eternal damnation did in a past time. In such a configuration, managers are not simply controllers but are controlled as much as any other group.

But the surveillance is not just of words and actions. With the battery of psychological (and chemical) tests – experts in attitudes, culture and bodily fluids – the corporation assesses the purity of one's mind and soul (see Hollway, 1984). But more importantly, employees self-assess on the corporation's behalf. The fear of someone seeing beneath the surface to detect a doubt or disloyalty or the fear that one's own gender or belief structure will be rejected, conspire to enforce the norms. The new age self-manipulations are often far deeper and more extreme than Huxley could dream of or than any corporation could explicitly require.

In several ways the 1960s' move of the 'backstage' (the hidden social order negotiation talk, professionalized by Goffman and the ethnomethodologists) into the open provided new areas of surveillance, particularly self-surveillance. For example, when common practices are totally taken for granted in traditional societies they discipline invisibly and completely, but they are also protected from manipulation by this same invisibility. As common practices are revealed as mere social conventions a measure of freedom is acquired since they can be enacted or not, or even openly negotiated. But as such they may be trained or manipulated. Goffman may have made visible the invisible disciplinary processes of culturally inscribed ways of managing appearances but in doing so he made a significant input to an industry of 'facial' surveillance and 'facial' production in the form of image management. Similarly in corporations, performance appraisals, designed to enable employee input into the formation of objectives, turn to open the personal to public appraisal. Not only is one's work being appraised, but also one's hopes, dreams and personal commitments. Most employees learn to bring these under prior assessment by their own private public eye. The failure of the 1960s movements to promote an understanding of the politics of the personal enabled disclosure of a constructed psychological state as freedom rather than promoting more autonomous self-development. In doing so, the rightness of the insides became a matter of public appraisal rather than of the politics of that rightness.

The conception of the workplace as a game rather than a structure of life can provide a cynical player who confidently hopes to both beat the game and remain untouched. But ultimately such a conception facilitates a game addict who is consumed by staying viable in the game, haunted by the prospect that he or she cannot control the self or others enough to win, yet unconcerned with the investment owing to an arrogance suggesting that it is merely a game and they could quit at any time. The impersonal and unlifelike quality of the workplace becomes reason enough not to critically investigate it.

The complicity of humanistic, cognitive and behavioural psychology in these processes should not be underestimated. Psychology has provided the study of the individual, especially the prediction and control of the individual. Fostered by the massive research support of the military and professional drive of therapy, it has been the ideal provider of the tools of the new 'discipline' of corporations (see Driskell and Beckett, 1989). As an academic discipline, psychology matches well what Scott (1985: 153) identified as the core beliefs of managerialism: 'People are Essentially Defective'; 'People are Totally Malleable'. The prospect of a well-integrated worker appropriately matched to the job, and the job to the individual, bespoke the harmony of managerial hope and the motives and confidence of self-manipulation. The centred self who knows who he or she is, and what he or she wants, provides the trustworthy person in control (well subject*ed*/sub*jected*). The testing/training programmes provide the mechanism of correction in a self-referential system oriented to control rather than autonomy. And significantly, the human self-understanding as malleable and values as subjective and learned, has discredited competing voices and glorified the secular and modern. The 'helping profession' could define healthiness based on social integration and lack of personal conflict, disqualifying radical voices and the fragmentation within and without. Adjustment and retooling could put problems, or at least the solutions to them, within the person. Both the individual and the corporation could be seen as gaining at once. The corporation is active in the production of a unitary personal identity armed with a science of the person. And all this is done in the realm of value-neutral social research, a discipline at its best.

Discipline is thus a configuration of power inserted as a way of thinking, acting and instituting. The disciplined member of the organization wants on his or her own what the corporation wants. The most powerful and powerless in traditional terms are equally subjected, though there is no doubt who is advantaged. But it is not as if either sees this advantage as 'rightful'. In fact its ideological rightfulness may well be contested. The struggle over sovereign rights can hide the discipline which situates the struggle (e.g. the existence of a labour union can create its opposite, a unified management). Contestation itself can follow practices which reposition the actors in terms of their difference and establish the resources of one as the preferred in the struggle. Concepts like ideology and interests are useful in enabling the identification of the difference and the manner of discursive moves, but the presence of specific identities and interests has to be situated in the disciplinary structure itself. They are produced there as well as playing a central role in its representation.

The political interpretation of organizational practices is to reproblematize the obvious. In some sense there is no surprise in showing power formations in discursive practices in organizations. Of course corporations are hierarchical, of course managers strategically deploy power. Control is the name of the game. But the self-evidence hides much. Why does management control rather than co-ordinate and how is that secured? Why isn't the co-ordination function seen as largely clerical and facilitative? To understand modern domination, we must take the routine, the commonsensical and the self-evident and subject them to reconsideration. The more distant dominations by the Church and kings were not simply forced on subjects but were routine and ritualized, reproduced in innumerable practices; they were consented to but not chosen. Reproblematizing the obvious requires identifying conflicts which do not happen, pulling out latent experiences which are overlooked, and identifying discursive practices which block value discussion and close the exploration of differences. Ideological critique can be useful to define the conditions necessary for the articulation of conflicts regarding access to speaking forums and information (as equality of opportunity), social relations (a critique of historically derived asymmetries), personal experience (as conflictual rather than unitary), and the claim of the subject matter (a critique of the reduction of the otherness of the external world to any single description) (see Habermas, 1984). But the politics of identity and knowledge construction requires a more complete understanding of discursive and non-discursive practices aided by the investigation of disciplinary power.

In sum, control of corporate institutions by democratic institutions is unlikely and less significant than the development of internal political democracy based on an understanding of micropolitics of disciplinary power and transformative communication practice at the corporate site. Meaningful democracy, which is positive in form and which invigorates the autonomy of citizens, can take place through corporate restructuring and the fostering of non-dependent rather than dependent and co-dependent ones within corporate practices. This becomes the leading political issue of the day. Such democracy would go well beyond simply more worker involvement in decision-making. It entails changes in the daily processes out of which identity, meaning and common sense are formed.

References

Abercrombie, N., Hill, S. and Turner, B. (1980) *The Dominant Ideology Thesis*. London: Allen & Unwin.

Althusser, L. (1971) 'Ideology and ideological state apparatuses', in *Lenin and Philosophy and Other Essays*, trans. Ben Brewster. London: New Left Books.

Alvesson, M. (1987a) *Organizational Theory and Technocratic Consciousness: Rationality, Ideology and Quality of Work*. New York: de Gruyter.

Alvesson, M. (1987b) 'Organizations, culture and ideology', *International Studies of Management and Organizations*, 17: 4–18.

Baudrillard, J. (1975) *The Mirror of Production*, trans. Michal Poster. St. Louis: Telos Press.

Bourdieu, P. (1977) *Outline of a Theory of Practice*. Cambridge: Cambridge University Press.

Burawoy, M. (1979) *Manufacturing Consent*. Berkeley: University of California Press.

Burrell, G. (1988) 'Modernism, post modernism and organizational analysis 2: the contribution of Michel Foucault', *Organization Studies*, 9: 221–35.

Cameron, K. and Whetten, D. (eds) (1983) *Organizational Effectiveness: A Comparison of Multiple Models*. New York: Academic Press.

Clegg, S. (1989) *Frameworks of Power*. Newbury Park, CA: Sage.

Deetz, S. (1990) 'Representation of interests and the new communication technologies', in M. Medicare, T. Peterson and A. Gonzalez (eds), *Communication and the Culture of Technology* Pullman: Washington State University Press. pp. 43–62.

Deetz, S. (1992) *Democracy in an Age of Corporate Colonization: Developments in Communication and the Politics of Everyday Life*. Albany: State University of New York Press.

Deetz, S. and Mumby, D. (1990) 'Power, discourse and the workplace: reclaiming the critical tradition in communication studies in organizations', in J. Anderson (ed.), *Communication Yearbook 13*. Newbury Park, CA: Sage. pp. 18–47.

Derrida, J. (1976) *Of Grammatology*. Baltimore: Johns Hopkins University Press.

Donzelot, J. (1979) *The Policing of the Family*. London: Routledge.

Driskell, J. and Beckett, O. (1989) 'Psychology and the military', *American Psychologist*, 44: 43–54.

Edwards, R. (1979) *Contested Terrain: The Transformation of the Workplace in the Twentieth Century*. New York: Basic Books.

Foucault, M. (1972) *The Archaeology of Knowledge*. New York: Pantheon.

Foucault, M. (1977) *Discipline and Punish: The Birth of the Prison*, trans. A. Sheridan. New York: Random House.

Foucault, M. (1980) *The History of Sexuality*, trans. R. Hurley. New York: Vintage.

Giddens, A. (1979) *Central Problems in Social Theory*. Berkeley: University of California Press.

Giddens, A. (1984) *The Constitution of Society*. Berkeley: Campus.

Gramsci, A. (1971) *Selections from the Prison Notebooks*, trans. Q. Hoare and G. Nowell-Smith. New York: International.

Habermas, J. (1984) *The Theory of Communicative Action, Vol. I: Reason and the Rationalization of Society*, trans. T. McCarthy. Boston: Beacon Press.

Habermas, J. (1987) *The Theory of Communicative Action, Vol. II: Lifeworld and System*, trans. T. McCarthy. Boston: Beacon Press.

Hollway, W. (1984) 'Fitting work: psychological assessment in organizations', in J. Henriques, W. Hollway, C. Urwin, C. Venn and V. Walkerdine (eds) (1984) *Changing the Subject*. New York: Methuen. pp. 26–59.

Knights, D. and Willmott, H. (1985) 'Power and identity in theory and practice', *The Sociological Review*, 33: 22–46.

Knights, D. and Willmott, H. (1989) 'Power and subjectivity at work: from degredation to subjugation in social relations', *Sociology*, 23 (4): 535–58.

Laclau, E. and Mouffe, C. (1985) *Hegemony and Socialist Strategy*, trans. W. Moore and P. Cammack. London: Verso.

Lukes, S. (1974) *Power: A Radical View*. London: Macmillan.

Mingers, J. (1989) 'An introduction to autopoiesis – implications and applications', *Systems Practice*, 2: 159–80

Morgan, G. (1986) *Images of Organization*. Newbury Park, CA: Sage.

Mumby, D. K. (1987) 'The political function of narrative in organizations', *Communication Monographs*, 54: 113–27.

Mumby, D. K. (1988) *Communication and Power in Organizations: Discourse, Ideology, and Domination*. Norwood, NJ: Ablex.

Pêcheux, M. (1982) *Language, Semantics and Ideology: Stating the Obvious*, trans. Harbans Nagpal. London: Macmillan.

Przeworski, A. (1980) 'Material bases of consent: economics and politics in a hegemonic system', *Political Power and Social Theory*, 1: 21–66.

Saussure, F. de (1974) *Course in General Linguistics*. London: Fontana.

Scott, W. G. (1985) 'Organizational revolution: an end to managerial orthodoxy', *Administration and Society*, 17: 149–70.

Smart, B. (1986) 'The politics of truth and the problem of hegemony', in D. C. Hoy (ed.) *Foucault: A Critical Reader*. Oxford: Basil Blackwell. pp. 157–74.

Thompson, J. (1984) *Studies in the Theory of Ideology*. Berkeley: University of California Press.

Weedon, C. (1987) *Feminist Practice and Poststructuralist Theory*. Oxford: Basil Blackwell.

Young, E. (1989) 'On the naming of the rose: interests and multiple meanings as elements of organizational culture', *Organization Studies*, 10: 187–206.

3

Critical Ethnography: On Fieldwork in a Habermasian Way

John Forester

Critical Ethnography and Professional Practice

When we walk into a meeting in a city hall, a church basement, or a dean's office, we do want to know who seeks which ends, who has which purposes, interests, wants and intentions, but we typically want to know more than that too. We want to know not only about the actors' likely decisions about costs, benefits and tradeoffs – in general, about utilities – but we want to know too about their allegiances and loyalties, their trustworthiness and integrity – in general about their political and social identities.

In Steven Lukes's terms, we want to know not just about their instrumental decision-making, but about their abilities to shape agendas and even others' senses of their own best interests (Lukes, 1974). We want to know how in shaping attention – and neglect – selectively, they will shape other people's senses of 'can' and 'can't', others' senses of what is and is not possible, and thus others' political senses of self, their political identities (Forester, 1989). As actors pursue ends, they reproduce social and political relations as well. As decisions are made, relations of power are reproduced too. When we decide what to say and what not to say, when to challenge and when not, we often consider both our immediate purposes and our future relationships, today's goals and tomorrow's prospects of acting with others, our 'strategic position'.

James March and Johan Olsen (1976: 52) put the point crisply, writing that

> choice situations are not simply occasions for making substantive decisions. They are also arenas in which important symbolic meanings are developed. People gain status and exhibit virtue. Problems are accorded significance. Novices are educated into the values of the society and organization. Participation rights are certification of social legitimacy; participation performances are critical presentations of self.

But how does all this happen?

When we examine it, ordinary action turns out to be extraordinarily rich. What passes for 'ordinary work' in professional-bureaucratic settings is a thickly layered texture of political struggles concerning power and authority, cultural negotiations over identities, and social constructions of the 'problems' at hand. As this chapter will illustrate by considering just a fragment of a professional staff meeting, the purpose of critical ethnographic work is to reveal the politics of this multilayered complexity. Such work is 'critical' in so far as it focuses on relations of power and hegemony and their contingencies – not because it provides any decision-rule or simple tool with which to 'measure' domination. Such work is ethnographic in so far as it is empirical and phenomenological: sensitive to socially constructed meanings, looking beyond distributions of utilities to the construction of identities (Marcus, 1986; Giddens, 1984; Willis, 1977; Foucault, 1980).

Critical ethnographic work in general, then, and fieldwork done in a Habermasian way in particular, should show us practically how much more than instrumental action, deciding which means to use to get to which ends, takes place in ordinary practice, and what difference this makes for questions of power and powerlessness, community and autonomy (Marcus and Fischer, 1986; Clifford and Marcus, 1986; Stacey, 1988; Habermas, 1984, 1987). Building on previous work, this chapter seeks to show, too, how Habermas's work can be fruitfully appropriated for empirically rich, politically acute, social research.

We tell ourselves far too easily that ordinary action must be understood 'in its context', but the very context itself is not given but made, inherited and appropriated in subtle political ways (Heritage, 1984). Too easily too we assure ourselves that the 'micro' and the 'macro' must fit together, that any action occurs on a structured stage, that to understand any action we must understand the particular historical stage on which it takes place. But the same stage can support a bewildering variety of actions, judgements, deceits, strategies and expressions. We certainly do not need to put issues of context, stage and political structure aside, but to look closely at practice, at careful action as it takes place. By looking closely, listening carefully, we can appreciate even the most apparently simple 'bureaucratic' interactions as entry points, as windows through which we might look to see the extraordinary political complexity of professional and organizational work (Knorr-Cetina, 1981).

This chapter, accordingly, will argue that one small part of critical social theory, Habermas's sociological analysis of communicative action, has a vast and yet unrealized potential for concrete social and political research, for critical ethnographic analysis. Unfortunately, though, the promise of such research has often been obscured in a flurry of narrower epistemological debates. We ought neither to devalue those philosophical debates nor to hold sociological and ethnographic inquiry hostage to their less than imminent outcomes.

As a window to a field setting, we consider below a simple twelve-sentence fragment of a conversation taken from a staff meeting of a small city's Department of City Planning. The staff meeting provides an example of a professional setting – a relatively non-controversial, ordinary, even 'boring' setting – in which we can explore the ongoing 'micropolitics' of city planning practice. The conversational sequence we shall consider here followed some forty minutes of discussion of all the data the staff might want from a potential new citywide information system.

In this small city, as in many other small municipalities, the planners have found themselves attempting to balance development pressures with neighbourhood preservation and environmentalist pressures. The staff have been working on studies of low-income housing needs, downtown transportation patterns, the redesign of the city's most important public park, the location of a farmer's market, and ongoing economic development needs. Unemployment has been relatively low, compared to other municipalities in the state. Local politics has largely been controlled by the Democratic Party, with increasingly strong challenges being mounted recently from a 'green' and no-growth coalition – whose leaders have routinely attacked the planners for doing too little, too late in the face of 'new development'. Planning staff turnover has been fairly low, but the planning staff typically feel overwhelmed with the number of projects and issues for which they seem to be held responsible.

After 'brainstorming' a long, long list of desired information, a junior planner, Helena, finally asks, 'So now that we know everything that we want (data-wise), how do we get it?' and the following stream of interactions had begun.

Field Data: Interaction in a City Planning Staff Meeting, City Hall, Northville

Helena (Junior planner): So now that we know everything that we want (data-wise), how do we get it?
Director [facetiously]: Oh, Peter's gonna take care of that!
Peter (Associate director): Yeah, that's a minor detail. . . .
Jack (Senior planner): Let John do it.
Kate (Senior planner): Is there any interest on the City Council to fund this sort of thing?

Director: Well, we're going to ask them for money . . .

Peter: And they're gonna give us a quarter of what we're going to ask for . . .

Director: Then we won't do it.

Jack: What kind of finance data would be appropriate for this?

Director: I don't know.

Jack: If we could interest people like Kano [another agency director], maybe we'd get a little support for this.

Director: That's an interesting idea. No, he's only interested in whether the numbers add up right . . .

What, then, do the staff do in this brief interaction? How do they reproduce social and political relationships? What forms of rationality do the staff exhibit? And, finally, so what?

These questions reflect the theoretical agenda of this chapter. We appropriate Habermas's account of the pragmatics of communicative action (Habermas, 1979) to examine how in practice the four pragmatic 'validity claims' Habermas discusses actually work. Developing accounts of John Austin and John Searle, Habermas suggests, roughly, that we can understand our actions by considering their practical-communicative dimensions. In particular, when we speak, for example, we typically make four practical claims on listeners simultaneously: (1) we refer to 'outer' states of affairs, which a listener may explore as truly or falsely existing; (2) we invoke contextual norms that legitimize the action we're undertaking, norms to which listeners may consent or alternatively challenge as inappropriate to the situation at hand; (3) we express 'inner' states of self, emotions and dispositions such as seriousness, anger, impatience or frustration, which a listener may trust or alternatively challenge as feigned or inauthentic; and (4) we represent the issues before us in a selective language, terminology or framework, which a listener may accept or challenge as possibly incomprehensible (Habermas, 1979; Forester, 1985, 1993). Listeners may challenge speakers or they may not, in a given setting, for no action is guaranteed. The point here is not to predict what listeners will do, but to understand how much is at stake when speakers speak and, more generally, whenever we act meaningfully, thus communicatively. Habermas's analysis of the dimensions of communicative action can help us empirically to explore just how complex, how contingent and how rich, social and political actions actually are.

Next, we can explore too what happens when these four pragmatic validity claims we've noted are in fact accepted, not challenged. As I have argued more politically, because much routine interaction enacts all four of these pragmatic claims simultaneously, such interaction (most of what we do!) reproduces four subtle yet power-full relations of social belief, consent, status and attention to problems (Forester, 1989, 1985). Because social and political interaction broadly have such a pragmatic communicative structure, this analysis can inform a far-reaching analysis of hegemony and discursive power (Giddens, 1984; Alvesson, 1987; Silverman, 1987; Davis, 1988; Mumby, 1988; Forester, 1989, 1993).

Let us return now to the meeting of our planners. What sort of pragmatic claims-making do they do? How can Habermas's attention to a claims-making structure of interaction help us? Once we have addressed those questions, we can turn to the issues of power and reproduction by asking what relations of belief, consent, trust and attention we see reproduced here.

What Do the Staff Do Here?

Notice that in the flow of the interaction at hand, whatever the role of communication may be, claims about 'what is true' are perhaps least important of all. In some frustration, Helena refers to 'everything we want', a list of information desired. The director responds by making a prediction – that Peter will accomplish the goal – which he and everyone else know to be patently false. The very untruth of his claim is central to its meaning and his action; taken literally, his words surely communicate nothing 'true'. The director's answer, 'Peter's gonna take care of that!' states a simple proposition, but it also enacts a far more complex performance. After all, everyone knows he's not trying to 'con' or lie to the assembled staff.

The same holds for Peter's response, 'Yeah, that's a minor detail.' This claim too is patently false, as everyone knows. 'Truth' is not the point of these communicative acts. Not conveying, describing or reporting facts here, the director and then Peter in turn are instead rebuilding their own working relationships – their moral order – in the face of a daunting and massive information-gathering problem. So, Peter will be in charge, even if the staff will never really get all the information they'd like.

And again, when Jack suggests that the summer intern, John, could do the job, his claim too is quite obviously untrue. But that, of course, is the point. Following up Peter's reference to 'a minor detail', Jack identifies the least experienced member of the staff, the new student intern, as a (hardly) potential solution to the problem, and in doing so he acknowledges ironically the immensity of the practical problem at hand.

Thus in the sequence of:

Director [facetiously]: Oh, Peter's gonna take care of that!
Peter (Asst director): Yeah, that's a minor detail . . ..
Jack (Senior planner): Let John do it.

the obvious untruth of what's said is far more important than the 'facts' of any state of affairs. Practical communicative action, obviously, involves far more than the communication of true information. Yet truth-claiming performances do matter. So Kate refers to a particular strategy of going to the City Council, and the staff predict the likely consequences of adopting that strategy. So too does Jack refer later to another strategy of involving another agency's director, Kano. The truth of the likely consequences of adopting these strategies – what's really likely to happen if the staff do one thing or another – does seem to matter. Knowing what's so and what isn't will help the staff gauge whose support they'll have, what they can, and what they can't, effectively do.

But the staff do much more than gauge and predict consequences of alternative strategies. They act politically and ethically, assigning responsibility, reproducing hierarchy, and conferring and challenging legitimacy too. Responding to Helena's call to action – essentially, 'Enough already! What're we going to do?' – the director says, in effect, 'Difficult projects are Peter's; difficulties like this are his responsibility.'

Peter's facetious response then suggests a subtle political point: since the task is so intractable, the data that the planners will ultimately get will largely be a function neither of community need nor of the merit of cases at hand, but rather of the administrative difficulties of gathering good data. Information is not free, Peter is saying, and the quality of the public planning and decision-making process will be affected as a result. In discharging our responsibilities, Peter suggests, the staff will have to, practically speaking – and ought to – 'settle for less' than the 'everything we want' that Helena has referred to.

When Jack suggests, 'Let John do it', he places John in a staff hierarchy as everyone's junior: for a job involving 'a minor detail', assign the least important, the most 'minor', member of the staff. John is new, relatively inexperienced and free of prior commitments. Identified as powerless and subordinate, John's difference from the rest of the staff defines them as much as it characterizes him: the other staff have prior commitments, ongoing obligations, and obviously higher status. No other member of the staff could have been as casually invoked to deal with 'minor details'.

The ensuing discussion of 'what ought to be done' is revealing too. Just as Helena intervened to set a new agenda for the staff by saying, in effect, 'Enough talk! What are we going to do?!', Kate then intervenes by bringing her colleagues back to strategic issues. Her question identifies the City Council as the authority to be approached first, and she legitimizes the council in that way. She tests staff support for the particular strategy of asking the City Council for its blessing. Yet as Peter predicts unhappy results, the staff explore the virtues of a second strategy: should they try to get support from Kano?

But the staff do more than evaluate, legitimize, and recommend strategies. For they reconstitute themselves, too, in part as a community of frustration, in part as a community of strategists. Helena asks in frustration, what now? The director passes the burden of responding to Peter. Peter satirizes the massive problem as a minor detail. Jack echoes Peter's sentiment. As the City Council's response is predicted to be inadequate, the director backs off, 'Then we won't do it', if we don't have the necessary support.

The staff frame the issue at hand in terms of task assignments, City Council's or another agency director's support, and issues of personality too ('No, he's only interested in whether the numbers add up right'). Surely this raises questions about other ways of addressing the issues: for example, addressing 'the merits' of gathering the needed information or organizing public, community support.

Consider too the three presumptive uses of 'we' in Helena's opening question, 'So now that we know everything that we want, how do we get it?' The first use presumes the recognition of shared knowledge: we the staff know something together. The second use presumes a set of collectively shared goals and desires, just what it is that we the staff want here. The third use, in 'how do we get it?' refers to shared activity: we're a community of actors. These uses of 'we' appear as the quite ordinary expressions, or presumptions – altogether unchallenged here – of staff solidarity in the face of the practical problems at hand.

In these ordinary ways the staff accomplish extraordinary work: evaluating strategies, building solidarity, reinforcing hierarchy, legitimizing courses of action, and adjusting their own expectations too. What we see here, then, is the many-layered practical significance of communicative action.

As actors speak together, they act together. To explore this ordinary world of action we must not just hear words, but listen to people. We must attend not only to what is said, but to what is being done in the saying – or in the gesture, or even in the silent refusal to speak. The same sentence, of course, can have multiple pragmatic meanings, as Habermas's delineation of the pragmatic 'validity claims' makes clear: each utterance can have significant referential, norm-invoking, feeling-expressing, and attention-framing aspects to it (Habermas, 1979). So, observing and probing a wide range of interactions, we can assess how communicative actors, in their actual performances of speaking, simultaneously make each of the four practical claims upon one another that we have referred to above. We can study the actual contingent production of claims that:

1 refer to states of affairs, so shaping the listener's beliefs;
2 invoke legitimate norms, so appealing to the listener's consent;
3 express the speaker's disposition, so appealing to the listener's trust; and
4 adopt a conventional way of representing issues, so framing the listener's attention in particular ways.

Accordingly, our twelve-sentence transcript could be explored as a series of four overlays, enabling us, then, to understand how, for example, a superficially factual claim ('Peter's gonna take care of that!') is at once untrue; responsibility-shifting; distance-creating; and problem-setting. As ordinary and natural listeners, of course, we are often able to interpret all four levels of such practical claims-making simultaneously.

Facing our transcript, then, we could ask after each utterance – if doing so were not so endless – a series of practical and ultimately political questions. First, what facts does the speaker refer to or seek to establish? Secondly, what norms of legitimacy does the speaker invoke? Thirdly, what inner dispositions does the speaker express? Fourthly, what categories are used by the speaker to frame attention to the issue at hand? In every communicative action, then, we might investigate issues of the control of information, the management of legitimation and consent, the presentation of self and the construction of trust, and the selective organizing or disorganizing of others' attention (for the analysis of professional practice, see Forester 1989).

Consider just two examples: the ways that we see the actors in our interaction, first, making practical claims to legitimacy, and so managing a moral order, and, secondly, making expressive claims, shaping both individual and collective senses of self.

Practical Claims to Legitimacy

Consider the claims to legitimacy made in just the first four lines:
L1: Helena argues, in effect, we're planners, so wanting data isn't

enough. We have to try to get that information so we can work with it. Shouldn't our wishes be tempered by what we can realistically do?

L2: The director passes the ball: Peter, as the Associate Director, will be in charge of this project; it'll be his responsibility to figure out what we should do.

L3: With his opening acknowledgement, 'Yeah', Peter says facetiously, in effect, 'I'm in total control', meaning, of course, that he is not. Further, with '*minor* detail' he implies that the data that will be available for planning purposes will be shaped by the *major* details of political-administrative considerations: the staff should appreciate the difficulties to be faced and so they should be prepared to accept a partial, limited, 'solution'.

L4: Jack, as we have noted, suggests that John, the student intern, is subject to assignment. In echoing Peter's reference to the 'minor detail', Jack further legitimizes Peter's and the director's professional judgements about the intractable character of the tasks at hand.

In four lines – four actions – we see, then, a call to action, the shifting of responsibility for that action, an argument about what the staff should settle for, and a supporting professional judgement. In the staff's ongoing work of making these claims we see a subtle and ordinary micropolitics of practical argumentation. Questions and claims regarding what ought to be done, and what norms, obligations, rules and judgements are to be respected, are continually at issue here, in the most ordinary moments of professional practice.

Consider now the expressive claims of selves in the same lines:

L1: Helena expresses a mixture of frustration and anticipation. She does not simply say, 'how do we get this information?' She begins, 'So . . .' to mark a turn, finally, in the conversation to an issue that she knows and feels needs attention: action. She also uses 'know everything that we want' and not 'know what we want' – again marking the close of the prior topic, emphasizing its completeness, and expressing some irritation perhaps that that earlier conversation has not yet addressed how the staff will get the data they need.

L2: The director defuses what could be a potential criticism of him – should he have addressed the feasibility question earlier? – by humorously claiming that Peter (his thus esteemed Associate Director) would take care of everything. In so doing, he acknowledges the point of Helena's question, expresses a confidence in Peter, and at the same time distances himself from the responsibility and desire to solve the problem. Even so he manages the staff – pointing to Peter, hoping Peter will have a strategy of response, and indeed shifting responsibility to Peter to come up with something. In one quick response, the director expresses distance, confidence, acknowledgement and respect for Helena, and scepticism about success too.

L3: Peter expresses both confidence and scepticism as well. His acknowledgement, 'Yeah', reconstitutes or maintains his status as Associate Director: of course I'll do it, whatever the task, that's who I am here. But of course he expresses his practical judgement too, by facetiously saying it's a 'minor detail' and meaning, of course, that it's a big deal! So he sympathizes with Helena and the director, acknowledges their concerns, shares them, and shows that he's the kind of person who's willing to take on projects and yet who's realistic and competent as a practical actor, too, one who shares the staff's concerns sympathetically while nevertheless being willing to laugh at their shared predicament. Notice that *both* the political difficulty, getting the desired information, and the substantive problem, lacking adequate data for public purposes, are internalized and then expressed in interpersonal humour, a building of solidarity among staff who face the same – collectively – exasperating conditions.

L4: Jack does not literally mean, 'Let John do it', even though that's exactly what he's said, for that would be absurd on the face of it: the problem is enormous and complex, and John has just arrived. Instead, Jack welcomes John to the staff, acknowledging that he is there to perform productive (but possible!) work in the coming months. Yet he also seconds the sense of the director and Peter: he shares – he claims – their sentiments about the scale and difficulty of the task at hand. So he expresses a level of quite moderated, tongue-in-cheek, hope (he's lowered expectations too), at the same time that he includes the new intern in the group while marking and defining as subordinate the intern's new status.

The line-by-line analysis illustrated here suggests the extraordinary richness of what the staff do with each quite ordinary utterance, with each action in speech. Of course, the virtues of such a method of close reading of social interaction also suggest its liabilities. How could we assess a two-hour meeting in this way, a meeting whose transcript would reveal many hundreds of pragmatic moves by the participants, each of which might be referred to later in potentially political and practical ways by other participants, 'Well, you said . . .'? This issue reflects in part the challenge of articulating mid-level analyses devoted to the structure and change of organizations – a level of research relatively more aggregate and 'macro' than that focusing on interaction, and a level quite a bit more 'micro' than that focusing on political-economic structures (Mumby, 1988; Forester, 1989). Yet the very plausibility of participants' later saying, 'Well, you did say . . .' suggests that participants in social interaction do routinely and quasi-naturally, ordinarily and tacitly, actually perform the intricate and detailed validity-claim analysis illustrated here. A critical ethnographic reading should do justice, of course, both to participants' interpretations and to the ongoing production of hegemonic relations, a topic to which we turn in a moment.

Notice here that the role of gender can be interpreted in quite different ways in this interaction. What are we to make of Helena's opening and Kate's suggestion that follows? At least two interpretations are possible. First, the actions of these two women appear authoritative, agenda-setting, effectively initiative-taking. The men in our excerpt seem to act satirically; the women can be interpreted as exerting leadership, referring to collective challenges and strategies. On this interpretation, neither Helena nor Kate are second-class citizens in this meeting or this staff. Yet another reading is possible too. Helena's intervention seems to be deflected and treated lightly by the director; Kate's suggestion is quickly superseded rather than discussed in any detail.

Which interpretation is correct? On the evidence before us, both might be right and actually far more compatible than they might first appear. It may well be that the staff is hierarchical, that Helena and Kate have neither the power nor the status of the director or associate director, and that they are able nevertheless to exert leadership, bringing the staff and their 'superiors' back to the pressing tasks at hand. To pursue the issue, we need more evidence of the interactions of the staff. We might then well be able to judge whether Kate's suggestions are deflected more than Jack's, whether Helena's participation is slighted or fully respected, and so on.

Now we could go beyond the first four lines of this one simple fragment to assess further norm-invoking and expressive claims, and we could, as well, probe the referential and attention-framing character of each utterance, each practical move in this meeting excerpt. But instead let us turn to consider how these same actions sustain and remake the very institutional setting in which the staff work.

What Social and Political Relations Do the Staff Reproduce?

The staff not only act with purposes, seeking ends, but they also reproduce the social and political order in which they work – learning about it, shaping it and changing it as they go. Habermas suggests that broad processes of social rationalization can actually be distinguished as learning processes in two dimensions, roughly instrumental and moral, which have systematic connections to the double structure of speech, to claims-making involving 'truth claims' on the one hand and 'legitimacy' and expressive claims on the other

(1979: 142, 1984). How do the staff in our meeting learn in such ways?

How, we can ask, do communicative interactions maintain or alter social structures – patterns of social action in which investments are made, identities are recognized, normative sanctions (e.g. regulations) are established, and beliefs and world-views are formed? To address this question, we must examine our transcript by focusing on the actors not as speakers, but as listeners. What, we should now ask, is being established, being contingently reordered, reproduced, as the staff talk and listen – as they act together? Consider, then, how the staff reproduce patterns of belief, consent, status and identity, and perceptions of 'the problem' at hand.

Patterns of Belief

How do the staff construct and reconstruct patterns of belief about the world? Helena makes the point that the issues of feasibility have to be faced: she has set out the topic, and as the following responses make clear, the staff recognize her problem as a serious one, one they share. The problem really is tough, the staff learn as they consider it together. Not only does Helena have the question, but the director, Peter and Jack confirm the level of difficulty here. The desired information is not to be had. The information obtained will be a function of politics, not need, of funding levels, staff time, negotiations perhaps, but not 'the merits' – they now come jointly to believe.

The exchange about who's to fulfil the task establishes another common belief: getting the data will be quite difficult; the staff won't be able actually to get what they need. The subsequent two exchanges, one about approaching the City Council and one about approaching Kano, develop strategic beliefs as the staff explore possible lines of action and practice. The City Council will be approached, but they're not likely to be helpful. So other strategies are necessary. What about Kano? An interesting idea, but perhaps not a good one. As these beliefs are developed, so the staff explore the world together and learn, factually speaking, about their common possibilities.

Patterns of Legitimacy: The Management of Consent

The opening exchange, before the City Council comes into the picture, also establishes the legitimacy of a quite modest, if not necessarily conservative, norm of action, a norm of politically bounded rationality. The staff construct their common problem to be concretely practical, context-bound and limited. They have no illusions about acquiring perfect information. Instead, they prepare themselves not only to settle for less, to desire less, but to accept, condone, legitimize and judge as proper, obtaining far less information than they would like, and far less, too, than their professional knowledge suggests would be good and proper to have.

These planners acknowledge conflicting norms. Thus they propose as legitimate – and mutually consent to – what they take to be a reasonable and balanced way of proceeding. The city's problems – seen abstractly – warrant and deserve more information than the staff will be able to get, but the obligations of practical action, acting in a timely manner with limited resources, justify settling for less.

The staff's attention to an evolving political order, one they are actively seeking to fashion themselves, does not stop here. They legitimize the City Council as the authority of first resort, and then they quickly undercut its legitimacy ('Well, we're going to ask them . . .'; 'And they're gonna give us a quarter of what we're going to ask for . . .'). Similarly, the staff legitimize a secondary strategy of possibly forming a coalition with agency director Kano. In so doing, these planners reconstruct their collective sense of political order – what authority is to be respected and what courses of action are appropriate or not.

So two problems arise: lacking likely council support, what should be done? The director knows as much about the City Council as Peter does. Sharing Peter's scepticism about their support, he nevertheless authorizes the move to go to the Council ('we're going to ask them') – for perhaps they will learn about the issue and the planning needs of the city. This much surely is to be expected of the planning staff, it seems, for they are, after all, on the public payroll.

Yet the staff also consider as legitimate the strategy of coalition-building with Kano – and so they explore another political game too: the more support for the data-collection project they can organize from other agencies, the greater the pressure (if not the moral claim) upon the City Council for support. Surely it is acceptable to join forces with Kano, should Kano's agency too need some of the information being pursued. This deceptively simple logic enables the planners to defend as politically legitimate a strategy of bureaucratic organizing to shape the very sentiments and responses of the City Council. So a political norm legitimizing the staff's turn to the City Council is first respected and then contested, resisted with the appeal to an additional norm which authorizes coalition-building with yet another agency responsive to a public constituency.

The director also protects the planning staff – claiming authoritatively that the staff will not take on work if they are not adequately funded. He authorizes basic norms of the staff meeting too. When he says, 'That's an interesting idea' he not only expresses his interest, he also authorizes and affirms the place of staff suggestions, ideas and proposals. In so doing, he characterizes his disposition, his willingness to listen, and so he recreates his working self, his reputation, the kind of person he can be taken to be – as we discuss in the following section (Gusfield, 1989; Frug, 1988; White, 1985).

Patterns of Status and Identity
As the staff joke about what to do, they also reproduce their own social order: the hierarchy of the director's and Peter's authority, Jack's seniority, and John's subordinate status. They also assess and project the practical identities of both the City Council and Kano, the agency director. The staff wonder, in effect, 'What can we expect of them? Who do we really have here, with whom we can work?' They suppose that the Council will not care sufficiently to support their work, and Kano may only be 'interested in whether the numbers add up right', not presumably in the broader public need for the information that the planners want.

The staff refashion themselves, as well, for they moderate their own desires. Beginning with 'everything we want', the discussion takes a sober turn: expectations of administrative difficulties being what they truly are, desire is to be moderated, what the staff 'really want' must be cut back. So the staff formulate their own expectations and commitments, what they will want, and thus they shape, in part, who – in some practical measure – they will be.

Notice, too, that although the director speaks often, each time that he does he responds to a staff member's initiative: he does not propose new lines of action. His judgements appear to have authority, but he presents himself – practically constructs himself – as a manager, not as a commander. From twelve sentences, of course, we can hardly 'type' the director, but notice that even from this conversational fragment we might be led to 'see him as' more managerial than authoritarian, more cautious than bold. The point of course is not whether *these* inferences are correct, but that our imputations of another's identity, 'who they are', are likely to derive in large part from our observation of what they do, act by act – rather than from, for example, their official titles, their self-descriptions, or even others' descriptions of them. Learning about others, we observe not just their pursuit of instrumental ends, but their display of virtue and character, their ongoing construction of self. So too more generally, as staff members must articulate their judgements in diverse settings will they appear competent or not in front of the City Council, pushy or not with Kano and other officials, sensitive or insensitive to community groups and popular leaders, and so on.

Patterns of Attention to Problem Formulation

Consider finally how the staff attend to the problem before them in three distinct ways. First, they discuss who's to be responsible: how the job is to be done in terms of formal staff assignments. The obvious limits of that discussion lead to a second focus: financial support – for more staff – from the elected body, the City Council. The limits of that strategy, in turn, lead to a focus on bureaucratic politics, the strategy of 'coalition-building with Kano'.

This all seems plain and obvious enough, but what's unsaid suggests the political framing of what seems otherwise all too plain. Notice that the staff have not posed the issue in terms of political goals, political needs, constituency organizations, powerful leaders, historically abiding problems, obligations owed by the City Council to campaign promises, and so on. Inevitably, any problem formulation will shape attention selectively and thus too neglect, in principle, an infinite number of alternative ways of posing the same 'problem'. The point is not just *that* such selective problem-framing occurs, but that our research and practice should be sensitive to *how*, culturally and politically, such selectivity operates.

The staff focus attention on bureaucratic rather than constituency politics, a concern for personality rather than group or class, a concern with available resources rather than with a network of social relationships which might be brought into play (Gusfield, 1981). Their focus on bureaucratic politics, resources and individual actors is rooted no doubt in experience and training; it reflects, in part, the resources they bring to the situation. We say that people with hammers look for nails; people with pens and pencils look for paper. So perhaps we should not be surprised that actors in a city agency respond as this staff does in our example. But that background, that training, that representational and rhetorical capacity to frame attention selectively matters, for the staff are creating a future – their own in part – for others. These representational capacities were suggested in Habermas's earlier (e.g. 1979) account of ordinary speakers' pragmatic claims to 'comprehensibility', an account curiously missing from his *Theory of Communicative Action* (Habermas, 1984, 1987). With such pragmatic claims, nevertheless, we orient ourselves and our listeners in particular ways, shaping the ways we attend to issues at hand (Edelman, 1988).

The staff here, then, not only act in complex ways, saying one thing and meaning another, interweaving practical arguments about strategies with expressions of distance, deference and respect. For they also re-elaborate and reproduce their own social organization as they shape patterns of belief, consent, identity and problem formulation. In so doing, the staff reproduce relations of power too.

Consider briefly, now, what sort of practical rationality the staff enact in this conversation.

Practical and Politically Bounded Rationality

The staff have no access to full information. So we can neither understand their action as focused on any optimization nor can we blame them for failing to be 'rational' economic men and women. Acknowledging the constrained nature of their actions, we should expect to find them practising a 'bounded rationality', but we know too little about the forms such rationality can take in political contexts like City Hall.

In the face of necessarily limited information-processing abilities, Herbert Simon argued long ago, skilled actors do and ought to lower their aspirations – to 'satisfice' rather than optimize. But Simon's account was concerned neither with the role social structures may play in a given case to bound rationality, nor with those bounds which might be otherwise, bounds that are 'unnecessary', alterable and contingent, not arguably part of being human. These distinctions – identifying bounds that are structural or not, necessary or not – suggest that appropriate practical actions will vary with the particular nature of the boundedness in the action situation at hand (Forester, 1989: 27–64).

In the light of these distinctions, the transcript suggests that the staff respond to a variety of constraints and match their strategies and actions accordingly. They do, as Simon says, lower aspirations. But they do more too. Facing a bureaucratically differentiated world, they look to Kano for support in a possible coalition. Facing a shifting political constellation of interests and support, they consider a negotiating position with the City Council: getting a quarter of what we need will not do, so we must strengthen our hand. Even in this fragment of the meeting, the staff show us a bounded rationality that is more politically sophisticated than a more conventionally social-psychological model of 'satisficing' might lead us to expect.

What's Distinctive about such Fieldwork in a Habermasian Way?

We have read our twelve-sentence transcript as a fragment of an ongoing flow of interaction. Our interpretation raises many more problems than it answers, but it is still instructive. By attending to the character of communicative action, we can explore a four-layered practical structure of social and political interactions shaping (more or less true) beliefs, (more or less appropriate) consent, (more or less deserved) trust, and (more or less aptly focused) attention. In so doing, we can identify subtle, yet powerfully pragmatic, moves of social actors who both seek ends instrumentally *and* yet continually reproduce social and political relations too. We can utilize but move beyond a strictly phenomenological analysis. We can move beyond a phenomenology of political frustration, and perhaps the political frustration of phenomenology too, to an analysis of discursive or communicative power – legitimation, the construction of selves, the framing of attention, and the resulting social and political reproduction of the social organization at hand – in its relationships to encompassing political structures of (in our case) the state (Deetz and Kersten, 1983; Alvesson, 1987; Mumby, 1988).

Doing fieldwork in a Habermasian way enables us to explore the continuing performance and practical accomplishment of relations of power. By refining Habermas's attention to a 'double structure of speech', we come to examine specifically the micropolitics of speech and interaction (Habermas, 1979). Quite contrary to prevailing misinterpretations of Habermas, we come not to expect any idealized truth-telling; instead we look closely at the ways in which appeals to truth (and quite differently, truthfulness) serve varied and significantly contingent, variable ends (Forester, 1985, 1991). We presume neither that truth always serves the powerful nor that truth necessarily shall set anyone free; instead we look at concrete communicative practices to see what differences they can and do make. Similarly, too, for the contingencies of consent, claims to legitimacy and cultural conventions, and the contingencies of trust and forms of attention.

We are given absolutely no *a priori* guarantees that anything approximating ideal discourse takes place empirically (Forester, 1991). Quite the contrary; fieldwork done in a Habermasian way leads us to look carefully and closely at the complex and largely uninvestigated ways that normative claims are actually made in practice – to shape obligation, senses of membership and self, consent and deference, patterns of future action. In such ways, a Habermasian fieldwork tells us and helps us to 'look and see', neither to assume determinate structures *a priori* nor to expect any idealized discourse, but rather to shift from abstract discussions of truth and power, discourse and Other, to assess actual flows of action that reshape our beliefs, consent, trust, and even more subtle frameworks of attention.

In so doing, a strategy of Habermasian fieldwork is immediately practical, making us more attentive listeners as we come to realize, walking into meetings, that we will soon witness and perhaps take part in the reconstruction of political, perhaps professional, relationships in complex and multi-levelled ways. We learn quickly that we are not only listeners but speakers too, not only observers and readers or writers of texts but actors as well. So we can appreciate the ways we must learn not only about interests but about character, not only about utilities but about identities, as these are expressed and articulated in everyday practice.

This chapter's analysis can only be illustrative and suggestive: illustrating an empirical appropriation of Habermas's theory of communicative action and suggesting dimensions of power to assess more closely. To explore further the fruits of doing fieldwork in a Habermasian way we must assess 'larger' streams of interaction located in their contingently structural contexts, and of course, we must compare our reading to other accounts (Van Maanen, 1988). Yet here, our analysis reveals the play of power and action, convention and performance, in flows of conversation – with multiple voices presenting and contesting facts, norms, selves, and representational styles too.

But does this analysis threaten to lose us in a multiplicity of voices, distracting us from power and the possibilities of emancipatory response? Quite the contrary, for we can now examine intimately four interwoven threads of action and meaning, power and resistance, rationality and politics as they are played out in concrete cases. No longer mistaking a Habermasian fieldwork to presume ideal conditions, we are freed to investigate the actual communicative practices shaping relationships of ever-contingent belief, consent, trust and attention (Forester, 1989, 1993).

Habermas's theory of communicative action has far too often been understood as predominantly – and typically, as necessarily – metatheoretical, having little to do with empirical cases and having less to say about what we might explore in such cases. Yet this reading – sketchy and preliminary as it is – suggests that if we seek an empirically grounded, phenomenologically sensitive and politically critical sociology, appropriating and building upon Habermas's theory of communicative action, then the rumours of the emptiness of this line of analysis are quite exaggerated. There's a good deal here to explore.

Note

Earlier versions of this chapter were presented at Cornell's College of Human Ecology and the University of Iowa's Project on the Rhetoric of Inquiry. Thanks for critical comments are due to Jennifer Greene, Paul Dillon, Ralph Cintron, Rich Horowitz, Mats Alvesson and John Jermier, none of whom is responsible for the flaws of the present account.

References

Alvesson, Mats (1987) *Organization Theory and Technocratic Consciousness*. Berlin/ New York: de Gruyter.

Clifford, James and Marcus, George (eds) (1986) *Writing Culture: The Poetics and Politics of Ethnography*. Berkeley: University of California Press.

Davis, Kathy (1988) *Power Under the Microscope*. Foris.

Deetz, Stan and Kersten, Astrid (1983) 'Critical models of interpretive research', in L. Putnam and M. Pacanowsky (eds), *Communication and Organizations*. Beverly Hills, CA: Sage.

Edelman, Murray (1988) *Constructing the Political Spectacle*. Chicago: University of Chicago Press.

Forester, John (ed.) (1985) *Critical Theory and Public Life*. Cambridge, MA: MIT Press.

Forester, John (1989) *Planning in the Face of Power*. Berkeley: University of California Press.

Forester, John (1991) 'Reply to reviewers of *Planning in the Face of Power*'. *International Planning Theory Newsletter*, Dipartimento Interateneo Territorio, viale Mattioli 39, 10125 Turin, Spring.

Forester, John (1993) *Critical Theory, Public Policy and Planning Practice*. Albany: State University of New York Press.

Foucault, Michel (1980) *Power/Knowledge*, ed. Colin Gordon. New York: Pantheon.

Frug, Jerry (1988) 'Argument as character', *Stanford Law Review*, 40(4) (April).

Giddens, Anthony (1984) *The Constitution of Society*. Berkeley: University of California Press.

Gusfield, Joseph (1981) *The Culture of Public Problems*. Chicago: University of Chicago Press.

Gusfield, Joseph (ed.) (1989) *Kenneth Burke: On Symbols and Society*. Chicago: University of Chicago Press.

Habermas, Jürgen (1979) 'What is universal pragmatics?' in *Communication and the Evolution of Society*. Boston: Beacon Press.

Habermas, Jürgen (1984) *The Theory of Communicative Action, Vol. I: Reason and the Rationalization of Society*, trans. T. McCarthy. Boston: Beacon Press.

Habermas, Jürgen (1987) *The Theory of Communicative Action, Vol. II: Lifeworld and System*, trans. T. McCarthy. Boston: Beacon Press.

Heritage, John (1984) *Garfinkel and Ethnomethodology*. Cambridge: Polity Press.

Knorr-Cetina, Karin (1981) 'Introduction: the micro-sociological challenge of macro-sociology: towards a reconstruction of social theory and methodology', in Karin Knorr-Cetina and Aaron Cicourel (eds), *Advances in Social Theory and Methodology*. London: Routledge & Kegan Paul.

Lukes, Steven (1974) *Power: A Radical View*. New York: Macmillan.

March, James and Olsen, Johan (1976) *Ambiguity and Choice in Organizations*. Oslo: Universitetsforlaget.

Marcus, George (1986) 'Contemporary problems of ethnography in the modern world system', in James Clifford and George Marcus (eds), *Writing Culture*. Berkeley: University of California Press. pp. 165–93.

Marcus, George E. and Fischer, Michael M. J. (1986) *Anthropology as Cultural Critique*. Chicago: University of Chicago Press.

Mumby, Dennis K. (1988) *Communication and Power in Organizations: Discourse, Ideology, and Domination*. Norwood, NJ: Ablex.

Silverman, David (1987) *Communication and Medical Practice*. Beverly Hills, CA: Sage.

Stacey, Judith (1988) 'Can there be a feminist ethnography?', *Women's Studies International Forum*, 11 (1): 21–7.

Van Maanen, John (1988) *Tales of the Field: On Writing Ethnography*. Chicago: University of Chicago Press.

White, James Boyd (1985) 'Rhetoric and law: the arts of cultural and communal life', in *Heracle's Bow: Essays on the Rhetoric and Poetics of the Law*. Madison: University of Wisconsin Press.

Willis, Paul (1977) *Learning to Labor*. Aldershot: Avebury, and New York: Columbia University Press.

4

The Organization of Pleasure

Gibson Burrell

'after death the heart assumes the shape of a pyramid'

(Barnes, 1989: 237)

From the physiological observation of the mammalian cardiac muscle once it ceases to beat one can take much insight. The classic organizational shape insinuates itself into the place where once a heart moved in its regular but dynamic rhythm. Organizational structures in their typical bureaucratic form adopt the morphology of that dead tissue which for centuries has been assumed to be the seat of life, emotion and love (Romanyshyn, 1982). Only when the heart has lost its capacity for life and love does the pyramid coagulate into existence. Only when life and love are finally extinguished does the hierarchy solidify into its defining state.

This chapter takes the tension between the emotions, the body and its key symbolic component, the heart, and the typical bureaucratic organization, its structure and its pyramidal shape as a deeply serious one. The corporeality of human beings within organizations has for far too long been ignored. What I intend to do is attempt to surface the bodily, the visceral, the carnal into full view and to suggest that a Critical Theory of organizations needs to embrace such issues much more fully than hitherto. Human emotions as well as the conscious must press their place on the agenda of Critical Theory. And nowhere is this more important than on the issue of pleasure.

Three Faces of Pleasure

'Pleasure' is on the agenda for both Critical Theory and management theory in the 1990s. The slow rise of postmodernism, seen by some as the cultural logic of late capitalism (Jameson, 1984), has brought joy and playfulness in many forms into focus as terms over which there is much contestation. Pleasure (and some kindred notions such as desire, love, *jouissance* and play) offers three faces: one to those charged with the management of large organizations where 'it' is seen as a reservoir of potential energy to be channelled, shaped and directed in the service of corporate goals (Orwell, 1949; Peters and

Waterman, 1982: 84). The second face is one of escape from reality and the acquisition of 'joyous serenity' (Boss, 1979). The third face is that reflected in the tradition of political liberation (Reich, 1942; Marcuse, 1962) where the pleasure principle rather than the reality principle is placed in the foreground. Here, pleasure is seen to be decidedly dangerous, threatening existing powers and the social order should it be given free rein. In the recent French bicentenary celebrations, the work of the Marquis de Sade featured prominently. Some sought to end the long process of diabolization to which his name had been subjected by proclaiming him as the 'true' revolutionary of that period because of his relentless pursuit of pleasure in its polymorphous forms. Precisely because he was deemed to be dangerous his besmirchment had been almost complete.

These three faces of pleasure *all* see the body as the site of sensation, emotion and love – even ecstasy. Where they differ, however, is in the use to which bodily feelings should be put, how 'pleasure' is perceived by others, how pleasure is perceived by the pleasure-seeker and what discourses of power create the conceptualization itself. In other words, 'pleasure and the body' become the site of much contestation between competing perspectives. Whilst there is agreement that the physical form of human life is a key element upon which to play within contemporary discourse, there is next to no agreement upon its significance, whether in theoretical or political terms. The politics of the body, as Foucault (1979) outlined, is rather important politics and cannot be peripheralized any longer by labelling those who discuss it as biological determinists or as followers of 'Parisian fashion'. Clearly, there is a strong element in French culture which elevates the human body to a very high level of importance whether in how it is dressed or how it is perfumed or how it is filmed or represented on canvas. French society is not alone in such preoccupations nor should we allow the crude stereotype to stand unchallenged (Jay, 1984) but it is clear that in the United Kingdom discussions of the body's role in social science are relatively underdeveloped.

As we shall see, pleasure has many meanings but so too has the body. The concrete physicality of our enfleshed skeleton may appear to allow us to divorce the body in its raw materiality from our understanding of culture but this would be a mistake. Romanyshyn talks of a medieval world in which paintings and sculptures represented pantomimic bodies, 'bodies whose gestures are inseparable from the emotional situation and the story they enact' (1989: 108). According to him, today we have changed the body to an anatomical one which we now see as more 'real', more technically correct than those bodies portrayed on medieval walls. These earlier 'gestural' bodies appear to us surreal or subjective compared to our modern objective understandings. But we have lost our tolerance for ambiguity and now disrespect differences. Nevertheless, we have invented, then reinvented the body, century after century. Rifkin argues that 'What Darwin discovered was not so much the truths of Nature as the operating assumptions of the industrial order' (J. Rifkin 1984, quoted in Romanyshyn, 1989: 110) Thus, 'we invent the body and the nature that we need' (1989: 111).

If this is correct, what kind of body and what kind of pleasure is required, encouraged, enthused and enshaped by the industrial order of the 1990s? Such evidence as there is points in the direction of the first face of pleasure.

The First Face of Pleasure

We shall begin, then, with the first face of pleasure, looking at it as a resource to be rendered up to chief executives for organizational use, allowing the powerful forces locked with 'joy' to be utilized in the interests of the enterprise.

The rise of 'management' from the aristocratic kitchen and stable (Mant, 1982) into the corridors of power has allowed some to talk of managers as if they were heroic figures. In the United Kingdom, for example, the growth in management education, the Thatcherite emphasis on the enterprise culture, the variety of reports calling for improved training for managers given their presumed importance to the economy, and the huge number of biographical and autobiographic accounts of 'successful' corporate executives (e.g. Harvey-Jones, 1988; Iacocca, 1985) has produced a climate in which managers have high status – supposedly.

There are the first signs, however, that this façade is crumbling. At a symbolic level, many senior executives refuse to have themselves called 'managers'. A semantic inflation has set in, in which 'manager' gives way to 'director' or those learning management disciplines claim to be Masters, not of management, but 'business administration'. The current trend towards 'delayering' large British organizations, where a 'liposuction' of middle management tiers takes place, threatens morale and encourages political resistance within the ranks of middle managers. Those who have already lived through such programmes speak of being in 'mourning' for their now absent colleagues. For many years, it has been suspected that blue-collar workers are unhappy with their employment situation and that large numbers enjoy their place of work despite the tasks they perform. The evidence is that these trends are now very visible in managerial groups (Reed, 1989). Scase and Goffee in *Reluctant Managers* (1989) studied 374 managers (including 51 women) in six large United Kingdom organizations. Most were unwilling to commit themselves psychologically to their employing companies. They deliberately limited their corporate attachment to protect themselves from 'failure', redundancy and redeployment. They expressed feelings of being undervalued, underutilized and overworked. In short, they were reluctant to give themselves wholly to the organization. And as most senior executives know, compliance and conformity are not enough. What is needed, more than anything else, is managerial and subordinate creativity.

Management consultants have realized in the last few years that the liberation of creativity requires the unlocking of pleasure. The leading exponents of Heathrow Organization Theory are articulate and highly professional in revealing a new key to this treasure house. In the 'shows' that Tom Peters performs, he usually asks the following kind of rhetorical question of chief executive officers (CEOs): 'How is it that your staff are the most enthusiastic, committed and energetic people – except for the 8 hours a day they work for you?' Here Peters (1987, 1990) reinforces the upper-managerial desire to channel and retain enthusiasm, skill and adrenalin within the workplace. Indeed, his shows employ techniques used by religious preachers, which deliberately generate commitment and release energy within the audience. In essence their key currency is adrenalin, which is thought to be a powerful supplier of pleasure.

Even today, chemical influences on the function between synapse and neuro-muscular activity in humans are not fully understood. The exciting effects of acetylcholine are well understood, but LSD's mimicking of naturally occurring chemicals is not as yet; however, the *biochemistry* of management is a topic which one rarely sees addressed. Of course it is not entirely new, for in Huxley's *Brave New World* (1955) the role of soma in suppressing activity is obviously a key one. Today, the pharmaceutical companies are still selling bromide to the Home Office for use in HM prisons for the reduction of sexual appetite in all inmates. Male sex offenders volunteering for 'chemical castration' welcome treatment with goserelin (Zoladex) when drugs previously used on sex offenders, such as Depo-Provera and Androcur, failed to work. US aircraft manufacturers are exploring brain-stem implants for fighter pilots to monitor their stress levels so that avionic computers can take over if biochemical signals suggest the low-flying pilot is likely to make wrong decisions. Given the role of avionic companies in developing CAD/CAM systems, how long will it be before the human-computer cyborg is at work on the production line? Pharmaceutical researchers are attempting to identify the single hormone which usually floods a pregnant woman's body just before parturition and creates that burst of energy sometimes called 'nest-building'. How long will it be before this is isolated and is sold to multinational manufacturers of goods for use throughout the organization? Successful MBA teachers stalk the aisles of large lecture theatres intimidating and cajoling students so that the gladiatorial atmosphere is physically tangible to the olfactory system of those who enter later. And when the smell of fear is at its highest so too is the student feedback.

The use of externally created substances to manipulate employee biochemistry is, of course, often frowned upon. Moderate use of tobacco and alcohol is tolerated but when this becomes 'chain-smoking' or 'heavy drinking' it is deemed to be a sign of adverse reaction to stress and therefore in need of disciplining. What is perceived to be the decline in worker and managerial motivation which comes from drug abuse is often met with dismissal. Thus, adrenalin is the most favoured form of drug for use by corporate employees – or is it? More important than adrenalin even, is libido – the visceral sexual energy which is a key part of human existence.

In *Nineteen Eighty-four*, Orwell recognized a fundamental tension between organized life and pleasure.

> With Julia, everything came back to her own sexuality. As soon as this was touched upon in any way she was capable of great acuteness. Unlike Winston, she had grasped the inner meaning of the Party's sexual puritanism. It was not merely that the sex instinct created a world of its own which was outside the Party's control and which therefore had to be destroyed if possible. What was more important was that sexual privation induced hysteria, which was desirable because it could be transformed into war-fever and leader-worship. The way she put it was:
> 'When you make love you're using up energy; and afterwards you feel happy and don't give a damn for anything. They can't bear you to feel like that. They want you to be bursting with energy all the time. All this marching up and down and cheering and waving flags is simply sex gone sour.' (Orwell, 1954: 118)

As I have attempted to argue elsewhere (Burrell, 1984), it is possible to dare to believe – even in these postmodern times – that a gradual process of desexualization has occurred within many organizational forms in the West over a long historical period (Hearn and Parkin, 1986). Whether one turns to monasteries, prisons, factories, the ship at sea or the commercial organization, there is evidence to suggest a managerial effort to repress sexual relations and expel them from the organization into the 'home'. The rationale for such an expulsion has differed over the centuries, sometimes taking the form of medically sound advice to employers based on a theory of equilibrium of bodily fluids, sometimes being based on religious notions, sometimes on the social mores associated with the civilizing process (Elias, 1983) and the suppression of violence (Freud, 1984) and sometimes on the need for better discipline as expressed in dressage, panopticism and normalization (Foucault, 1977).

Whatever the rationale, the expulsion and repression of sexuality have been key management goals. Nowhere is this rejection of tenderness more evident than in Weber's work on the development of rational bureaucracy. Roslyn Bologh in *Love or Greatness* (1990) attempts to provide a fresh reading and critique of the work of Max Weber. Her title self-consciously parallels Marcuse's book *Eros and Civilisation* (1962) and she seeks to maintain that 'For Weber love and greatness were incompatible' (Bologh, 1990: 291). His voice, she maintains, was masculine, masculinist and patriarchical. Weber disparaged mere happiness and well-being for they are associated with contented passivity. Greatness, on the other hand, is the responsibility of the heroic figure and is all about 'discontented activity'. It is from this bias towards action and the renunciation of the desire for happiness and contentment that dynamism and development spring forth. The charismatic breakout to greatness will be led by someone who has turned his or her back on love and embraced, instead, greatness. Weber's own biography is testament to this rejection of erotic love and sociability. It is almost as if he wishes us to *celebrate the celibate*.

But the separation of love from greatness, eros from civilization, the pleasure principle from the reality principle are not simply theoretical notions. They have affected, now affect and will continue to affect organizational members in their day-to-day lives. That employers and the state have recognized the tension between bureaucratic organization on one hand and sexuality on the other for millenia is amply testified in Hassard and Porter's paper, 'Cutting down the workforce' (1990), in which the role of the castrati in many oriental bureaucracies is discussed. In the fact-based movie, *The Last Emperor* (1987), one sees the Palatial male administrators being allowed to be buried with their hacked-off organs, which had been carefully stored and labelled for such an eventuality. Clearly then, in all rationality there is more than a hint of deprivation.

I do not claim, of course, that the de-eroticization of the workplace has succeeded. Even in the case of the eunuch, libido has not been totally transmogrified into work of a productive kind. In a thought-provoking passage, Gonzalez-Crussi tells us

> The cruel practice of creating Eunuchs showed them [the Chinese] that the resolute make do with less than the apportionment of nature. They entrusted the custody of the emperors' harems to those unfortunates whom they made men 'minus the peccant part,' as the orientalist Richard

Burton says referring to the equivalent metier among the Arabs. But despite the atrocious mutilations, seductions went on. The seducer availed himself of whatever remnant the ferocity of his captors had spared; if none, technical ingenuity took the place of the missing wherewithal. (Gonzalez-Crussi, 1989: 129)

Thus there never has been achievement of a total desexualization in an organizational context but considerable efforts have been made in that direction, including the encouragement of linguistic conventions within the populace.

Everyday language, for example, recognizes the widespread assumption that sexual satisfaction is inimical to good, effective administration in phrases which describe system failure and inefficiency such as 'it's buggered', 'what a cock-up', 'it's fucked' and so on. Unfortunately, our own disciplines reflect this expulsion of the erotic from the organization. Sexuality is to be discussed in private, not on the pages of journals; it is to be enjoyed in the bedroom (a euphemism, of course) and certainly not in our offices. Even in the security of the home and in our leisure activities, however, the organizing forces of bureaucratic society are increasingly visible (Elias, 1978, 1983).

As Cohen and Taylor (1973) and Rojek (1985) argue, there are forces at work which mean that the bureaucratization of leisure is developing apace. G. Blitz, the person who developed Club Méditerranée in the early 1950s, saw these camps as primitivist, communal centres for pleasure and recreation, where the money economy was suppressed for as long as you were within the confines of the club. By 1990, the clubs had become commercialized, disciplined, modernized and heavily dependent upon monetary exchange. The regimentation of leisure (as superficially evidenced by pop mobility) brings with it pacification, commercialization and de-eroticization. The release of dopamine that supposedly accompanies hard physical exercise such as long-distance running is reputed to create pleasurable feelings within the body but this excitation has also led to an intense commercialization of road running and its related equipment. Individual and interpersonal enjoyment have become the target for commodification – a process made much easier once pleasure has been expelled from the workplace.

Thus, after centuries of desexualization, modern organizations have expelled to a major, though not complete, extent, the erotic, the libidinous, the pleasurable from within their confines. With modernity came surveillance, bureaucratization and desexualization (Dandeker, 1990). With postmodernity, Adorno's earlier demonstration of how the original use value of goods is lost in the rise of exchange value, allowing the original to take up an ersatz or secondary use value, is even more powerful. Romance, exotica, desire, beauty, fulfilment can thus be attached to the mundanities of motor cars or Mars bars. Pleasure under postmodernism is not only used to sell commodities; more importantly 'it' becomes a commodity (Featherstone, 1990). Management consultants such as Peters and Kanter have recognized the powerful forces locked within pleasure and seek to render them up to chief executives for organizational use – but they may be following earlier examples.

Calas and Smircich (1991) have written an insightful deconstruction of four management texts, each of which celebrates leadership. These are by Barnard, McGregor, Mintzberg, and Peters and Waterman. Calas and Smircich entitle the article 'Voicing seduction to silence leadership' and seek to silence the monotonous babble of leadership talk with its all too obvious attempt to seduce people to commit themselves to the organization. Following the French feminist, Luce Irigaray (1985), they juxtapose an interpretation of what is said to the words themselves. For example, they attempt to 're-mark' the seductiveness of Mintzberg's ten managerial roles. They focus on the words 'head', 'sound', 'infuse', 'neglect', 'relationship', 'physical', 'charismatic', 'vested', 'permeate', 'encourage', 'capacity', 'inhibit', 'anxious', 'probe', 'meddle', 'integration', 'potent(ial)', 'weld', 'liaison' and 'horizontal'. By displacing the text the rearticulation reveals a 'true confession' of the close links between seduction and leadership – and, incidentally, the hidden role of the body in organizational discourse.

Of course, Calas and Smircich have been accused of 'obscene distortions' and of besmirching Mintzberg's innocence, but to my mind, the notion of the leader as a seducer is very revealing. Much of the literature on leadership *clearly* refers to the leader's ability 'to stir emotion' and 'elevate others', without necessarily re-marking such work in a more detailed way. And in similar prurient vein, it should be noted that in American argot the name 'Tom Peters' implies the 'double phallus' – which has a seductive potency some might unconsciously respond to.

The use of sexuality in selling commodities, of course, is a well-recognized phenomenon. Featherstone (1990) has recently argued that a legitimate focus on consumer culture would be one where it was possible to ask 'the question of the emotional pleasure of consumption, the dreams and desires which become celebrated in consumer cultural imagery and particular sites of consumption which variously generate direct bodily excitement and aesthetic pleasures' (Featherstone, 1990: 5). This question is not simply theoretical. There are examples drawn from current practice where this is all too obvious. One well-sketched exemplar may suffice.

one initiative associated with the HRM umbrella has been the introduction of customer care policies. One of our PhD students has studied the major supermarket chains' current fashion for 'training' check-out operators to smile at customers as part of such policies. (When I shop, someone smiles at me, therefore I am attractive/sexy.) The staff, although compliant, have not taken to it with much enthusiasm and the practice has not always been 'read' correctly by the customers – one woman attacked a check-out operator for 'flirting' with her husband; there have been numerous examples of obscene phone calls to operators. (Keenoy, 1990)

So there are dangers in seeking to use pleasure to control producers, customers and workers but the 'excellence' literature seems unaware of these problems. With *their* exemplars, drawn often from Silicon Valley in the early 1980s, the need is expressed for 'changemasters' (Kanter, 1983) not to suppress play but to utilize it for their own benefit. The point of production is seen as the legitimate place for such energy and adrenalin – otherwise it is wasted and change is not brought about.

It is here, fortunately, that we confront a second and very different tradition of pleasure and joy: one based on a radical, critical stance in which the bureaucratization of leisure, the commodification of pleasure and the canalization of libido are looked upon with deep suspicion – not, however, as targets for change but as hostile forces from which to escape. For example, Barthes wished to study the decomposition of bourgeois consciousness which he saw as leading to the bliss of *jouissance*. Whilst there is no direct translation in English the word means enjoyment, the rights of privilege, pleasure, sexual climax, delight and loss (Rojek, 1985: 146). It has a mystical flavour to it and it firmly implies merging with the world *as it is* rather than trying to change it. It is, in other words, 'contented passivity'. It is very unlike the notions of play and joyfulness which Kanter (1983) expresses in the *The Change Masters*, which, on the contrary, are expressions of 'discontented activity'.

The Second Face of Pleasure

Historically, there has been a strong tradition of contented passivity in which escape rather than challenge has been valued. D. M. Levin in *The Opening of Vision* (1988) concludes with a critique of ego-logical vision. With the development of the ego there comes an inevitable agitation of mind which structures the way in which we see the world in very rigid, narrow and restricted ways. Ego-logical vision is assertive and always tends to follow the straight line of 'desire'. It is necessary for human beings to survive but there is a parallel and alternative version of vision by the *seer*. The seer must first relax and lessen the grip of normal anxieties and tensions. Without the constant obsessive monitoring of the ego a more calm, restive and open vision is possible which allows the possibility of 'ecstasy'. This appears superficially similar to that notion of Husserl – epoché – where reality is bracketed in the interest of introspection. Marcuse said 'there are modes of existence which can never be true because they can never *rest* in the realization of their potentialities, in the *joy* of their being'. This is what the existential psychiatrist Boss has described as 'joyous serenity' and is the province of all who are 'seers' (Russell, 1967). He maintains that 'Because the composed, joyous serenity opens a human being to the broadest possible responsiveness, it constitutes happiness as well' (Boss, 1979: 112).

According to Levin (1988), Boss's description is very similar to that of Nietzsche in discussing Epicurus in *Joyful Wisdom* (1960) and to Heidegger's analysis of a vision marked by clear serenity. But there are other sources for contented passivity, in poetry for example.

In the work of Samuel Taylor Coleridge (1772–1834), there are clear signs of the vision of the seer and not of ego-logicality. At one time keen to set up a utopian community in the USA, based on pantisocracy, he was later to become less concerned with 'activity'. Paradoxically, he became very interested in persons and characters supernatural, or at least Romantic. In 1797 Coleridge stayed at a farm near Porlock in Somerset. According to a note he wrote in 1816, one evening he took opium (in the form of laudanum) and fell into a reverie where he 'read' a long poem about the Kubla Khan. On waking he began to write it down but was interrupted by 'a person . . . from Porlock', and lost the thread of the story.

What we have in Kubla Khan is a beautiful, exotic and enigmatic escape from ego-logical vision. It begins with the famous lines:

> In Xanadu did Kubla Khan
>   A stately pleasure-dome decree:
> Where Alph, the sacred river, ran
> Through caverns measureless to man
>   Down to a sunless sea.

Within this visionary dream we have the highly explicit and orgasmic verses of the section below. It is punctuated by exclamation marks, which the first reading to oneself might not fully communicate. It is worth repeating the exercise.

> But O, that deep romantic chasm which slanted
> Down the green hill athwart a cedarn cover!
> A savage place! As holy and enchanted
> As e'er beneath a waning moon was haunted
> By woman wailing for her demon-lover!
> And from this chasm, with ceaseless turmoil seething,
> As if this earth in fast thick pants were breathing,
> A mighty fountain momently was forced.

This verse is certainly powerful and explicit on the place of the pleasure-dome but may be a little phallocentric for some tastes. Nevertheless, the 'person's' intervention and the return to ego-logical vision unfortunately robbed us of the conclusion to Kubla Khan and a full articulation of the pleasure-dome and its erotic menace. In the poem and the reverie which brought it forth, Coleridge achieves the fusion of serenity and ecstasy which these two passages communicate. The achievement of joyous serenity and ecstasy that creates vision of this magnitude sadly is one which organization studies appears to have neglected. Surely there is very little sense of the utopian, the Romantic, the poetic, the visceral on the pages of our leading journals. As Calas and Smircich might show us, it may well be lying there unseen and unintended, waiting to be re-marked. But the cultural achievement of previous generations, however basely rooted, rarely gets a mention at the level of *conscious* content (Barthes, 1975).

Here again, Weber's insights continue to amaze each new generation of scholars. Bologh (1990) is to be thanked for bringing to our attention Weber's interest in ecstasy as an object of theoretical interest. For Max Weber, ecstasy is accessible only on occasion, usually in the orgy and the intoxication of alcohol and the dance (Weber, 1978). However, these acute ecstasies are transitory and leave very little trace behind them. Everyday behaviour carries on. In order to achieve lasting change through a new meaningful relation-ship with the world, Weber argues that milder forms of euphoria through mystical illumination or active conversion are necessary. Acute ecstasy in the form of 'possession' is seen as possible, but this is spiritualized or sublimated erotic love. Weber cites the Hindu doctrine of love as tinged with eroticism. Four levels of contem-plation are recognized, each being a different type of love. These are servant love, friendship love, filial/parental love and, at the highest level, definite eroticism. Whilst ecstatic feelings are possible in any type of 'love' relationship, Weber focuses on definite eroticism. Bologh's chapter on 'Erotic love as coercion' demonstrates Weber's acceptance that 'every lover know himself [sic] to be freed from the cold skeleton hands of rational orders, just as completely as from the banality of everyday routine' (Weber, 1946: 347). Moreover, 'this boundless giving of oneself is as radical as possible in its opposition to all functionality, rationality and generality' (ibid.).

Erotic love offers a salvation which requires neither devotion to the rational ethics of a God nor rejection of the body and its desires. The sublime meaning within erotic love transcends mere physical sensation. It is, in other words, 'absolutely incommunicable'. But it is also full of coercion. It is coercive because it involves imposing one's desire upon the other. The other may be unaware of this but erotic love necessarily involves self-expression *and* social attachment simultaneously. To the extent that the former dominates the latter, erotic love will be coercive of one's partner. Thus Weber does not encourage the development of erotic love except as a transitory, non-traceable escape from the iron cage of bureaucracy. One leaves it tonight but by the morning one is self-incarcerated yet again.

But in the same way as the utopian imagery of William Blake (1979) or Coleridge (1973) or Rabelais was critical without manufacturing far-reaching political activity, the retreat from rationality towards bliss in the tradition of contented passivity is open only to those who already have the freedom to escape. The critics' social position suggests the acquisition of some degree of freedom from prevailing norms and values anyway. As Marx said, the point is not to interpret but to change the world and direct confrontation with the bureaucratic tendencies in organizational life, leisure and our private lives is much more difficult than individualized escape attempts (Cohen and Taylor, 1973).

The Third Face of Pleasure

The Frankfurt School, of course, addressed the whole issue of leisure within contemporary capitalist society (Jay, 1973). In opposition – or at least parallel – to orthodox Marxist analyses of production, they began to focus on consumption, culture and leisure. Adorno and Horkheimer (1979) coined the term 'culture industry' to describe the major forms of mass entertainment. The person 'with leisure has to accept what the culture manufacturers offer' her. The culture industry's allotment of administered pleasure and calculated distraction is condemned by the School because it paralyses critical self-reflection. But in the same way as desexualization is never successful, the culture industry cannot suppress critique and questioning. The work of the film director David Lynch, for example, is commercially successful but quite deeply questioning of prevailing cultural values. The negativity of *One-Dimensional Man* (Marcuse, 1962), where leisure and work are both seen to be permeated by bureaucratic rationality, contains within it the notion of change of a fundamental kind developing through the provocation of critical consciousness. Subcultural reaction, particularly by the underclasses, appears to offer some hope to Marcuse of progress and change.

Here then we meet the third face of 'pleasure'. Its second face is dangerous to capital and its functionaries because it signals retreat from delivery of energy in the interests of large organizations. But the third face is very dangerous because it implies change and transformation. An organization, or a society which has *re-eroticized* itself will be totally destructured. Pleasure in this sense is the most potent weapon human beings possess (De Sade, 1959; Nietzsche, 1960; Reich, 1942).

What I have in mind by re-eroticization is similar in part to Bologh's articulation of 'erotic love as sociability' (Bologh, 1990: 213–39), Irigaray's (1985) notion of an 'amorous language', Vance's (1989) politics of pleasure and danger and Rojek's (1985) call for a sociology of pleasure. The following sections rest heavily upon this body of literature.

By re-eroticization I do *not* simply mean a resexualization of human relations where this merely concerns heterosexual or homosexual penetrative acts. Such an image carries with it no understanding of the polymorphous and historically specific nature of human 'sexuality', which has to be seen as a plurality of relativistic notions in time and space (Hearn et al., 1989). Additionally, such an image implies the likelihood of increased sexual harassment within the organized world based, as it is, upon ego-logicism (Levin, 1988) and obviously in no way do I wish to encourage that sort of reaction. Re-eroticization is a term used here to suggest a more joyous, playful attitude to life and to fellow humans, where sensuality and feeling are enhanced and where the erotic plays a more central role in our day-to-day lives but where 'erotic' is seen to be very widely conceived. It does not simply mean more orgasms. Indeed, the preoccupation with penetration and orgasms we see today is symptomatic, arguably, of a dis-ease with the sexuality of the human body (Lasch, 1979).

Bologh, for example, defines eros as the totality of pleasure-directed life instincts whose energy is derived from libido (1990: 213). Similarly Gonzalez-Crussi quotes Sartre on desire – 'the organic totality of a body and its consciousness in a special relation to the world and to the subject who experiences desire' (Gonzalez-Crussi, 1988: 13). In other words we must be conscious that 'the hallmark of sexuality is its complexity: its multiple meanings, sensations and connections' (Vance, 1989: 5). It is to be closer, perhaps, to sensuality rather than sexuality that we seek.

'Re-eroticization' has as its aims the enhancement and development of the 'erotic' in social life. As we have seen, human eroticism is much more than a set of physiological reactions by which the species is perpetuated. Indeed, it lies, for some, at the centre of the ontological problem. It is not enough to say that eroticism is a form of relating to others. So too is the market. We must clarify the relationship more than this (Gonzalez-Crussi, 1989). Sexual desire is not the want of coition. It is more and less than this. 'Desire in no way implies by itself the sexual act, does not pose it thematically, does not even sketch it' (Sartre, quoted in Gonzalez-Crussi, 1989: 13). Re-eroticization is the attempt to reintroduce serious polymorphic emotions into human organization at any level. It involves spontaneous involvement of the masses and their willingness to experiment with many forms of social organization – collectives and co-operatives, communes and communal acts. Life is lived by recourse to the pleasure principle. For Freud (1984) the human subject is animated by 'the pleasure principle' in which pleasure is sought and unpleasure avoided. It expresses the inclinations of the life instinct. On the other hand, the reality principle seeks to maintain balance and equilibrium by 'keeping the quantity of excitation present in the mental apparatus as low as possible or at least keeping it constant' (Freud, 1984: 277). Civilization depends upon this principle of constancy in which the pursuit and attainment of pleasure are constantly regulated. The reality principle, then, 'does not abandon the intention of ultimately obtaining pleasure but it nevertheless demands and carries into effect the postponement of satisfaction, the abandonment of a number of possibilities of gaining satisfaction and the temporary intolerance of unpleasure' (Freud, 1984: 278).

The path of re-eroticization, however, would reject the call for the postponement of gratification as a ploy for shoring up *industrial* civilization on behalf of an elite group who are able to say when and how the unpleasured majority may take gratification. Renunciation of gratification is stratified, for as Freud revealingly said 'the masses are lazy and unintelligent' and are unwilling to renounce pleasure in a controlled form. The principle of inversion, so often found in the medieval carnival for example, cries out for the embracing of pleasure wholeheartedly and not some submission to an instruction to follow an unpleasured existence in the foreseeable and austere future. The medieval carnival, then, is one social locale in which the eroticization of life was well expressed and it may be appropriate to consider briefly the essential elements of these events.

Emmanuel Le Roy Ladurie in *Carnival in Romans* (1981) describes the events within parts of the Rhone Valley in the period 1579–80 which culminated in a people's uprising in February 1580. According to Ladurie, 'all things duly considered, the Dauphine phenomenon in 1579–80 is a sort of open-air museum of every form of social organisation – abstract collectives, leagues, ruling and co-operative groups, associations, corporate groups' (Ladurie, 1981: 279). It must be noted that there is no contemporary parallel, certainly in the West, to the spectacle and meaning of this sort of carnival. Rojek (1985) uses the work of Bakhtin (1968) heavily in his discussion of the role of the carnival in the Middle Ages. He maintains that the carnival represents a period of unrestrained merrymaking where work is suspended. The hierarchy of the official order is overturned and the lowly are able to mock the high. For days on end, jesting, drollery and pleasure-seeking dominate social relations (Cleugh, 1963). There was in evidence a 'second life' which expressed a 'universal spirit' in that there was an embodiment of a sense of immediacy and spontaneity. Typical were lewdness and vulgarity, with an emphasis on grotesque exaggeration and colourful clowning. There was a low level of control over bodily and natural forces. The tabooed and the fantastic were possible. Reciprocity and mutuality were expressed through the interdependence of carnival members trusting each other for mutual safety, well-being and pleasure (Rojek 1985: 26–8). Very often, carnivals were fun because they were crowd efforts in which everyone was included, everyone was an accomplice. They represented anti-structure and *communitas* (Featherstone, 1990). Very often they relied upon the *principle of inversion* where high and low, for a short time, were in reverse locations (King, 1977). But the more we understand the carnival, the more we can see that they have now disappeared from view. The annual miners' picnics in the north-east of England never approached such liberation. In no meaningful way does the Notting Hill Carnival fulfil such a role. It is not allowed to, nor does there seem to be articulated demand for such a 'love-in'. It is much more like the medieval *fair*, in which commodification, exchange and money-making were the *raison d'être*. The 'carnival' was a monument to pleasure – not economic activity.

A key feature of the carnival in Romans was the whole variety of organizational forms which developed in response to the admittedly pre-industrial but nevertheless bureaucratizing society in which it was placed. The features of subcultural reaction by the underclass to efforts by a powerful superordinate class to impose a single world-view which led to a bloody uprising are those which Marcuse might well have welcomed. Although Marcuse did not speak of carnivals it would have strengthened his case had he done so. The explosion of organizational forms allows pleasure to disrupt, question and subvert bureaucratic practices. Pleasure in this tradition is *very* dangerous. According to Rojek 'in the industrial-urban societies today, the experience of raw pleasure is confined only to infants and individuals bidden by certain forms of madness' (Rojek, 1985: 82). As Meakin (1976) and Anthony (1977) both show, the contemporary work ethic enhances such feelings and privations. With re-eroticization, raw pleasure would spill all over the confining bonds of industrial capitalism, would be embodied by organizational subordinates and embraced with a high level of intensity.

Of course, the *second* face of pleasure would not be excluded from this vision of eroticization. Ecstasy through joyous serenity and the emphasis on *being* rather than doing would be perfectly at home within a context of social interaction moving towards full eroticism. Perhaps those who had embraced joyous serenity would have played little role in the movement, one suspects, with their concern for quietism and resigned acceptance but the individualized responses to pleasure outlined by Barthes, Coleridge, Russell and Boss would normally fit within re-eroticized human interaction as envisioned here.

Discussion

Now all this may sound like something from the 1960s. How archaic a 'love-in' sounds today. Nevertheless, I do not apologize should it do so, for it stems in part from a conviction that there is a curious cyclicality in ideas, and 'the myth of the external return' is bringing forth features from that period back into mainstream thinking. Elsewhere, it has been argued that if we go 'back to the future' (Burrell, 1991) we self-evidently need to understand history and its vaguely repetitive nature even if it is merely in the forms of tragedy and farce forever intermingling their lights. Thus I have contended that certain features of so-called 'anti-organization theory' with its roots in critical theory, its emphasis on the shaman or seer, its ecological consciousness, its ready acceptance of the liberating effects of drug use (*not* abuse), its dependence on the arts and humanities, the novel and the poem for its inspiration, its search for alternative forms of organization, and above all its celebration of pleasure and excitement in many polymorphous ways is about to re-emerge after years of neglect. Re-eroticization is one process which this re-emergence may well take seriously as an issue.

A key point to make at this juncture is that the dormant perspective of anti-organization theory rejects the notion of privileging the organizational level of analysis. Indeed, in some versions it rejects the concept of 'organization' altogether, since this is equated with bureaucratic, patriarchal forms of control. Thus, if we were to re-eroticize our lives would we start at the organizational level and move outwards from there? Clearly, the notion of 'totality' implies that one cannot expect developments at the organizational level to have any chance of success unless one is able to expect 'detotalization' of the whole social structure. Re-eroticization of any organization can only be possible if there is re-eroticization of the totality.

In most versions of anti-organization theory there is a commitment to rupturism and caesurism (Martins, 1974) in which fundamental cleavage lines within the social fabric slip and distort, allowing opportunities for radical transformation of the human totality. If we are to wait for such a seismic happening then re-eroticization is unlikely to be witnessed anywhere. Indeed, pleasure will follow leisure (Rojek, 1985) into the maw of bureaucratic surveillance (Dandeker, 1990). It will become safe, clean and healthy – in other words, controlled. Re-eroticization is not about control. It is spontaneous, messy and complicated – in other words, dangerous. It is made even more unsafe because it will have to be found in isolated pockets of joy and *jouissance* whose chances of survival cannot be judged to be good. These may not be conventional organizational forms. Re-eroticization is much more likely within the growing number of alternative organizational forms now appearing, whether inspired by anarchism, syndicalism, the ecological movement, the co-operative movement, libertarian communism, self-help groups or, perhaps most importantly, by feminism.

I have written the sections above from an attempted stance of pro-feminism, but it would be surprising if feminists from any number of perspectives did not regard re-eroticization as a very problematic concept. A female colleague described the notion as 'spooky', 'because women spent a lot of time trying to de-eroticize the workplace'. She made her point forcefully and eloquently. In what follows I will attempt to allay some of these fears by looking at some recent feminist writing in which 're-eroticization' may be part of the agenda.

Vance maintains, not quite in line with my colleague, that 'the tension between sexual danger and sexual pleasure is a powerful one in women's lives' (1989: 1). My focus on pleasure and gratification would seem to ignore the patriarchal structure in which women act. Violence, brutality and coercion in the form of rape, incest and exploitation as well as everyday cruelty and humiliation make the pleasures pale by comparison. Vance, however, allows for the possibility of sexuality being positive. Explorations of the body, curiosity, intimacy, sensuality, adventure, excitement, human connection, basking in the infantile and non-rational are seen by her not only as worthwhile but as energy-sustaining. Thus, it is too easy to see one side of the equation rather than the other. Sexuality is at one and the same time pleasurable *and* dangerous.

Re-eroticization is not a process that would aim to enhance victimization, to emphasize danger, to rely upon anxieties, to instil terror. It would seek to remove pleasure from its hiding place as the great guilty secret among feminists (Vance, 1989: 7) and allow women's sexual pleasure to be spoken about safely, honestly and completely. If this process were to develop more fully then re-eroticization might cease to be so 'spooky'.

Nevertheless, the issue of phallogocentrism is still crucial. This is a term used by Luce Irigaray (1985) to describe the very strong Western tradition which relegates the feminine to the position of matter, material or object against which the masculine defines itself. Thus the feminine is consigned to the economy of exchanges between males (Burke, 1989: 226). In short, those with a phallus govern discourse and exchange, the worlds of communication and economy. If re-eroticization were to take place within phallogocentrist assumptions then feminists might well argue it would be worse than where we are now.

So the organization of pleasure with the carnival as the metaphor must ask the question: *whose* pleasure? The ecstatic oneness of which many men speak is probably a phallocentric oneness, given, shaped and assessed from within this perspective. Luce Irigaray has called for a new language with which to understand these issues – an amorous language not based on the morphology of the phallus as *the* signifier but on an interplay of a revitalized female body and a male body newly aware of its interrelation to the female partner (Burke, 1989: 230). The Eastern tradition is perhaps more open to such a notion, especially in the dialogue between Siva and his wife which forms the Tantra and led to Tantrism. Irigaray, within the Western tradition, says

> Historically [men] have chosen sex and language against or in spite of the body. It would be necessary for women to be recognised as bodies with sexual attributes, desiring and uttering, and for men to rediscover the materiality of the bodies. There should no longer be this separation. Sex/language on the one hand, body/matter on the other. Then, perhaps another history would be possible. (Irigaray, 1985: 76)

In the construction of this amorous language, Irigaray advocates not *tête-à-tête* relationships based on cognition and cerebration but visceral ones based on a physical *corps-à-corps*. Her amorous language is built upon this relationship or interplay, which she calls nuptials. Her search for a terminology with which to describe exchange, social organization and love is often poetic and exclusively unsystematic. It is postmodern in the sense that it relies upon instabilities and slipperiness; it celebrates undecidability. It offers severe difficulties for even those willing to follow the path of undecidability.

The *corps-à-corps* approach to opposites sees them as meeting in a creative encounter rather than within a seductive power play. Resonating with or perhaps embody-ing Habermas's notion of communicative competence, Irigaray presents a picture of exchange built upon a form of desire which does not seek to seduce or consume. Rather than use linguistic categories given by the phallus it emphasizes the caress and the corporeal. From within the physical relationship between the bodies develops a space between – *l'entre deux* – an intermediate area where both parties can meet in mutual admiration and respect. This is not so much either/or – rather both/and.

Irigaray's notion of an amorous language is quite central here. In placing so much emphasis on pleasure as a locus of contestation, it behoves us to give consideration to what an 'amorous language' might look like. For only if we develop a form of cultural exchange between men and women through which true liberty is possible to envisage, would it then become possible to talk of organizing 'pleasure' in a fully-fledged sense. Without such a language, 'pleasure' under postmodernism becomes another ersatz value.

Roslyn Bologh has also written about non-masculine forms of erotic love. For her, 'erotic love involves the greatest personal risk but also the greatest possibility of communion. Hence erotic love can produce the most intense agony and ecstasy' (Bologh, 1990: 217). In other words, she accepts Vance's dichotomy between pleasure and danger. To reconcile this polarization she looks at 'erotic love as sociability'. It is supposedly this movement which distinguishes the feminist model of erotic love as sociability from the patriarchal model of erotic love as coercion (Bologh, 1990: 220). Self and the other are powerful *and* vulnerable not powerful *or* vulnerable. The sociability of this erotic love comes from its avoidance of phallogocentrism in that the male is not subject and the female object. Embodying the argument that Levin (1988) develops, both are seen as both subject and object, spirited bodies and embodied spirits, self-determined and compliant. Bologh says that this is *not* a utopian model of love and good feeling (Bologh, 1990: 235) for violence can occur and there will be negative passions provoked by these sensitive interpersonal dynamics. Nevertheless, the ultimate value is life itself and the warrant of that value is other lives. Bologh concludes her discussion with the following section.

> Erotic interest creates sociability as mutual empowering and mutual pleasuring through the playful move back and forth between assertion of difference and surrender to one-ness, an ongoing conversation of self-assertion and self-surrender among individuals, communities and nations . . . and erotic interest makes it possible to reconcile differences and be ironic and playful about them. (Bologh, 1990: 238)

Re-eroticization here in *Love or Greatness* is seen as possible and not utopian and highly dependent upon the role, skill and perseverance of women.

However, it would be foolish to pretend that phallogocentrism will be easy to topple and that erotic love as sociability or an amorous language will be easy to install in its place. The utopianism in Irigaray is as plain as it is in Habermas when he talks of 'communicative competence'. The utopianism in Bologh is as it is in the anarchist communists whose vision of sociability and mutual aid (Kropotkin, 1975) looks much like her own. But what is wrong with utopianism? Without a model of some (past or) future society to guide praxis there is little beyond the individualistic escape attempts we saw in the second face of pleasure. Utopias are a key illuminatory device of those interested in re-eroticization, for without them the all-encompassing blanket of phallogocentrism seems complete.

Concluding Remarks

What I have attempted to do in this chapter is to raise the issue of sex and language as they intersect over 'pleasure' and invite us to rediscover the materiality of our bodies. In the face of phallogocentrism – of which this chapter may be part – we need to construct an amorous language. But can a man escape long enough to recognize this and enter 'a fecund caressive language that respects the bodily contours and inwardness of the other, seeking to know the other as a corporal being within elemental forms of nature' (Hunter, 1989: 9)?

Perhaps not. Perhaps gender is inescapable, as are the structures of patriarchy, but if pro-feminist men can begin to conceptualize the possibility of an amorous language, is this a sign of *enhanced* phallogocentrism or reduced phallogocentrism? Is it a threat or an opportunity for women? Can re-eroticization be gender-neutral – or are our gender identities so strong as to render the task impossible?

But contradictions of this kind are typical in this field. We risk them simply by being alive (Gonzalez-Crussi, 1988: 89). Consummation *and* consumption, being 'blissed out' *by* primeval spastic responses of the body; Kiros as intense periods of activity *alongside* regular uninterrupted time (chronos); sadism and masochism as mysterious paradoxes (Gonzalez-Crussi, 1988: 89; Hearn et al. 1989: 176–7) which *imply* one another; pleasure *as* enslavement; pleasure as escape; pleasure as the focus of the identical *subject-object* (Bologh, 1990). This list of paradoxes is a long one but they all lie on the terrain of 'joy', 'play', 'pleasure' and 'excitement'. However, the very existence of such conflict and terminological turmoil is indicative of deep debate and should encourage us to seek understanding rather than turn our backs on this babel of confusion.

The words themselves, as well as the reality they portray, represent the battleground between organizational development and anti-organization theory. Organizational Development has attempted to use the techniques of transactional analysis, team-building, outdoor activities and so on to reintroduce pleasure into the organization. But this is neo-human relations and the postwar search for contented workers, supervisors and managers revisited. It is development for livelihood not development for life. In *Eros and Civilisation*, Marcuse argued that bureaucracy had contracted the libido from a concern with the erotic to mere sexual gratification. In this he probably wildly underestimated the 'progress' made. The libido has been contracted more radically from a concern with the erotic to 'marching up and down and cheering and waving flags' (Orwell, 1949: 109). It is energy for use.

People's reserves of energy are now the target as they have never been before. Play and playfulness have joined other terms as the focus of contestation. If we offer no struggle these concepts will enter the lexicon of Newspeak in a bastardized, sterilized form. If we remain true to the theory of pleasure, as outlined by those besmirched writers such as Rabelais and De Sade who gave up their reputations in fighting against the reality principle, then there is hope that our practice can be enriched by it. In the end there is, as Turner maintains, not the symbols and words but there is '*the body*'.

So there are signs that 'pleasure' will come back on to the Critical Theorist's agenda in the 1990s, having disappeared for twenty years or so. Indeed, looking at Reaganite economics and Thatcherite politics, one might describe the 1980s as the decade of 'unpleasure'. The reality principle is under attack and the 'pleasure principle' is again whispered about as if it still existed but was rightly hidden from our view. In search of a label, some commentators are beginning to speak of the 'Naughty Nineties'. Postmodernism in architecture, the arts and humanities celebrates witty disjunctures, playfulness and the colourful. The advent of New Times in the place of Modern Times, a movement which *Marxism Today* has done so much to bring into consciousness, carries with it a turning away from the serious business of modernity. But postmodernism in some of its gutted forms is serious business to the pedlars of 'excellence'. It is a cultural movement which they seek to tap and channel for better performativity in what is a wonderful irony. Supposedly predicated on the rejection of performativity (Lyotard, 1982), postmodernism becomes a source for its improvement.

Anti-organization theory (Burrell and Morgan, 1979) was almost postmodern *avant la lettre*. The discussions of such a position were predicated upon a critique of and opposition to orthodox organization analysis. Part of the debate had been located earlier in the

Freudian antithesis of the reality principle and pleasure principle and this again is coming to the fore (Hearn et al., 1989; Levin, 1988; Bologh, 1990). The terrain of battle between the two may well consist in the immediate future of the proprietorial rights over the words 'joy', 'play', 'pleasure' and 'excitement'.

In recognizing *three* faces to pleasure, I have attempted to prevent pleasure from being seen in organization studies from only one stance, namely as a commodity to be exploited. This viewpoint is the new position of those now seeking to manipulate such ideas within late capitalism. They are often self-employed consultants seeking to provide the expensive but quick fix to an industrial and commercial audience who, ever hungry for novelty, are eager to consume different ideas before turning greedily to a newer fad in the relentless pursuit of busyness. Thus, just as critical discourse re-emerges back into the future it becomes open to many uses, many degradations, many abuses. This chapter is an attempt to retain 'pleasure', 'joy', 'play' – indeed our own 'body' – as concepts, words and signifiers for our own use before they too become consumed by Heathrow Organization Theory in its many guises. I am not confident that this is possible, for the straws in the wind point to the appropriation of such words in the old tradition of Newspeak on an international scale. Without wishing to exaggerate the point, in true cyclical fashion the organization of pleasure is yet again about to become the battlefield where the personal meets the political. If so, we need to be aware that pleasure has two other faces: that of passive resistance and that of radical transformation. Of one thing we can be sure. If we offer no struggle, pleasure will be lost to many of us in both its second and third faces.

References

Adorno, T. and Horkheimer, M. (1979) *Dialectic of Enlightenment*. London: Verso.
Anthony, P. (1977) *The Ideology of Work*. London: Tavistock.
Bakhtin, M. (1968) *Rabelais and his World*. Cambridge, MA: MIT Press.
Barnes, J. (1989) *A History of the World in 10½ Chapters*. London: Picador.
Barthes, R. (1975) *The Pleasure of the Text*. New York: Hill & Wang.
Blake, W. (1979) *The Works of William Blake*. Oxford: Oxford University Press.
Bologh, R. (1990) *Love or Greatness*. London: Unwin Hyman.
Boss, M. (1979) *The Existential Foundations of Medicine and Psychology*. New York: Aronson.
Burke, C. (1989) 'Romancing the philosophers: Luce Irigaray', in Dianne Hunter (ed.), *Seduction and Theory*. Urbana: University of Illinois Press.
Burrell, G. (1984) 'Sex and organisational analysis', *Organizational Studies*, 5 (2): 97–118.
Burrell, G. (1991) 'Back to the future?', in M. Reed and M. Hughes (eds), *Rethinking Organisation*. London: Sage.

Burrell, G. and Morgan, G. (1979) *Sociological Paradigms and Organisational Analysis*. London: Heinemann.

Calas, M. and Smircich, L. (1991) 'Voicing seduction to silence leadership', *Organizational Studies* 12 (4): 567–602.

Cleugh, J. (1963) *Love Locked Out*. London: Hamlyn.

Cohen, S. and Taylor, L. (1973) *Escape Attempts*. Harmondsworth: Penguin.

Coleridge, S. T. (1973) *The Works of Coleridge*. Oxford: Oxford University Press.

Dandeker, C. (1990) *Surveillance, Power and Modernity*. Cambridge: Polity Press.

Elias, N. (1978) *The Civilising Process Vol. I*. Oxford: Basil Blackwell.

Elias, N. (1983) *The Civilizing Process, Vol. II*. Oxford: Blackwell.

Featherstone, M. (1990) 'Perspectives on consumer culture', *Sociology*, 24 (1): 5–22.

Foucault, M. (1977) *Discipline and Punish*. Harmondsworth: Penguin.

Foucault, M. (1979) *The History of Sexuality, Vol. I*. Harmondsworth: Penguin.

Freud, S. (1984) *On Metapsychology: The Theory of Psychoanalysis*, ed. A. Richards. Harmondsworth: Penguin.

Gonzalez-Crussi, F. (1988) *On the Nature of Things Erotic*. London: Picador.

Harvey-Jones, J. (1988) *Making it Happen*. London: Collins.

Hassard, J. and Porter, R. (1990) 'Cutting down the workforce', *Organizational Studies*, 11 (4): 555–67.

Hearn, J. and Parkin, W. (1986) *'Sex' at 'Work'*. Brighton: Wheatsheaf Books.

Hearn, J. Sheppard, D. L., Tancred-Sheriff, P. and Burrell, G. (eds) (1989) *The Sexuality of Organization*. London, Newbury Park and New Delhi: Sage.

Hunter, D. (ed.) (1989) *Seduction and Theory*. Urbana: University of Illinois Press.

Huxley, A. (1955) *Brave New World*. Harmondsworth: Penguin.

Iacocca, L. (1985) *Iacocca: an Autobiography*. London: Sidgwick and Jackson.

Irigaray, L. (1985) *Speculum of the Other Women*. New York: Cornell University Press.

Jameson, F. (1984) 'Postmodernism, or the cultural logic of late capitalism', *New Left Review*, 146: 53–92.

Jay, M. (1973) *The Dialectical Imagination*. London: Heinemann.

Jay, M. (1984) *Marxism and Totality*. Cambridge: Polity Press.

Kanter, R. (1983) *The Change Masters*. London: Allen & Unwin.

Kanter, R. (1989) *When Giants Learn to Dance*. London: Allen & Unwin.

Keenoy, T. (1990) Personal communication reporting research at Cardiff Business School.

King, A. (1977) 'A voluntarist model of organization', *British Journal of Sociology*, 28–30: 363–74.

Kropotkin, P. (1975) *Mutual Aid*. London: Porter Sargent.

Ladurie, E. L. (1981) *Carnival in Romans*. Harmondsworth: Penguin.

Lasch, C. (1979) *The Culture of Narcissism*. New York: Norton.

Levin, D. (1988) *The Opening of Vision*. London: Routledge.

Lyotard, J.-P. (1982) *The Postmodern Condition*. Manchester: Manchester University Press.

Mant, A. (1982) *The Rise and Fall of the British Manager*. Harmondsworth: Penguin.

Marcuse, H. (1962) *Eros and Civilisation*. Boston: Beacon Press.

Marcuse, H. (1964) *One-dimensional Man*. London: Routledge & Kegan Paul.

Martins, H. (1974) 'Time and theory in sociology' in J. Rex (ed.), *Approaches to Sociology*. London: Routledge & Kegan Paul.

Meakin, D. (1976) *Man and Work*. London: Methuen.

Nietzsche, F. (1960) *Joyful Wisdom*. New York: Ungar.

Orwell, G. (1954) *Nineteen Eighty-Four*. Harmondsworth: Penguin.

Peters, T. (1987) *Thriving on Chaos.* New York: Macmillan.

Peters, T. (1990) 'Towards the Entrepreneurial and Empowering Organization'. London: Royal Lancaster Hotel, February 13.

Peters, T. and Waterman, R. (1982) *In Search of Excellence.* New York: Warner.

Reed, M. (1989) *The Sociology of Management.* Hemel Hempstead: Harvester Wheatsheaf.

Reich, W. (1942) *The Function of the Orgasm.* New York: Noonday.

Rojek, C. (1985) *Capitalism and Leisure Theory.* London: Tavistock.

Romanyshyn, R. (1982) *Psychological Life: From Science to Metaphor.* Austin: University of Texas Press.

Romanyshyn, R. (1989) *Technology as Symptom and Dream.* London: Routledge.

Sartre, J.-P. (1957) *Being and Nothingness.* London: Methuen.

de Sade, D. A., Marquis (1959) *The Complete Works of Sade.* Paris: Pauvert.

Scase, R. and Goffee, R. (1989) *Reluctant Managers.* London: Unwin.

Vance, C. (ed.) (1989) *Pleasure and Danger.* London: Pandora.

Weber, M. (1946) *The Theory of Social and Economic Organization.* Glencoe, Ill.: Free Press.

Weber, M. (1978) *Economy and Society*, 3 vols. New York: Bedminster Press.

5
Technical, Practical and Critical OR – Past, Present and Future?

John Mingers

Introduction to Operational Research and Critical Theory

The aim of this chapter is to view the history and possible future of Operational Research (OR) through the lens of Critical Theory, in particular the work of Habermas on the three knowledge-constitutive interests. To do this we must introduce briefly both OR and Habermas's ideas.

As the majority of the chapter will explore OR, it need only be briefly characterized now. Operational Research is essentially concerned with improving the effectiveness of decision-making and problem-solving in organizations. It does not cover a particular functional area like marketing or finance, but provides a general approach together with a range of mathematical and computer-based techniques. The approach is based on the idea of scientific research and generally involves collecting data, building a model of the situation and then using the model to evaluate the best ways of meeting objectives. OR has to some extent developed differently in Britain and the USA. American *Operations* Research tends to be more technical and mathematical, British more pragmatic. The above is a very partial description of OR, as the rest of the chapter will show.

Habermas's theory of knowledge-constitutive interests (Habermas, 1972, 1974) is the core of his whole work. It deals with the problem of epistemology – that is the question of the validity of our knowledge of the world. In historical times valid knowledge was based on religion and myth. However, since the Enlightenment, knowledge has been judged in terms of reason and rationality. In particular, the spectacular success of natural science culminated in the idea of positivism, that the *only* valid knowledge, indeed the only meaningful thought at all, was that which matched the canons of the scientific method – i.e. universal laws based on objective and value-free empirical testing. Habermas challenges this supposed monopoly of positivism by arguing that there are different domains of knowledge with their own different criteria of validity. He justifies this by showing that knowledge is never 'pure', for itself, but always serves some deep-rooted *interest* of the human species. The particular interest leads to or *constitutes* the form of knowledge in a particular domain. Thus the term 'knowledge-constitutive interests'.

Habermas identifies three interests – the *technical* interest in the control and manipulation of the physical world; the *practical* interest in communicating with and understanding other people; and the *emancipatory* interest in developing and freeing ourselves from false ideas. These can be seen to arise within the development of the species. The need for physical survival leads to the development of knowledge about and control over the environment. This has been supplied by natural (or empirical-analytical as Habermas calls it) science, which is fundamentally instrumental. In humans, the development of language led to entirely new domains of communicative and social interaction. Here the necessity is for *understanding* – making sense of what others mean – and, through discussion and argument, reaching agreement and consensus. This leads to the interpretive or cultural sciences such as *hermeneutics*.

Finally, Habermas argues, humans have an interest in self-development and autonomy based on revealing the true from the false: to be critical of the prevailing orthodoxy and develop a genuine autonomy rather than a false one based on illusion and untruth. This requires *critical science* and *philosophy*, which operate in both the other domains. Within the natural sciences it must reveal the positivist illusion of objectivity, and within the cultural sciences it must critique the distortions in language and communication, the ideologies that reinforce existing power structures.

These three knowledge-constitutive interests and their characteristics are summarized in Table 5.1.

The rest of this chapter will show how the development of OR/systems can be seen as successively embodying these three views. Section 1 traces the early days of OR, when it developed as

Table 5.1   *The three knowledge-constitutive interests*

Type of science	Cognitive interest	Social domain	Purpose
Natural science (empirical-analytical)	Technical	Work	Prediction/control
Cultural science (hermeneutics)	Practical	Language/culture	Understanding/ consensus
Critical sciences	Emancipatory	Power/authority	Enlightenment

technical knowledge concerned with the manipulation and control of an objective world, selecting efficient means of reaching pre-defined ends. Section 2 shows that lack of success with this approach led to the development of 'Soft OR' in which attention switched to the subjective world of individual beliefs and perceptions, mirroring the practical domain of hermeneutics and phenomenology. Section 3 addresses the inadequacies of this view alone, looking towards developments of critical OR/systems.

Related to OR is what is known as 'the systems approach', which involves viewing the world as interconnected systems or wholes (Checkland, 1981). From the perspective of this chapter, they are best seen as complementary (Mingers, 1989a; Flood, 1989b). A critical approach to systems is documented elsewhere (Jackson, 1985; Oliga, 1988; Flood, 1990a, 1990b; Flood and Jackson, 1991a, 1991b; Jackson, 1991). Where both are implied, the term 'ORS' will be used.

Technical OR and Systems

There are numerous histories of the origin of both OR and systems (summarized in Checkland, 1983; Rosenhead, 1989) and only a brief recapitulation is necessary here. The very name Operational Research betrays its origin as research into military operations before and during the Second World War. Scientists such as Bernal, Blackett and Watson-Watt began to apply their scientific approach to investigating operational problems such as the effective use of the newly invented radar; determining the best convoy size to minimize losses; or increasing the effective availability of aircraft. What characterized this early work was the choice to view these operations as if they were objects of scientific study; an emphasis on observation and the collection of empirical data; and the use of modelling and experimentation as if in a laboratory – in short, the adoption of the prevailing rationality of natural science rather than tradition or common sense.

It is less well known, however, that many of the founders of OR were socialists or communists (relatively common for intellectuals in the 1930s) who saw science as a progressive force for the common good. Bernal, in an influential text called *The Social Function of Science*, wrote: 'Science, conscious of its purpose, can in the long run become a major force in social change' (Bernal, 1939: 410), while in the same book Blackett wrote 'socialism will want all the science it can get. . . . Scientists have . . . to make up their minds on which side they stand' (1939: 396). It is possible to see OR in the forefront of this commitment of science to the social good, as the application of science not just to technology but to society itself.

Traces of such a socially committed view of OR can be seen in its later history (Parry and Mingers, 1990), for example the current development of the Community OR initiative. However, the practice of OR soon became engulfed in the purposive spheres of industrial and state organizations. It was taken up by large companies and nationalized industries and utilized in a tactical way to improve efficiency by analysing recurrent problems such as stock control, machine replacement and queues (Tomlinson, 1971). The classical mathematical techniques of OR – such as mathematical programming, queueing theory and simulation – were developed, and extensive use was made of computers. A number of unfortunate trends can be seen (Ackoff, 1977, 1979a). As the gifted and innovative founders were replaced by the less able, and companies required quick solutions, careful and often innovative scientific analysis became replaced by the development and application of packaged techniques. Messy and complex problems were reduced to that which the technique could handle, and people were just another component of the system, like machines and money. OR's 'solutions' gained their legitimacy through their supposed scientificity as embodied in the idea of optimality.

OR practitioners had to face and deal with practical problems but gained little help from theoretical developments, which were largely mathematical. Methodology, as *briefly* discussed in the many OR textbooks, became a question of specifying objectives, collecting data and building a model of the situation, experimenting with the model to find the best solution to achieve the objectives and finally implementing the solution. In practice, little attention was paid to the first and last stages, with the result that the rate of successfully implemented projects was often very low. ORS thus became the embodiment *par excellence* of Habermas's idea of *decisionism* – dealing only with efficient means of reaching pre-specified ends (Checkland, 1983). It was seen essentially as a technical subject employing scientific analysis in a neutral way, leaving politics to the politicians:

> Taking operational research into government is not taking operational research into politics . . . the statement of objectives is a political problem, to be solved through the democratic process, and the use of operational research in government will show the means to a popularly chosen end. So many of our political arguments are about means; but the man on the Clapham omnibus cannot be expected to select means. (Rivett, 1963)

A critique of this self-misunderstanding is presented in Section 4.

In philosophical terms, the approach is best seen as part of the broad area of empiricism and in particular can be described as naive realism. It emphasizes the measurement and collection of data, and assumes the objectivity of its results (Mingers, 1989b). Like positivism, it assumes its own value-freedom and neutrality, but unlike Humean empiricism and positivism it adopts a basically realist stance. This can be seen both in its view of models as models *of* reality and in emphasizing that initial concerns may only be symptoms of deeper, underlying problems.

Practical OR and Systems

After early success in the 1950s and 1960s, disillusionment set in within the OR community. OR was not meeting the success at higher levels of management that had been expected. Many projects were never implemented and there was an increasing divorce between the pragmatics of OR practitioners and the mathematization of OR teaching and journals. Strongly written critiques were produced and OR was said to be in crisis (Dando and Bennett, 1981). In response to this, a number of new approaches developed which, in various ways, countered the traditional assumptions of objectivity, value-freedom and neutrality, and took seriously the distinctive nature of human beings. In so doing they can be seen to embody the practical interest in understanding and the exploration of people's ideas and meanings. It is common (e.g. Jackson, 1982; Oliga, 1988) to discuss soft ORS as if it were an homogeneous area, but in fact a distinction can be drawn between those who aim to rectify certain aspects of technical ORS within an essentially objectivist paradigm, and those, such as Checkland, who espouse a full-blown subjectivism.

Objectivity, Interests and Uncertainty

Several approaches can be seen as developments of traditional ORS, going some way to recognizing subjectivity, interests and their conflicts, and the essential commitment of OR. These include hypergames (Bennett et al., 1989); strategic choice (Friend, 1989; Friend and Hickling, 1987); decision conferencing (Phillips, 1982); whole systems dialectics (Churchman, 1979) and idealized planning (Ackoff, 1974, 1977, 1979a, 1979b). Only Ackoff's work will be described here. Ackoff, one of the postwar founders of OR, was perhaps *the* critic of technical OR. His criticisms can be summarized by the title of one of his papers 'Optimization + objectivity = opt out'. OR has failed because of its mistaken belief in objectivity and optimization. One can optimize models but not reality, for reality does not consist of isolated and tractable *problems* but complex, ever-changing interrelated *messes*. Objectivity does not come about through the supposed value-freedom and neutrality of an analyst;

instead it results from the social interaction of many, committed, individual subjectivities. OR should aim to manage complex messes rather than solve problems. It should be adaptive and conscious of aesthetic values and should ensure that the interests of all those affected by decisions are represented in the process.

All of this is to be achieved by a process called *interactive planning* based on three principles – that it should be a continuous activity, that it should involve the active participation of those affected, and that it should be holistic. The actual stages – structuring the mess, planning the ends and means, generating the resources, managing the process and implementing the results – are unexceptional except for the second one. This is the heart of Ackoff's vision – *idealized design* which aims to 'design a desirable future and invent ways of bringing it about' (Ackoff, 1979a: 103). This is to be done by generating a consensus among the stakeholders as to what would be an ideal design if they were free from outside constraint. All that must be considered is that the design be technologically feasible and operationally viable in itself. The design should incorporate learning and adaptation mechanisms. Having agreed an ideal, the rest of the process aims to get as near to this as possible. Ackoff recognizes that there may initially be conflicts in the interests of the stakeholders, but believes that the focus on ultimate values, and the actual process of participation, will overcome short-term differences in objectives and means.

Subjective Idealism
The above writers have all in their way pushed back the doors of objectivism to let the light of inquiry shine upon values, interests, uncertainty and subjective viewpoints. They have not, however, been so thoroughgoing in their subjectivism as Eden (1989) and Checkland.

Checkland's work developing the Soft Systems Methodology (SSM) has probably been the single most important influence in legitimizing soft approaches. SSM has been taken up in a wide variety of disciplines and has been very fruitful in provoking further work. It has been extensively documented elsewhere (Checkland, 1981, 1989; Checkland and Scholes, 1990), and in broad terms is based on Vickers's (1965) concept of appreciative systems and Churchman's (1971) use of *Weltanschauung* in dialectical inquiry. Checkland (1983) sees SSM as very clearly moving the intervention process away from the real world towards the conceptual world. If there are a reality R and a methodology M, then hard systems (and OR) sees R as systemic, and M as systematic, while the soft view is to see R as problematic (we do not have clear access to the nature of reality) but M as systemic. We apply systems ideas to our thinking, not to the world.

we have no access to what the world is, to ontology, only to descriptions of the world, that is to say, epistemology . . . we should never say of something in the world; 'It is a system', only: 'it may be described as a system'. (Checkland, 1983: 671)

Summary
In their different ways, all these approaches and techniques reflect a shift from the technical to the practical. They move away from a belief in modelling and manipulating a single objective reality towards exploring and expressing individuals' subjective meanings in order to achieve understanding and consensus.

However, it should not be thought that soft OR has in some way replaced technical OR; that a paradigm shift has occurred. Quite the contrary, certainly in the practice of OR, where soft techniques are seldom more than names. In a recent survey (Mingers, 1991) among heads of OR groups in companies concerning the content of OR courses, SSM was rated lowly because few had even heard of it. OR practitioners still deal with practical problems in a largely common-sense and untheoretical way.

Critical ORS

The main purpose of the previous sections has been to reach the point where we can consider current developments of a Critical ORS. Alvesson and Willmott (1988), and Chapter 1 of the present book, provide a view of Critical Management Science in general, but we are concerned with the application of CT to ORS. ORS is, above all, concerned with taking action, solving problems, improving situations, and so our interest is in methodologies and theories oriented towards action not simply description or analysis. This section will describe work which can be seen as part of Critical ORS under a number of headings. First, work which provides critiques of the prevailing theories and methodologies, particularly the technical and practical rationalities of hard and soft ORS; secondly, work which creates the space for a Critical ORS and debates its future development; thirdly, work which moves away from Habermas's high-level theorizing to the development of specific action-oriented methodologies. A conclusion of the methodology section will be that the greatest weakness is the lack of an adequate conceptualization of power, and this will be addressed in the final section.

Critiques of Traditional ORS
A critical view of ORS, whether in the form of pure criticism, or more positively as the development of a critical approach, has its own

Technical, Practical and Critical OR   97

history (Keys, 1987). There are two broad strands – a Marxist-based critique within OR and more recently a CT-inspired development within systems.

The Marxist view was initially espoused by Hales (1974), discussed by Wood and Kelly (1978) and developed as 'A materialist analysis of OR' by Rosenhead and Thunhurst (1982). It includes a critical debate with Ackoff (Ackoff, 1974, 1975; Chesterton et al., 1975; Rosenhead, 1976) and other work by Bevan and Bryer (1978) and Tinker and Lowe (1984). The main arguments concern what I have here called technical OR. First, OR is mistaken in its own self-understanding. It sees itself as a neutral, and indeed beneficial, harnessing of science to the common good, initiated by the radical ideas of a few individuals. In fact, this view is both ahistorical and idealist. In reality it is part of the development of the means of production, simply another step in the history of the employment of science by capitalism. As such it is, of course, not neutral but committed to improving the effective use and control of the workforce. Its employment in the state sector of nationalized industry and services such as health is no better, both because the state itself exists for capital rather than workers, and because the specific contribution of OR tends to be concerned with efficiency and cost reduction rather than with eliciting and supplying people's needs. Finally, OR serves an ideological function (as analysed by Habermas) in suppressing discussion of ends and objectives in favour of a technical choice of means by 'scientific technicians', all in the name of science.

The debate with Ackoff focuses specifically on the nature of interests and conflict in society and foreshadows central issues in the critique of practical OR. Ackoff argues that OR does have a social responsibility to involve all those affected by decisions and planning. Although there will be conflicts in interests and values, Ackoff believes that these conflicts can always be reconciled in some way, that some idealized plan can be found which everyone can support. His critics argue that *real* structural conflicts of interest exist, which cannot be resolved; that his approach ignores the asymmetries of power between different parties; and that therefore his 'solutions' are bound to favour one side and support the status quo.

These Marxist critiques have mainly concerned technical OR, and certainly the development of soft approaches marks an improvement in moving away from the belief in objectivity and optimization towards recognizing differing interests and perceptions. However, soft approaches have been equally subject to critique by Jackson, Mingers and Oliga.

The first main attack was that of Jackson (1982), which grouped together the work of Churchman, Ackoff and Checkland as 'soft', and criticized it as both subjective and regulative. This prompted some debate (Ackoff, 1982; Churchman, 1982; Checkland, 1982; Jackson, 1983), which is analysed by Willmott (1989). Jackson argues that these approaches are essentially regulative (Burrell and Morgan, 1979) – that is, unable to bring about radical change. This is partly because of their inherent subjectivism. In focusing on actors' ideas and perceptions they are unable to theorize the causes and preconditions of such *Weltanschauungen*, or the constraints of power and interest. They lack a social theory. Any change they bring about will therefore be limited by the distorted nature of the prevailing situation. Checkland, in response, argues that as SSM is a learning system aimed at changing people's ideas it could *in principle* bring about radical change. He also deploys the subjectivist argument that it is illegitimate to refer to 'social systems' and 'objective social reality'.

Mingers (1984) argued, concerning SSM, that the primary problem was subjectivism and that the regulatory nature of the methodology followed from its subjective idealism. Taking this as the primary target, Mingers aimed to 'refute the implication, inherent in subjectivism, that social theory is inevitably limited to the exploration of individuals' commonsense, and equally valid, understandings and conceptions'. This debate clearly mirrors the arguments within social science, and CT in particular, about how to overcome the relativity inherent in subjectivism. Finally, Oliga has analysed from a critical perspective the assumptions made by various systems methodologies concerning power (Oliga, 1989a) and ideology (Oliga, 1989b).

The Possibility of Critical OR

Given the critiques of both technical and practical OR, the question must be asked as to whether there can be any legitimate possibility of *critical* ORS, or whether it is irretrievably capitalist and managerialist? The view taken here is that critical OR is possible, as a number of writers demonstrate, although Knights (1989) has raised a strong criticism from a Foucauldian perspective, which will be discussed below.

First, however, we must distinguish two different possibilities: ORS in an emancipated society, and ORS in an oppressive society. From a Habermasian perspective, all knowledge is ultimately committed to use and action in the world. Communicative action itself is grounded, not in understanding per se, but in the need for the co-ordination of action which then requires understanding (Habermas, 1987, ch. 5). The problem is not purposeful activity itself, but the distortions and inequalities which have developed historically.

CT is only required because of this, and if it is successful will make itself redundant. In such a truly rational society there will still be a need for the effective co-ordination of action, and a properly constituted ORS should have its place. What is not so clear is the nature of a critical ORS at the moment. What part can ORS play in the transition to a rational society?

Rosenhead and Thunhurst (1982) suggest various technical tasks which could be performed, such as exposing and critiquing official plans, generating counterplans based on working-class interests, and assisting working-class movements in planning their own struggles. Rosenhead (1987) also outlines a possible alternative OR based on characteristics opposite to those of managerialist OR (e.g. supporting rather than replacing judgement, treating humans as active subjects, accepting conflict and uncertainty as endemic), but recognizes that such ideas can only have real effect if they are taken up by groups or movements with a genuine interest in change and struggle.

Moving to more CT-inspired arguments, Mingers (1980) initiated the debate by comparing CT and SSM, outlining similarities – for example that both criticized hard systems analysis and aimed to bring rationality to the domain of values and interests – and differences. Later work critiquing SSM (outlined above) shows that the differences are probably greater than the similarities. In terms of the necessity of a critical ORS, the main arguments stem more from the limitations of hard and soft OR in problem-solving than from seeing ORS as helpful in transforming society. Jackson (1985) was the first to explicitly advocate Critical Systems Theory (CST), suggesting that it was necessary for situations characterized by disparities in power and resources, and a lack of understanding and control. In describing what CST might involve he drew on Habermas's (1974: 32) brief discussion of the organization of theory and praxis. Here three stages are outlined – the development of critical theories about the nature of the social situation; their employment in enlightening concerned actors (and thereby also the validation of these theories); and the actual political struggle carried out by the enlightened social group. These form the basis of a methodology developed by Laughlin (1987) in accounting, to be discussed below.

Further work has developed into what might be termed a contingency approach to applied systems without developing actual methodologies. Jackson and Keys (1984) and Jackson (1987, 1988, 1989a) developed a system of system methodologies. This is a classification of *problem contexts*, that is 'the individual or group of individuals who are the would-be problem solvers, the system(s) within which the problem lies and the set of relevant decision makers' (Jackson and Keys 1984: 473), in terms of two dimensions, the

complexity of systems involved and the relationship between participants. Two degrees of complexity are distinguished – mechanical
systems and systemic systems, while the relationship between
participants may be unitary (i.e. one of consensus), pluralist
(involving differing, but fundamentally reconcilable interests) or
coercive (in which agreement depends on the exercise of power).
Combining these dimensions gives six different types of problem
context and provides a way of classifying ORS methodologies. For
example, technical OR is seen as unitary/mechanical, while SSM is
pluralist/systemic. No methodology is found entirely suitable for the
coercive contexts, although Ulrich's (1983) Critical Systems Heuristics is at least critically inspired.

Jackson uses this tool not only to classify methodologies but to help
with methodology choice. If a particular situation can be identified
with one of the problem contexts then an appropriate methodology
can be chosen. Going further, he argues that the existence of these
different problem contexts therefore requires that there be different
methodologies. Thus the 'crisis' in OR identified by Dando and
Bennett (1981) is not a problem of different and incommensurable
paradigms, indeed it is not a problem at all. Rather the situation is
seen as one of increasing competence through the development of
new methodologies able to cope with differing situations. This
supports Jackson's (1989b) views about the future development of
ORS and its different approaches. He identifies four possible
strategies (based on Reed, 1985) – *isolationist* where the different
strands develop in isolation; *imperialist* where it is assumed that one
particular approach is superior; *pragmatist* where theoretical differences are ignored and a tool-kit of techniques is developed; and
pluralist where a number of approaches are developed in a mutually
informing and respecting way. For Jackson the pluralist approach is
to be preferred. Flood (1989a) has critically developed these ideas
and provisionally supports a pluralist development.

A number of criticisms of Jackson's work may be made. As Oliga
(1988) points out, in a generally favourable review, the idea of
problem contexts can easily slide into the positivist fallacy that they
are objective features of the world. Jackson does explicitly recognize
that the definition of a problem context is actually the result of the
participants' perceptions and interactions. This, however, seems to
raise even more problems. What if the participants cannot agree
about a definition of the situation? Even if they do this does not
necessarily mean that it is correct. Is it not in fact very much part of
the problem defining what the nature of the problem is? Are the
powerful in a coercive situation likely to define it as coercive? Are
they not more likely to define it as a unitary situation (and have their

definition accepted)? Do not all situations actually have all these characteristics, particularly power? Should not a methodology begin by assuming the worst and only ignore features when this can be justified? Interestingly, Keys (1988) has developed a methodology to use the problem contexts for choosing a methodology, and completely omits the coercive contexts! In short, I would suggest that defining a situation as being a particular problem context is itself a major problem which needs to be addressed by a successful methodology, not assumed in order to choose a methodology.

There are more general problems with a contingency approach. First, the nature of the underlying dimensions is always in question. Why these particular ones? Are there not others to be considered? Are the categories within a dimension suitable? An adequate justification requires a deep theoretical analysis – for example much of Habermas's work on communicative theory is an attempt to do just that for CT – and such a theory is certainly not provided by Jackson. Secondly, this pigeonholing approach leads to an uncritical acceptance of the pigeonholes themselves and an unreflective and mechanical selection of approach. Used as a pragmatic heuristic, or as a way of distinguishing methodologies, the classification is helpful, but a proper analysis of problems and problem situations must follow from a comprehensive social theory, not replace it.

This section has considered the work of those who have made a case for the necessity of Critical ORS. What is conspicuous by its absence, however, is precisely a *critical methodology* from either a systems or OR perspective. The difficulties of this task will be taken up in the next section.

Towards Critical Methodology

Given that the main task of ORS is bringing about effective action and change, a practical methodology must be the central concern. Yet little progress has been made within ORS although critical methodologies have been developed in other areas such as accounting (Laughlin, 1987) and information systems (Lyytinen and Klein, 1985). Habermas's work itself is of little direct help because it has been at such a general and abstract level, far removed from the realities of an individual in an actual organizational situation. In this section a number of possible directions forward will be explored, illustrated where possible by methodologies that have appeared.

Critical Methodology as a Development of Previous Methodologies   The first approach, implicit in the work of Jackson and Flood, is to examine the deficiencies of current methodologies, particular soft approaches, to see what they lack. The conclusion, discussed above, is that they lack a social theory. In restricting themselves to exploring subjective meanings they cannot elucidate how and why particular views have come about, why some are more dominant than others, and what wider effects they have: in short, how subjects are constituted by society and how society is reconstituted through the interactions of its subjects. This, in turn, means that subjective approaches cannot deal with the barriers which impede change, both in the individual and in institutions and society. Central to this concern is the role of power in both creating and sustaining a particular social reality.

Before discussing a specifically critical approach, developments within the soft methodologies, in particular SSM, should be mentioned. In response to criticism, more consideration is now given to social and political aspects of an intervention. This occurs mainly in the initial 'finding out' stage, which now consists of three analyses (Checkland, 1989). Analysis One concentrates on the nature of the intervention – the client, the problem-solver; Analysis Two 'looks at the "social system" – using that phrase in its everyday language sense' (Checkland, 1989: 85), describing roles, norms and values within the situation. Analysis Three considers the situation politically by looking at the distribution of power. The particular approach here is based on work by Stowell (1989), who visualizes power as a commodity that is used by individuals to control and secure their immediate environment. Whilst any movement in this direction is to be welcomed, these particular developments do not really overcome the limitations of SSM. The 'commonsense' analysis of social structure remains precisely that, individualist and lacking any form of social *theory*, whilst the power as a commodity metaphor, although potentially useful as a heuristic device, is overly voluntarist and rather simplistic in comparison with the theories of power to be described later.

Ulrich's (1983) Critical Systems Heuristics (CSH) is one approach that is certainly critically inspired. It is developed from the dialectical and whole systems approach of Churchman, but incorporates critical ideas from Habermas and Kant. It focuses on a particular area, that of planning, which is done *by* technical specialists *to* ordinary people in a way which often obscures and mystifies the underlying interests and assumptions. CSH is concerned to open up such assumptions to criticism and debate by those affected by planning. In any plan or design, boundaries must be drawn; there must come points where rational argument finishes and justification breaks off. It is these points where the unarticulated assumptions and their consequences occur, and it is these which CSH seeks to explicate. Ulrich describes three key concepts in his approach.

First, the judgements concerning the boundaries of the design must be made explicit and be agreed by all those involved and affected. They must be normative – i.e. what *should be* according to the purpose of the design, not what is or has been. Secondly, a framework of practical reason is provided to identify and examine the justification break-offs and their consequences. This is a series of twelve 'ought to be' questions, such as who ought to be the beneficiary? What ought to be the purpose? Who ought to be a witness on behalf of the citizens? Who ought to be the controller? These are then compared with the corresponding 'is' questions. Third, boundary judgements are used in a polemical way as a tool to expose the dogmatic character of experts' judgements. This is done by those affected putting forward their own judgements not as being necessary, but as being desirable, and forcing the expert to say why not ('I would like it to be like this, why shouldn't it be?').

While this approach does have a critical intent, and is aimed directly at exposing the way in which perceptions and definitions of problems are controlled by the particular powers of certain groups, it is not sufficient to serve as a general critical methodology. First it is overly specialized in applying to a particular type of situation but, more importantly, it has no way of ensuring its own employment. To be used it requires at least a commitment by the planners and experts to renouncing dogmatism, and yet this is the very condition that it aims to combat (Willmott, 1989). This is because it has no adequate theory of how and why such situations arise, nor how they are maintained through the exercise of power.

A general caution about the 'critical methodology as a corrective' approach should be mentioned. That is, it may well lead to the development of methodologies which help the powerful as much as the powerless. A logical extension of Jackson's contingency position is that if there are problem situations which current methodologies cannot handle (for example, because they concern the exercise of power) then managers are just as likely as workers to be interested in improved methodology, and the result may be just as managerialist and regulative as soft methodologies. It is important therefore that any critical methodology must have a genuine and explicit emancipatory intent within it.

Critical Methodology Based on Habermas – Linking Theory and Practice A second approach to developing a critical methodology is to base it on one of Habermas's (1974) few discussions of the practical organization of theory and practice. This involves (as mentioned above) three stages. First, the development of critical theories about the nature of the social situation in terms of the position and true interests of actors within a social structure. Secondly, the use of these theories in enlightening concerned actors as to their position, leading to 'authentic insights' and changed attitudes. It is only success at this stage that provides the validation of the theories. Thirdly, the choice of tactics and strategy in the actual political struggle carried out by the enlightened social group. Such action cannot be predetermined by theory, but must emerge in the practical discourse of the group.

This forms the basis for Laughlin's (1987) critical approach to accounting systems. This incorporates both the concept of systems/lifeworld and of speech acts. Unfortunately, there is not the space for the detailed analysis that it deserves. The task of the methodology is to assist in understanding and changing accounting systems within actual organizational settings. It has three stages corresponding to those described above and in each tries to aim for an ideal speech situation. In the first, the *researchers* develop critical theories about the accounting systems and the often hidden roots of its current existence. The second stage involves discussing the results with the *researched* (i.e. actors in the situation). The aim is to critically assess these theories and to enlighten the researched, leading to a consensus on the historical, technical and structural roots of the system. The final stage involves suggesting, evaluating and acting on possible changes to the situation based on the enlightened consensus achieved in the first two stages.

In broad terms, Laughlin's methodology is certainly worthy of development and could easily be broadened to encompass the analysis of non-accounting systems. There are, however, weaknesses with the approach, some of which are recognized by Laughlin. First, the question of who are the researched and what is their interest in using a critical methodology is left largely unexamined. As argued above, such a methodology must be premised on emancipation, yet Laughlin suggests that the researched should be '*those who have power to effect change in the phenomena being investigated*' (1987: 490) [emphasis added]. Surely such people will be precisely those interested in maintaining the status quo? This is related to a second problem. If the researched *are* chosen to be a group without power then it is not at all clear that the methodology could ever start. Why should an organization allow itself to be researched in such a way? The methodology seems to be driven by the desires of the researchers rather than the needs of the researched (Freire, 1986). These problems are symptomatic of the third difficulty – a general lack of attention to the political and structural aspects of the situation and particularly to the issue of power. This is hinted at – 'the reality is that a vast range of constraints may prevent the steady movement between stages and reduce the insights gained and actions forthcoming' (Laughlin,

1987: 497) – but never dealt with. It is a crucial issue, however, for the exercise of power, both conscious and unconscious, continually shapes the process of inquiry and action.

Conclusions on Critical Methodology

Although there has been much interest in the development of a Critical ORS methodology, no substantive approach has emerged. Those which have developed have useful features, but the main shortcoming in each case is the lack of an adequate conceptualization of power, either in the constitution and maintenance of the current situation, or in enabling those who wish to bring about change. This, I would argue, reflects a general weakness within CT itself and requires us to consider other theories of power. All action-orientated methodologies aim to bring about change and thus alter the status quo in some way. Generally these are used on behalf of the powerful within a situation to improve it in their perceived interest. This may sometimes involve conflicts and thereby the exercise of power. However, by its nature, a *critical* approach sets out to challenge the status quo in a more radical way, aiming to change it in favour of the disadvantaged. It is therefore highly likely to have to deal with the resistance of those benefiting from the current situation.

Theories of Power

The previous section identified a major shortcoming of existing critical (and other) methodologies as a lack of explicit methods for dealing with power in situations of change. This leads us to review current theories of power as a first step in developing more satisfactory methodologies.

Possibly the one agreement between current writers on power is the immense difficulty in correctly defining and theorizing it. A number of recent reviews (Clegg, 1989; Oliga, 1989a; Robson and Cooper, 1989; Alvesson, 1989) reveal the wide disparity of approaches and, indeed, methods of classifying these approaches. In overview, approaches to power can be described as subjectivist objectivist, or relational depending on where they locate the main focus of power. Subjectivist approaches concentrate on individuals and groups of people exercising power in a relatively conscious way. Examples are elitism (Mills, 1956; Bachrach and Baratz, 1963), pluralism (Dahl, 1961) and radicalism (Lukes, 1974). Objectivist approaches, by contrast, concentrate on power as a structural phenomenon either constraining and oppressing (Poulantzas, 1973; Therborn, 1980) or creating order in society (Parsons, 1951). Finally, relational approaches emphasize, in different ways, that power must be seen as a relational concept, concerned either with the interaction of groups or interests, or of subject and structure (Giddens, 1984; Jessop, 1982; Foucault, 1977, 1982; Clegg, 1989).

One other point of implicit agreement between the reviews of power, particularly important for us, is the absence from these surveys of theories based on Habermas. This reflects the almost total lack of a sustained discussion of power in Habermas's work. To judge by his writing that has been translated into English, his views on the nature of the process of bringing about change are overly idealist. Change is seen essentially as a matter of changing people's attitudes and understanding. The main problem is defined to be distortions in communication, leading to false beliefs and a constrained level of rational discussion. It is almost assumed that subjects, once enlightened and correctly seeing their position, will be able to change their objective circumstances. The ideal speech situation is described, but little attention is paid to the problem of bringing it about.

For a Critical ORS, what is important is not a theoretical analysis of power per se, nor even the correct treatment of power in CT, but a conception of power from which may be derived useful operationalizations as part of action-orientated methodologies. The result must be able to be used practically in everyday situations of power by, and on behalf of, ordinary citizens (perhaps we should just buy everyone a copy of Machiavelli!). For this purpose we should not wait for some consensus on the nature of power to develop, but take the most fruitful of the current approaches, many of which have important if limited insights, and construct and test various methodological devices. This chapter can only outline some important features of an adequate conceptualization of power, and discuss briefly some potentially valuable theories.

Conceptualizing Power
Within the debates about power there are a number of underlying disagreements – for example, it is seen as either coercive or else enabling; as only intentional and explicit or also as unintentional and implicit. I would argue that power is most adequately conceptualized as an elusive, but above all multi-faceted phenomenon and it is this latter characteristic that we must look for in suitable theories. Rather than asking is power *either* X *or* Y, we must see it as *both* X *and* Y. In particular, power is both coercive, oppressive and constraining (power over), and enabling, productive and empowering (power to). Its effects are both visible, in altering states of affairs, and invisible, in maintaining states of affairs. It can be both conscious and intentional, and unconscious and unintentional. Finally it must be analysed both from the perspective of agency that acts and from the perspective of

structure that preconditions and enables. In other words, it must be seen as relational.

Particular Theories of Power

Clegg's 'Circuits of Power' Clegg (1989: 211–39) has developed a multi-level model of 'circuits of power'. At the top level are the day-to-day episodes of power in which agencies, with different resources and interests, interact in a complex network of semi-causal effects. This level draws on and reproduces social relations of signification and production which have become fixed through the history of interaction. Sometimes, however, changes can occur at the deeper levels, in particular the level of social integration which fixes meaning and membership, or system integration where changes in the technology of production and discipline can alter the balance of empowerment and disempowerment. These feed up to alter the rules and resources in the first circuit of power.

One of the main sources of the model is the work of Callon, Latour and others (Callon, 1986) who study and map out the actual practice of scientists as they attempt to control their environments and carry forward their research. In particular, they see scientists engaged in practical activities such as generating common interests, gaining allies, constructing allegiances, getting control of resources and so on within a structure which is itself the result of previous networks of such activity. They thus demonstrate empirically how such structures of interest and power are generated and reproduced.

Foucault on Power Foucault is concerned to describe power not as an abstract theoretical entity but in terms of its operation – what actually happens in the exercise of power. Power can best be observed in institutions such as prisons and asylums, which magnify its operations, but the practices involved spread throughout society. Indeed, this is a major characteristic: power is not exercised centrally by the state above society, but it is immanent throughout all the levels and activities within society. Power is only manifest as 'micro-power' on a localized basis. Equally, however, all our activity is involved in and shaped by power. Power is intentional, in that its exercise has intended consequences, but there is no overall guiding subject, no coherent structure or strategy. Its effects escape intentions – 'people know what they do; they frequently know why they do what they do; but what they don't know is what what they do does' (quoted in Dreyfus and Rabinow, 1982: 187). Power is intimately connected with knowledge. Foucault refers to 'power/knowledge', arguing that power relations lead to the development of knowledge, and know-ledge enables the exercise of power. In recent history this has manifested itself in techniques of power that Foucault describes as *disciplinary* (a word with several critical connotations including control and regulation, punishment and a body of knowledge), controlling, classifying, routinizing, scrutinizing people's every ac-tivity, and ultimately constituting individual subjectivity through self-disciplining.

Power is to be seen as relational and based in action. It is in fact constituted in the relations between whole networks of actions and reactions. It is the way one set of actions affects or conditions other actions. Power is not all or nothing, but a complex continuum from influence to violence, from easing to constraining, which channels and guides rather than forces and blocks, structuring the possibilities for action within the network of ongoing social practices. Power relations may be all-embracing but they are not overwhelming. The exercise of power brings into being resistance to power, and indeed power as a relation implies some space of freedom against which it is exercised. Bringing about change is thus possible, but only by local resistance within the power network, not by attempts to change the whole.

Foucault does become quite specific about the analysis of power relations (1982: 223), suggesting that it is necessary to establish a number of elements – the system of distinctions and differences that power draws upon; the varied objectives pursued by agencies; the means of creating power relations, e.g. force, language, rules, secrecy; the way they are institutionalized; and the degree of rationalization, that is effectiveness, of the techniques. Such analyses are useful in the continual struggle in and against power, but power can never be removed for it is implicit in our actions: 'to say there cannot be a society without power relations is not to say either that those which are established are necessary, or . . . that power constitutes a fatality at the heart of societies' (Foucault, 1982: 223).

Conclusion on Power
There does seem to be a convergence of theories towards a relational view, seeing power as manifest in localized networks of activity which draw on and reproduce/transform structures of meaning and disci-pline. These seem to me to provide a suitable basis for the further development of critical methodologies. There are a number of ways in which this might occur. First by extending or modifying existing methodologies such as those of Ulrich, Laughlin or even Checkland. Secondly, by developing wholly new approaches specifically con-cerned with power, which could be used in conjunction with or

instead of others. Thirdly it is possible that a more comprehensive and practical view of power might be developed within Critical Theory itself which would yield the basis of a methodology.

Conclusions

This chapter has sought to show that the history of ORS can be seen to reflect a movement from the technical, through the practical towards the critical. This movement, however, is very much in the academic world – the practice of OR is still almost exclusively technical. A space has been created for Critical ORS but this space has yet to be painted in with practical critical methodologies. It has been argued here that the main difficulty is an inadequate treatment of power, and suggestions have been made as to fruitful directions for such work.

References

Ackoff, R. (1974) 'The social responsibility of operational research', *Operational Research Quarterly*, 25: 361–71.

Ackoff, R. (1975) 'A reply to the comments of Keith Chesterton, Robert Goodsman, Jonathan Rosenhead and Colin Thunhurst', *Operational Research Quarterly*, 26(1): 96–8.

Ackoff, R. (1977) 'Optimization + Objectivity = Opt Out', *European Journal of Operational Research*, 1: 1–7.

Ackoff, R. (1979a) 'The future of operational research is past', *Journal of the Operational Research Society*, 30: 93–104.

Ackoff, R. (1979b) 'Resurrecting the future of operational research', *Journal of the Operational Research Society*, 30: 189–200.

Ackoff, R. (1982) 'On the hard headedness and soft heartedness of M. C. Jackson', *Journal of Applied Systems Analysis*, 9: 31–3.

Alvesson, M. (1989) 'Power, conflict and control', in M. Jackson, P. Keys and S. Cropper (eds), *Operational Research and the Social Sciences*. New York: Plenum Press.

Alvesson, M. and Willmott, H. (1988) 'Critical Theory and the Sciences of Management', paper presented at the 'Frankfurt School: How Relevant is it Today?' conference, Erasmus University, Rotterdam.

Bachrach, P. and Baratz, M. (1963) 'Decisions and non-decisions: an analytical framework', *American Political Science Review*, 57: 641–51.

Bennett, P., Cropper, S. and Huxham, C. (1989) 'Modelling interactive decisions: the hypergame focus', in J. Rosenhead (ed.), *Rational Analysis for a Problematic World*. Chichester: Wiley.

Bernal, J. (1939) *The Social Function of Science*. London: Routledge & Kegan Paul.

Bevan, R. and Bryer, R. (1978) 'On measuring the contribution of OR', *Journal of the Operational Research Society*, 29: 409–19.

Burrell, G. and Morgan, G. (1979) *Sociological Paradigms and Organisational Analysis*. London: Heinemann.

Callon, M. (1986) 'Some elements of a sociology of translation: domestication of the scallops and the fishermen of St Brieuc Bay', in J. Law (ed.), *Power, Action and Belief: A New Sociology Of Knowledge?* (Sociological Review Monograph 32). London: Routledge & Kegan Paul.

Checkland, P. (1981) *Systems Thinking, Systems Practice*. New York: Wiley.

Checkland, P. (1982) 'Soft systems methodology as process: a reply to M. C. Jackson', *Journal of Applied Systems Analysis*, 9: 37–9.

Checkland, P. (1983) 'OR and the systems movement: mappings and conflicts', *Journal of the Operational Research Society*, 34: 661–76.

Checkland, P. (1989) 'Soft systems methodology', in J. Rosenhead (ed.), *Rational Analysis for a Problematic World*. Chichester: Wiley.

Checkland, P. and Scholes, J. (1990) *Soft Systems Methodology in Action*. Chichester: Wiley.

Chesterton, K., Goodsman, R., Rosenhead, J. and Thunhurst, C. (1975) 'A comment on "The social responsibility of operational research"', *Operational Research Quarterly*, 26: 91–5.

Churchman, C. W. (1971) *The Design Of Inquiring Systems*. New York: Basic Books.

Churchman, C. W. (1979) *The Systems Approach and its Enemies*. New York: Basic Books.

Churchman, C. W. (1982) 'Reply to M. C. Jackson', *Journal of Applied Systems Analysis*, 9: 35.

Clegg, S. (1989) *Frameworks of Power*. London: Sage.

Dahl, R. (1961) *Who Governs: Democracy and Power in an American City*. New Haven, CT: Yale University Press.

Dando, M. and Bennett, P. (1981) 'A Kuhnian crisis in management science?', *Journal of the Operational Research Society*, 32: 91–103.

Dreyfus, H. and Rabinow, P. (1982) *Michel Foucault: Beyond Structuralism and Hermeneutics*. New York: Harvester Press.

Eden, C. (1989) 'Using cognitive mapping for strategic options development and analysis (SODA)', in J. Rosenhead (ed.), *Rational Analysis for a Problematic World*. Chichester: Wiley.

Flood, R. (1989a) 'Six scenarios for the future of systems "problem solving"', *Systems Practice*, 2 (1): 75–99.

Flood, R. (1989b) 'OR and systems: "management of messes"', in M. Jackson, P. Keys and S. Cropper (eds), *Operational Research and the Social Sciences*. New York: Plenum Press.

Flood, R. (1990a) 'Liberating systems theory: towards critical systems thinking', *Human Relations*, 43 (1): 49–75.

Flood, R. (1990b) *Liberating Systems Theory*. New York: Plenum.

Flood, R. and Jackson, M. (1991a) *Creative Problem Solving*. Chichester: Wiley.

Flood, R. and Jackson, M. (1991b) *Critical Systems Thinking: Directed Readings*. Chichester: Wiley.

Foucault, M. (1977) *Discipline and Punish: The Birth of the Prison*. Harmondsworth: Penguin.

Foucault, M. (1982) 'The subject and power', in H. Dreyfus and P. Rabinow, *Michel Foucault: Beyond Structuralism and Hermeneutics*. New York: Harvester Press.

Freire, P. (1986) *Pedagogy of the Oppressed*. New York: Continuum.

Friend, J. (1989) 'The strategic choice approach', in J. Rosenhead (ed.), *Rational Analysis for a Problematic World*. Chichester: Wiley.

Friend, J. and Hickling, A. (1987) *Planning under Pressure: the Strategic Choice Approach*. Oxford: Pergamon.

Giddens, A. (1984) *The Constitution of Society*. Cambridge: Polity Press.

Habermas, J. (1972) *Knowledge and Human Interests*. London: Heinemann.

Habermas, J. (1974) *Theory and Practice*. London: Heinemann.

Habermas, J. (1984) *The Theory of Communicative Action, Vol. I: Reason and the Rationalization of Society*, trans. T. McCarthy. Cambridge: Polity Press.

Habermas, J. (1987) *The Theory of Communicative Action, Vol. II: Lifeworld and System*, trans. T. McCarthy. Cambridge: Polity Press.

Hales, M. (1974) 'Management science and the "second industrial revolution"', *Radical Science*, 1: 5–28.

Jackson, M. (1982) 'The nature of "soft" systems thinking: the work of Churchman, Ackoff and Checkland', *Journal of Applied Systems Analysis*, 9: 17–29.

Jackson, M. (1983) 'The nature of "soft" systems thinking: comment on the three replies', *Journal of Applied Systems Analysis*, 10: 109–13.

Jackson, M. (1985) 'Social systems theory and practice: the need for a critical approach', *International Journal of General Systems*, 10: 135–51.

Jackson, M. (1987) 'New directions in management science', in M. Jackson and P. Keys (eds), *New Directions in Management Science*. Aldershot: Gower.

Jackson, M. (1988) 'Some methodologies for community operational research', *Journal of the Operational Research Society*, 39: 715–24.

Jackson, M. (1989a) 'Which systems methodology when?: initial results from a research program', in R. Flood, M. Jackson and P. Keys (eds), *Systems Prospects: The Next Ten Years of Systems Research*. New York: Plenum.

Jackson, M. (1989b) 'Future prospects in systems thinking', in R. Flood, M. Jackson and P. Keys (eds), *Systems Prospects: The Next Ten Years of Systems Research*. New York: Plenum.

Jackson, M. (1991) *Systems Methodology for the Management Sciences*. New York: Plenum.

Jackson, M. and Keys, P. (1984) 'Towards a system of system methodologies', *Journal of the Operational Research Society*, 35: 473–86.

Jackson, M. and Keys, P. (eds) (1987) *New Directions in Management Science*. Aldershot: Gower.

Jessop, B. (1982) *The Capitalist State: Marxist Theories and Methods*. Oxford: Martin Robertson.

Keys, P. (1987) 'Traditional management science and the emerging critique', in M. Jackson and P. Keys (eds), *New Directions in Management Science*. Aldershot: Gower.

Keys, P. (1988) 'A methodology for methodology choice', *Systems Research*, 5(1): 65–76.

Knights, D. (1989) 'Intervention and change', in M. Jackson, P. Keys and S. Cropper (eds), *Operational Research and the Social Sciences*. New York: Plenum.

Laughlin, R. (1987) 'Accounting systems in organizational contexts: a case for critical theory', *Accounting, Organizations and Society*, 12(5): 479–502.

Lukes, S. (1974) *Power: A Radical View*. London: Macmillan.

Lyytinen, K. and Klein, H. (1985) 'Critical theory of Jürgen Habermas as a basis for a theory of information systems', in E. Mumford, R. Hirscheim, G. Fitzgerald and T. Wood-Harper (eds), *Research Methods in Information Systems*. Amsterdam: North-Holland.

Mills, C. W. (1956) *The Power Elite*. Oxford: Oxford University Press.

Mingers, J. (1980) 'Towards an appropriate social theory for applied systems thinking: critical theory and soft systems methodology', *Journal of Applied Systems Analysis*, 7: 41–9.

Mingers, J. (1984) 'Subjectivism and soft systems methodology – a critique', *Journal of Applied Systems Analysis*, 11: 85–103.

Mingers, J. (1989a) 'Systems criticisms of OR: a response', *Systemist*, 11 (4): 8–16.

Mingers, J. (1989b) 'Problems of measurement', in M. Jackson, P. Keys and S. Cropper (eds), *Operational Research and the Social Sciences*. New York: Plenum.

Mingers, J. (1991) 'The content of OR courses: results of a questionnaire to OR groups', *Journal of the Operational Research Society*, 42 (5): 375–82.

Oliga, J. (1988) 'Methodological foundations of systems methodologies', *Systems Practice*, 1 (1): 87–112.

Oliga, J. (1989a) 'Power and interest in organizations', paper presented at the 33rd Annual Meeting of ISSS, Edinburgh, 2–7 July.

Oliga, J. (1989b) 'Ideology and systems emancipation', paper presented at the 33rd Annual Meeting of ISSS, Edinburgh, 2–7 July.

Parry, R. and Mingers, J. (1990) 'Community operational research: its context and its future', *OMEGA* 19 (6): 577–86.

Parsons, T. (1951) *The Social System*. Glencoe, Ill: Free Press.

Phillips, L. (1982) 'Requisite decision modelling: a case study', *Journal of the Operational Research Society*, 33 (4): 303–11.

Poulantzas, N. (1973) *Political Power and Social Classes*. London: New Left Books.

Reed, M. (1985) *Redirections in Organizational Analysis*. London: Tavistock.

Rivett, B. P. (1963) 'Opening address: OR Society Annual Conference', *Journal of the Operational Research Society*, 14: 1–11.

Robson, K. and Cooper, D. (1989) 'Power and management control', in W. Chua, T. Lowe and S. Puxty (eds), *Critical Perspectives in Management Control*. London: Macmillan.

Rosenhead, J. (1976) 'Some further comments on "The social responsibility of operational research"', *Operational Research Quarterly*, 27: 266–72.

Rosenhead, J. (1987) 'From management science to workers' science', in M. Jackson and P. Keys (eds), *New Directions in Management Science*. Aldershot: Gower.

Rosenhead, J. (1989) 'Operational research at the crossroads: Cecil Gordon and the development of post-war OR', *Journal of the Operational Research Society*, 40: 3–28.

Rosenhead, J. and Thunhurst, C. (1982) 'A materialist analysis of operational research', *Journal of the Operational Research Society*, 33: 111–22.

Stowell, F. (1989) 'Organizational power and the metaphor commodity', in R. Flood, M. Jackson and P. Keys (eds), *Systems Prospects: The Next Ten Years of Systems Research*. New York: Plenum.

Therborn, G. (1980) *The Ideology of Power and the Power of Ideology*. London: Verso.

Tinker, T. and Lowe, T. (1984) 'One-dimensional management science: the making of a technocratic consciousness', *Interfaces*, 14: 40–56.

Tomlinson, R. (1971) *OR Comes of Age*. London: Tavistock.

Ulrich, W. (1983) *Critical Heuristics of Social Planning. A New Approach to Practical Philosophy*. Berne: Haupt.

Vickers, G. (1965) *The Art of Judgement*. London: Chapman & Hall.

Willmott, H. (1989) 'OR as a problem situation: from soft systems methodology to critical science', in M. Jackson, P. Keys and S. Cropper (eds), *Operational Research and the Social Sciences*. New York: Plenum.

Wood, S. and Kelly, J. (1978) 'Towards a critical management science', *Journal of Management Studies*, 15: 1–24.

6

Critical Theory and Accounting

Michael Power and Richard Laughlin

A recent cultural critic claimed that we live in a world of 'pseudo events' and 'quasi-information'. The categories of truth and falsehood have been displaced by predominantly instrumental conceptions of information. Knowledge has been replaced by information which 'sounds' true and establishes transient claims to credibility. On this view the value of such information therefore lies in its capacity to influence and mobilize rather than to represent (Lasch, 1978).

Such thoughts are relevant when we consider the status of accounting and its informational aspirations. Is accounting a system of pseudo-information? Are its claims to represent economic reality hollow? In this chapter we respond to these questions in the light of Habermas's Critical Theory and, in particular, his theory of communication (Habermas, 1984, 1987). If accounting is a practice which increasingly 'sounds true' it is nevertheless a powerful force in economic reasoning. Notwithstanding crises and scandals in which the failings of accounting are briefly evident, it retains its credibility as a whole. Indeed when accounting 'fails', the solution invariably involves an investment in new or better accounting; such is its irresistible logic. If we are to control complex modern societies then we seem to require ever more elaborate forms of economic calculation, of which accounting is a dominant instance.

This chapter provides a tentative introduction to Critical Theory and its implications for accounting. It is by no means exhaustive in its treatment and the reader is referred to a number of other relevant studies. However, we have tried to capture the essential elements of Habermas's recent work in order to explore an alternative theoretical conception of the role and function of accounting. In the next section we begin with a broadly critical analysis of the view that accounting somehow represents economic reality. In the third section we articulate a perspective based upon Critical Theory within a field of different theories of accounting and its informational characteristics. This is intended to soften the ground for the reception of some of Habermas's ideas in the fourth section. In the fifth section we consider the position of accounting as a 'steering medium' in

Habermas's sense and in the sixth section we consider the role of accounting and its potential as a medium for enabling or distorting communication.

Overall, the arguments are suggestive of a conception of accounting in which there is a need both to recover the public dimension of its legitimacy and also to comprehend its possible effects on human subjects. This requires a richer theoretical perspective than dominant instrumental conceptions of accounting provide.

Contesting the Nature of Accounting

What counts as accounting? This question does not arise, for at least two reasons. First, it tends not to be asked because of an overwhelming presumption that the answer is obvious. Secondly, if it gets asked at all it is usually in the context of some crisis in our understanding of accounting. Clearly there is a tension between these two reasons for a lack of fundamental questioning about accounting. If the occasions of crisis and/or scandal multiply it becomes increasingly difficult to sustain the obviousness of accounting, analogous perhaps to the 'discovery' of epicycles to sustain an increasingly suspect Ptolemaic cosmology. But the durability of the belief in the utility of existing forms of accounting also suggests a more appropriate analogy with the poison oracle of the Azande (see Winch, 1964). Here reality itself is constructed to bring it into line with the tribal practice.

Traditionally, accounting is defined as a technique of quantification or calculation which is an important prerequisite for the smooth functioning of modern businesses. Accounting is therefore understood largely as 'work' rather than 'interaction' in Habermas's (1971: ch. 6) sense. Of those practices such as accounting that are commonly regarded as being merely technical we can say that they 'work' well or badly in a given context. Our criteria of appraisal are thereby limited to the instrumental success or otherwise of the technical attributes in achieving some pre-given end, for example supplying relevant information. In other words we can say that accounting is traditionally subsumed under a model of purposive rationality, 'Zweckrationalität' in Weber's (1978: 24–6) sense. It functions as a merely *formal* set of procedures whose techniques are neutral and incontestable. On this view accounting may supply guidance on appropriate means and methods to achieve given informational ends but cannot determine those ends themselves. This image of accounting as technique also supports a conception of accounting as an extension of common sense. It is an image of accounting as something that we can take for granted and that does not merit theoretical elaboration.[1]

The contemporary version of this slightly caricatured image of accounting is found in connection with the goal of decision-making. In 1966 the American Accounting Association published *A Statement of Basic Accounting Theory* (ASOBAT) in which it was stated that 'accounting information must be useful to people accounting in various capacities both inside and outside of the entity concerned' (American Accounting Association, 1966: 8). Despite widespread criticism of ASOBAT this conception of accounting has remained durable and has informed subsequent thinking; see, for example, Financial Accounting Standards Board (1978), Accounting Standards Steering Committee (1975). Accounting students learn very quickly to distinguish between accounting for internal decision-making purposes, i.e. management accounting, and accounting for external decision-making purposes, i.e. financial accounting. But although there are very different technical elaborations appropriate to each form of accounting (e.g. budgeting, variance analysis and costing for management accounting; recognition, valuation and disclosure conventions for financial accounting) there is a single common vision: accounting provides information that is *useful* to users of that information.

This textbook image of accounting as information for economic decision-making is promoted as sensible and robust. What else could accounting be for? Corresponding to such an image the accountant emerges as a worthy under-labourer, a 'worker' and perhaps an expert in technical niceties but with no pretence to pass value judgements on the goals of decision-making. His or her role is neutrally facilitative and, in a sense made popular by the media, rather dull.

If this is an exaggerated image of accounting it is not wildly so. However, it is an image which has increasingly been subject to critical scrutiny and redefinition as the commonsense view that accounting simply 'represents' economic reality in an unbiased fashion has been questioned from a number of directions. In what follows we shall look briefly at the problem of accounting as a representational practice and explore some of the ways in which accounting theorists have voiced doubts about it. These approaches share a broad critical purpose in that they refuse to take for granted accounting concepts and practices on their own terms. However, they are also profoundly different from each other in many respects.

Information supposedly tells us something new ('supposedly' because, as we shall see, information is often used in practice for a variety of purposes, such as to reassure or confirm expectations and preconceptions). It is assumed to achieve this by (re)presenting in some way events which are relatively independent of the representational system. In the case of accounting we might wish to call these independent events 'economic reality'. So here we have two crucial elements of accounting as information: novelty and representation. On the question of newness we shall have little to say.[2] As far as representation is concerned, criticism has come from many different sources. At a very simple level, the very possibility of 'creative' accounting practices suggests that the image of accounting as a simple mapping of an independent reality is naive, although it is worth adding that the idea of creativity presupposes the existence of some 'objective' benchmark against which it can be evaluated. Hence a more radical critique of the representationalist credentials of accounting would see it as a practice that was 'creative' in a much deeper sense, i.e. not as a deviation from an objective standard but as a practice *without* objectivity.

In the context of financial accounting there is much more at stake than double-entry bookkeeping. Group accounting and the setting of provisions are examples of areas which are constantly open to judgement and negotiation. Accounting authorities such as the Financial Accounting Standards Board (FASB) in the USA, and the Accounting Standards Committee (ASC) in the UK (replaced by the Accounting Standards Board (ASB) on 1 August 1990) have attempted to stem the tide of creativity by reducing areas of judgement and negotiation (a move which effectively involves institutionalizing and privileging certain 'official' judgements over others). Recently in the UK this has concerned the area of 'Off Balance Sheet Finance',[3] although such regulative moves run the risk of buying the virtue of consistency at the expense of being arbitrary. More significantly these bodies have in addition been subject to considerable pressure and lobbying by parties who believe that the particular representational convention chosen will have important economic consequences for them (Zeff, 1978; Solomons, 1986).

In the context of management accounting the position is similar. The determination of 'true' cost in some representational sense is a myth that the questions of overhead allocation or transfer pricing have done much to explode. To take the example of transfer pricing, most textbooks acknowledge that it is as much an issue of organizational power and politics as optimal costing/pricing technique. Historically, accounting, like many social practices and disciplines, has aspired to an objectivity both grounded in common sense and also theoretically justified. The search for 'true' income and 'true' cost indicate a representational ideal of accounting as a purely formal or procedural activity which has not been entirely expunged. The hope seems to be that if only we can refine or improve our set of accounting techniques then 'cost' and 'income' will be revealed.

Elsewhere, the very measurement convention on which account-ing has been based has also been an important focus for the question of representation. The apparent objectivity of historic cost account-ing has, in times of inflation, come to look obviously suspect. Alternative systems of accounting for changing prices have effec-tively multiplied the possibilities for the unit of economic measure-ment, thus undermining this objectivity further. Yet, as we noted above, the traditional image of accounting and its allegiance to the historic cost convention have proved remarkably durable.

Given these internal tensions and contradictions in the idea of accounting as a representational practice it should come as little surprise to encounter bolder critiques, which break with the notion of representation entirely. They hold that there is no independent economic reality. Rather, accounting is implicated in *creating* that reality. Hopwood (1987) has argued that management accounting systems provide a medium through which the organization becomes 'visible' to itself. That which is newly 'visible' is not a representation of an independent reality but the creation of a new domain of economic facts. Accounting therefore creates the economic facts that it purports to represent. Hines (1988) has argued in a similar fashion in the context of financial accounting. The communication of economic 'facts' in financial statements is simultaneously their construction *as* facts. No doubt these are strange and difficult ideas and they seem to violate our deepest 'objectivist' and 'realist' intuitions. But we must take seriously the possibility that these intuitions in the context of accounting are simply mistaken.

Accounting Information and Decision-making

The problem of representation suggests that there is no single way to account for economic reality despite a continuing rhetoric to the contrary. Given this inevitable indeterminacy or subjectivity there has been a variety of theoretical responses. These can be differen-tiated both according to their respective perceptions of the role and nature of accounting information for decision-making and also according to the explanatory level at which these perceptions are articulated. Figure 6.1 provides a very simple classification of these theoretical endeavours across both dimensions. In common with classifications of this kind, it must be understood as a simplification, a useful one but a simplification nevertheless. The figure provides an 'epistemological map' as a basis for articulating the relative theoreti-cal commitments of different perspectives. However, it must always be borne in mind that each perspective would not see itself in this way as one of a number of options but would attempt to criticize and

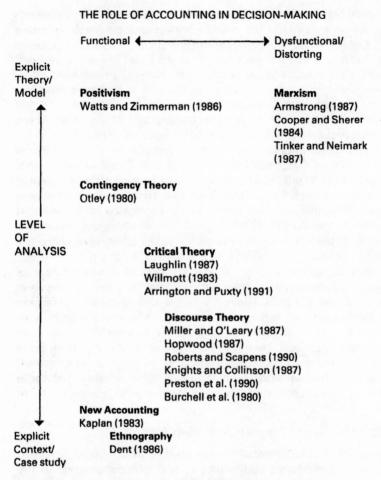

Figure 6.1   *Approaches to accounting information*

undermine those around it. The figure is thus a form of meta-overview. Far from being fixed and static, it is a 'field of force' which is always threatening to collapse into one of its 'moments'. With this in mind it can still fulfil a very useful heuristic purpose.

Figure 6.1 characterizes an important normative dimension of accounting thought in the horizontal dimension. This concerns whether accounting is to be regarded as enabling and facilitative or as merely coercive and distorting. The vertical dimension concerns the level of contextual specificity at which theoretical insights are articulated, i.e. whether the theoretical structure can be articulated relatively independently of specific contexts or whether such contexts play an explicit role in the theorization process. The point concerns the degree of analytical commitment to something like 'richness' of specific context. With this matrix in mind we can tentatively 'position' various approaches to accounting relative to an understanding of Critical Theory.

The idea of accounting for decision-making purposes seems so obvious that it is almost inconceivable that it could have any other role. But do we have a clear conception of what decision-making involves and how it takes place? What is a decision and what is it about? From Figure 6.1 it is apparent that there are different degrees of criticism or scrutiny of these questions in terms both of the degree of contextualization of the decision-making process and of the relative evaluation of accounting as a facilitating technology. A number of positions such as contingency theory (Otley, 1980) and positivism (Watts and Zimmerman, 1986) are located for completeness but we do not discuss them directly.

Close to the level of professional and industrial interests, e.g. as articulated by ASOBAT, are functional concerns about the *quality* of the decision-making purpose. Are we making optimal decisions? Do we have sufficient information for this purpose? There is an extensive body of research around these questions. A prominent strand of current research is the context-based criticism offered by Kaplan (1983) of traditional management accounting. In short he argues that traditional accounting culture has inhibited strategic decision-making. He proposes 'activity based' systems of costing as an aid to optimal product decisions.

Although Kaplan is critical, he accepts the decision-making framework as somehow functionally unproblematic: accounting as an enabling practice is merely in need of improvement. However, other studies have questioned the very nature of decision-making itself by confronting this ideal role for accounting with its actual functioning in organizational settings. The study by Burchell et al. (1980) attempts to enrich our conception of the role of information systems. Decision-making will only correspond to the enabling ideal where there is *high* certainty of the objectives or ends to which the decision is orientated together with *high* certainty concerning the causal relation between decision and action. However, this is only one possible (and rare) instance. In contrast, accounting information can also serve to rationalize and justify decisions *ex post* or can be used as 'ammunition' in organizational politics. These context-dependent roles are equally significant as the enabling ideal and, it is claimed, much more prevalent in practice. Following this critical initiative, numerous studies in the management accounting area have sought to analyse accounting in action and its consequences, not all of which, in contrast to the ideal, will be intended.

For example, studies of accounting innovation in organizational contexts have documented the sense in which accounting meets resistance to and possible transformations of its original purpose. Berry et al. (1985) document the resistance of one organization in the UK coal industry to the introduction of new financial controls. Ansari and Euske (1987) provide a similar study in the context of a US military enterprise. The ideal of improved decision-making, the official rationale for accounting innovation, encounters numerous pressures in organizational contexts. This suggests that accounting is less important as a functional resource for decision-making than as a symbolic resource for the organization as a whole (March, 1987).

An important extension of this contextualist research goes further and claims that whether accounting serves the decision-enabling role or not, it nevertheless has profound effects on human subjects, who are constructed as 'calculable' and 'calculating' individuals within the organization (Miller and O'Leary, 1987). Accounting distorts to the extent that individuals are subsumed within accounting regimes with important behavioural consequences in local organizational contexts (Knights and Collinson, 1987; Roberts and Scapens, 1990).

Radically orientated studies such as those by Tinker and Neimark (1987), Armstrong (1987) and Cooper and Sherer (1984) articulate the sense in which accounting is a *fundamentally* distorting practice in so far as it represents and promulgates the interests of capital. Hence accounting is one important dimension of an economic system considered as a repressive totality. Such neo-Marxist perspectives attempt to express the complicity of traditional accounting with modes of exploitation in general by treating labour simply as one cost 'above the line' amongst others. From this point of view, even if accounting does fulfil its functional mission for management it is nevertheless profoundly dysfunctional for labour.

In terms of Figure 6.1, Critical Theory occupies what might be described as a 'middle' position. In our opinion this has a number of attractions. Perhaps most important is the recognition that the enabling or distorting status of a practice such as accounting is an open empirical question, which is nevertheless guided by a distinctive theoretical model. This is the mode of analysis implicit in recent studies by Laughlin (1987) and Arrington and Puxty (1991), a contextual orientation within a more general critical framework. As there is very little accounting research in the Critical Theory tradition other than these two studies we need to consider this framework in more detail.

Accounting and the Rationalization of the Lifeworld

According to Habermas, Weber (1978) argued that purposive rationality is at the heart of the modernization process. Indeed, bookkeeping seemed to represent and symbolize rationality itself (Weber, 1978: 92–3). In contrast, Habermas (1984, 1987) contests Weber's identification of instrumental reason with the rationalization characteristic of modern life. He argues that rationalization is in substance a process of differentiation in which traditional forms of society develop relatively autonomous spheres of culture. The emergence of instrumental reason is just one possible sphere of development, and Habermas is concerned to render this visible. He identifies three cultural spheres or worlds each with its distinctive style of learning, cognition and institutional practice. Thus the objective world, the intersubjective world and the subjective world correspond broadly to the practices of science, politics and art. Habermas is attempting to construct a model of the rationalization process as the release of specialized experience in these three domains, which represent distinctive rationality complexes: instrumental reason, practical reason and affective reason respectively.

This model, if plausible, permits Habermas to argue that it is this differentiation in general rather than instrumental reason in particular which characterizes modernity. It also opens the way for a critique of modernity in which one particular form of reason, the instrumental, has dominated at the expense of others. Hence we must distinguish Habermas's brand of Critical Theory sharply from romanticist critiques of capitalism for which rehumanization is only possible as a rejection of technology itself (see Marcuse, 1986). Against the pessimism of his Frankfurt School predecessors Habermas attempts to articulate a basis for reconstituting social life and institutional action as the recovery of a balance between the three fundamental spheres of social development. Modernization is therefore not rejected but reappraised. The theoretical contours of this reconstruction depend on the concepts of 'lifeworld', 'system' and 'steering media', which we shall now consider.

The concept of the 'lifeworld' is intended to provide a relatively unproblematic characterization of the domain of everyday experience (although from certain Marxist perspectives, such as that of Althusser, it is profoundly problematic and ideological). The concept expresses a level of pre-theoretical practical experience in which social integration is effected by a largely unreflective cultural tradition. According to Habermas, the lifeworld exists both logically and historically prior to those processes of rationalization and differentiation which characterize modern societies. One of

Habermas's deepest themes concerns the extent to which we have forgotten the collective symbolic structures of the lifeworld which actually enable and inform those predominant but narrow and specialized systems of action, such as accounting.

In contrast to the lifeworld, Habermas's concept of 'system' is that of a functionally definable arena of action such as the economy or, on a micro scale, an organization. Systems emerge from the lifeworld as a consequence of processes of functional and cognitive differentiation. According to Habermas they rapidly develop an autonomous developmental logic of their own. Weber's (1978) analysis of domestic production provides an illustration of the point: traditional patterns of motivation and work are gradually replaced by more explicitly economic forms of organization and behaviour. Gorz (1989) has described this as the 'economic rationalisation of labour' whereby the (lifeworld) contexts of an integrated relation between work and life give way to an autonomous economic domain of work. In an accounting context Hopwood (1987) has argued similarly for the historical role of accounting in installing a new realm of microeconomic facts in place of more traditional patterns of organizational control.

Habermas's Critical Theory is largely an attempt to recover and articulate the dependence of the system on the lifeworld. But he is no backward-looking romantic. For him, the emergence of autonomous systems is a potentially positive force which is not necessarily distorting. To this extent, Habermas can be regarded as a systems theorist with a difference. The systems-theoretic framework is premised upon a broadly functional view of social organization: societies consist of systems and subsystems which are governed principally by survival imperatives and react and adapt to their environments to this end. Habermas has always questioned the analogy between social and biological systems which, he believes, sustains the many versions of systems theory. Thus Habermas is critical of Luhmann (1982) and others because their functionalist orientation fails to reflect upon the historical origins of the problems that systems theory addresses. For Habermas the problem of social 'survival' is not a quasi-biological matter but concerns the guiding symbolic structures of the lifeworld and their capacity to steer subsystems, such as the economy, rather than be colonized by them.

The concept of 'steering' plays a pivotal role in this theoretical structure by providing the link between lifeworld and system. Habermas's model of balanced social development posits the possibility that systems receive 'symbolic guidance' from the lifeworld via mechanisms of steering which are grounded in, and controlled at, the level of the lifeworld. However, according to Habermas, this order of dependence of system on lifeworld has in fact become 'distorted' and effectively reversed. Systems and subsystems of increasing complexity have emerged which threaten to colonize the lifeworld itself. Guided by the steering media of 'money' and 'power' the domain of instrumental reason has come to smother and eclipse both the lifeworld and other possible orders of reasoning, e.g. politics and subjectivity. This results in what Habermas calls the 'inner colonization of the lifeworld' (though he is ultimately more optimistic than Weber concerning the possibilities for intervening in this process): 'The thesis of internal colonization states that the subsystems of the economy and the state become more and more complex as a consequence of capitalist growth and penetrate ever deeper into the symbolic reproduction of the lifeworld' (Habermas, 1987: 367).

This theory of social development must be understood in the context of Habermas's broader theory of communicative action. Borrowing from speech act theory, Habermas does not draw a sharp distinction between language and action. Language is itself a form of action and establishes relations of interaction in the process of communication. The categories of language and action are therefore not analytically distinct. Habermas has argued that in all speech 'acts' there are implicit claims raised with varying degrees of emphasis. These are 'validity' claims to truth, normative rightness (or justice), truthfulness (or sincerity) and comprehendability. These claims are rarely made explicit in everyday life, notwithstanding that they lie at the heart of the communicative process. So when the waiter offers more coffee one normally assumes that there is coffee available, i.e. that an implicit truth claim or *warrant* can be accepted. However, there are occasions in ordinary social interaction when such implicit claims may be explicitly questioned. Specialized practices such as science seek to institutionalize this form of critical questioning but, according to Habermas, they nevertheless presuppose truth claims as a basis for sustainable communication.

According to Habermas, communication always anticipates the possibility that implicit truth claims may be questioned and justified in an ideal speech situation. This philosophical structure is a 'necessary counterfactual'. By this Habermas means that even though it cannot be realized in an empirical sense the idea of such an ideal speech situation plays a deeply constitutive role in communication because it expresses an underlying ideal goal or direction to discourse. Indeed it provides a basis for a theory of communicative action to illuminate pathological or 'distorted' forms of communication which violate the conditions of this ideal. In general such distortion consists in severing the institutional link to the possibility of discursive justification of implicit validity claims, a loss of reflection in which the communicative foundation of all forms of action is obscured from view.

In this sense the process of the colonization of the lifeworld by narrowly instrumental system imperatives is also a process of 'systematically distorted' communication. The lifeworld is a primary communicative resource which has become colonized by the functional dictates of system and subsystem. An example might be an economic system in which profitability, not necessarily maximized, is the predominant goal. Such a goal tends to negate and inhibit institutional possibilities for questioning and justifying itself. This means that the lifeworld is no longer capable of communicatively steering a complex economic system which has generated its own functional goals. The current concern with the alarming environmental effects of economically 'rational' action provides a dramatic illustration of the thesis. The rationalization of the lifeworld as a process of differentiation is not inherently distorting. But the discursive demarcation of specialized contexts of individual and collective action also brings the risk that such complex systems advance their own limited operational imperatives at the expense of others, with urgent consequences for social and global welfare.

Having sketched the contours of Habermas's theory of communication we need now to consider the position of accounting in relation to it. First we need to consider the role of accounting as a steering medium in Habermas's sense. Following this we need to consider the conditions under which accounting is a form of 'distorted communication' or an 'enabling' practice.

Accounting as a Steering Medium

As we have seen above, the concept of 'steering' has its origins and meaning in a systems theory perspective. To the extent that Habermas is attempting to restore the legitimate steering function of the lifeworld he can be regarded as a 'critical' systems theorist. Steering media in this ideal sense provide communicative mechanisms to facilitate system maintenance and/or adaptability.

In order to comprehend the phenomenon of accounting we must elaborate Habermas's account a little further in directions that he does not pursue. It makes sense to distinguish initially between steering media which may be *internal* to particular systems or organizations (such as management accounting) and those which are external to such systems (such as financial regulation). However, this distinction between internal and external steering media is by no means absolute. Indeed one version of the colonization thesis focuses on the increasing internalization of external steering media. On the one hand we might call this 'regulatory capture' whereby systems increasingly internalize the capability for their own regulation. But, on the other hand, external regulatory initiatives may have important internal effects on an organization. Preston (1989) has provided an interesting analysis of the colonizing effects of the UK tax regime. Hence steering media such as accounting and the law do not have a fixed position in the lifeworld-system complex and may be increasingly subsumed and internalized within systemic imperatives. Colonization can go both ways.

Can this notion of steering illuminate accounting? First we need to recall the image of accounting as information for decision-making. We can now see that, in Habermas's terms, this concerns accounting and its function in steering economic activity. Accounting has often been called the language of business; and economic calculation presupposes a basis in accounting through which those calculations are effected. Management accounting 'steers' the economic decision-making of managers; and financial accounting 'steers' the economic decision-making of the investing community.

But we saw above that steering in this ideal sense of decision facilitation is a special case in a complex process. Therefore steering in Habermas's sense is much messier and more problematic than the functionalist account would lead us to believe. Yet the thesis of the internal colonization of the lifeworld remains relevant to the accounting context. One way of demonstrating this is to develop some of Habermas's remarks on the law and his concept of 'juridification'. Here we shall find a richer theoretical model for understanding a transformation in the steering potential of practices such as law and accounting which corresponds to the colonization of the lifeworld.

The concept of juridification describes the tendency to an increasing complexity and formality in the legal process. Juridification expresses not merely the expansion of the volume of law but also, and more crucially, the *expansion of its domain*. Legal process increasingly filters into new domains of social life and this is paralleled by a fragmentation of that process into specialisms which can control the definition of the problems that they purport to address. This conception is at the heart of Habermas's criticisms of the 'violent abstraction' of the juridification process:

> In the end the *generality* of legal situation-definitions is tailored to *bureaucratic implementation*, that is, to administration that deals with the social problems as presented by the legal entitlement. The situation to be regulated is embedded in the context of a life history and of a concrete form of life; it has to be subjected to violent abstraction, not merely

because it has to be subsumed under the law, but so that it can be dealt with administratively. (Habermas, 1987: 362–3)

There are strong parallels here with some of the suggestions made above concerning the manner in which accounting creates new visibilities and factualities within an organization and thereby controls the definition of its environment. Accounting, like law, is much more than its technical elaborations, and its formal rationality is illusory. Weber (1978: 215) talks of the rational-legal authority of the law, the sense in which the law is at the very heart of the bureaucratic process. In a similar sense accounting is also a potential mode of juridification.

In order to pursue this idea further we need to consider Habermas's distinction between the 'regulative' and 'constitutive' functions of the law.

> From this standpoint we can distinguish processes of juridification according to whether they are linked to antecedent institutions of the lifeworld and juridically superimposed on socially integrated areas of action or whether they merely increase the density of legal relationships that are constitutive of systematically integrated areas of action. (Habermas, 1987: 366)

In other words, Habermas appears to be distinguishing between two possible senses of steering for, in his case, law. First it may steer in a 'regulative' sense as a *supplement* both to lifeworld and system contexts. Secondly, following processes of juridification, the law 'steers' in a more 'constitutive' and colonizing sense. With increasing complexity, accounting also comes to provide the very definitions of the areas that it regulates (Hines, 1988). Steering in the regulative sense corresponds by analogy to the ideal model of information for decisions, an ideal that Habermas wishes to preserve while recognizing the risk that it may transform itself into steering in the second, constitutive, sense. Figure 6.2 represents the dynamics of this model.

Thus the transformation from regulative to constitutive steering functions represents the process of the inner colonization of the lifeworld in which 'sub-systems of the economy and the state become more and more complex and penetrate ever deeper into the symbolic reproduction of the lifeworld' (Habermas, 1987: 367).

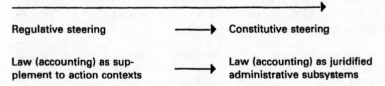

Figure 6.2   *The internal colonization of the lifeworld*

Although this is an abstract analysis, support for it is strongly suggested by a number of accounting studies in organizational contexts. Dent (1986) documents processes of financial and accounting colonization within railway and engineering industries. Despite initial resistance to change, accounting emerges as a new organizational language which displaces a previously dominant culture. Although this study is not informed by the lifeworld/system structure, it provides a good illustration of the colonization thesis. The colonizing power of accounting consists less in its manifest claims to information-based rationality than in its capacity to capture organizational self-understanding and to reframe it in accounting terms. Accounting becomes in this sense a 'disciplinary power' (Roberts and Scapens, 1990), which colonizes by virtue of its capability for creating a new ontology of economic facts. Gorz (1989) has rather clumsily called this 'economicization' but the point is the same: the rendering of increasing areas of social life within an economic language.

A context in which this is particularly evident in the UK at the present time is the public sector in general and the National Health Service (NHS) in particular. Hopwood (1984) has drawn attention to the significance of organizational transformations made in the name of 'efficiency' which have served to intensify internal investments in accounting in the public sector. However, studies by Bourn and Ezzamel (1986, 1987) and Laughlin (1988) seem to indicate that accounting in the NHS, universities and the Church is subsumed under a dominant culture of the 'sacred', whether this is expressed in terms of clinical, academic or spiritual freedom. Whether accounting can be restricted to a facilitating role in these contexts is an empirical matter but there is evidence to suggest that in the area of health care the sacred domain of clinical action is becoming influenced, although not yet comprehensively transformed, by accounting initiatives despite complex forms of resistance (Preston et al., 1990). As the accounting language of budgeting attempts to occupy clinical discourse it has the potential to control significant definitions of the hospital environment.

Much more could be said in detail about the colonizing role of accounting but in the context of Habermas's claims it is necessary to return to a question of fundamental importance. We saw above that Habermas conceives, albeit ideally, of a *balanced* process of rationalization and differentiation. Within this overall picture we also saw that the colonization process accelerates where a steering function changes from being 'regulative' to becoming 'constitutive' and therefore in some sense dysfunctional or distorting for the particular action-sphere, such as an organization.[4] Thus, as Habermas conceives of it, the 'critical' mission emerges as the need to:

protect areas of life that are functionally dependent on social integration through values, norms and consensus formation, to preserve them from falling prey to the systemic imperatives of economic and administrative subsystems growing with dynamics of their own, and to defend them from becoming converted over, through the steering medium of the law, to a principle of sociation that is, for them, dysfunctional. (Habermas, 1987: 372–3)

How then can we limit the systemic imperatives of a subsystem such as accounting? As accounting is the medium which enables economic calculation, this is also a question about how we can limit economic thinking, or at least particular versions of it. Is there a sense in which we can retrieve a non-colonizing, non-distorting role for accounting? Can accounting be authentically, if modestly, communicative? It is to these questions that we turn in conclusion.

Accounting, Users and Communication

According to Habermas, communicative processes may be 'systematically distorted' when they either strategically ignore or repress contexts of possible validity claim redemption such as spheres of public discourse (see Forester, Chapter 3 in this volume). It is not our intention to give a detailed elaboration of Habermas's theory of communication beyond what has already been said. But it is important to note the sense in which it provides a model of *procedural* rationality embodied in the possibility of discourse. Thus, when we come to think about what an 'undistorted' or 'new' accounting would look like, Habermas's theory will give us little of substance. An 'undistorted' form of accounting will be whatever emerges from consensually based discursive procedures at the heart of a revitalized public domain of discussion (see Deetz, Chapter 2 in this volume). It is from this public domain as the expression of the lifeworld that accounting systems and regimes will emerge and to which they will be accountable. Hence those looking for a substantive blueprint for, for example, a new environmentally conscious accounting may find Habermas's procedural conception anaemic. However, we shall attempt to identify a number of possible issues. Before this, we reconsider the sense in which accounting is a colonizing and hence distorted form of communication.

We have seen that it is plausible to see both managerial and financial accounting in terms of processes of juridification. This is not surprising given the close, if variable, relations between accounting and the law (Napier and Noke, 1992; Miller and Power, 1992). Increasing refinements of costing and budgeting systems, the proliferation (particularly in the USA) of detailed pronouncements on financial accounting practice and the emergence of specialisms within the accounting profession all testify to a growing density and complexity of accounting knowledge. Thus, the decision-making model is increasingly refined and detailed in its aspirations. With this density and complexity, the capacity of accounting to question its own mission and purpose is increasingly eroded, since questions of means and technique multiply at the expense of these ends. Although there is some evidence of attention to fundamentals at the level of standard setting, such as the conceptual framework project by the FASB in the USA, in general the articulation of detailed technical practices has proceeded in such a way that their ultimate legitimation remains a matter for an expert culture or profession and not a broader public. Hence the process of juridification is intimately bound up with the expert culture of accounting. This fragments the possibility for public discourse by expert capture of a range of policy issues.

One example of this expert capture concerns conceptions of 'users' of accounting information. In raising questions about the nature of accounting as information for decision-making we are necessarily led to question the constituency of claimed users of accounting data. We can distinguish two levels of critical inquiry in this respect. First there is the level which retains a broad commitment to the logic of economic decision-making and seeks to extend the range of parties entitled to accounting information within this framework. Secondly there is the level which more radically departs from the framework of economic reason and concerns itself with different possibilities for accountability relations. On this second approach the idea of the 'user' and the strictly instrumentalist conception of its relation to accounting information give way to richer conceptions of human agency (Arrington and Puxty, 1991).

It is not always easy to distinguish these levels. For example, the corporate social reporting literature tends to occupy a grey area between the two (for a good survey see Gray et al., 1987). The very idea of users of accounting information for decision-making is in any event a relatively recent one. Historically , accounting has tended to serve a stewardship purpose, which is certainly a use value but not one that is concerned with the assessment of something like economic performance. The rise of the user is closely tied to the rise of a corporate culture and capital markets with an interest in performance assessment; hence the priority of investor and creditor user populations over other groups. Indeed, citing other users of accounting information, such as employees or the public, only superficially extends the constituency. In the absence of richer models of what these groups might want from accounting information and the basis of their entitlement, this extension in fact requires that they be assimilated into the economic decision-making model. Other possible users of accounting information must, to count as users, be constructed as economic agents with economic interests and decision potential (for example the idea that labour can only be a user for wage-bargaining or job security purposes).

The idea of a user is therefore relative to the model of accounting for decision-making. Raising doubts about this model automatically implies a need to rethink the status of the agents for whom accounting data may have, in some broad sense, consequences. Indeed, following Habermas, we need to consider those dimensions of accounting as a social practice with consequences for subjects that remain invisible if we simply retain the decision-making model.

Arrington and Puxty's (1991) arguments parallel the concerns of this chapter and follow Habermas's theory of communicative action. They argue that accounting has three domains of contestability: the domains of instrumental reason, of public norms, and of subjective experience. Notwithstanding the ambiguity of accounting's instrumental aspirations which was noted above, the domain of economic reasoning has eclipsed the possibility of contesting the normative context of accounting and its possible consequences for a subjectivity that cannot be conceived merely as an end user.

Increasing accounting-based specialization engenders a control of information which is much more than the appropriation of knowledge; it is more generally the monopolization of modes of reason. The expert culture of accounting, rather than its particular elaborations, propagates an economically based discourse which can control the public definitions of social and organizational reality and hence the 'problems' and 'needs' of those domains. According to Habermas, the rise of such an 'Expertenkultur' transforms citizens into clients and is responsible for 'socially structured silences'. It is in the nature of an economically grounded concept such as 'efficiency' that no one can be against it; it exhausts the space of possible discourse.

Colonization via the agency of expanding expert cultures involves the generation of new forms of dependency on lawyers, accountants and others as an administrative elite: 'specialists without vision', as Weber has called them. Within such a context regulatory structures of accountability, such as auditing, provide only pseudo-legitimation of corporate activity, its mere conformity to accounting rules and practices, and not a more widely based justification of the corporate sector. Similarly, financial accounting as information for the investing public can be regarded as a form of pseudo-communication because:

1 The investing public cannot be identified with the public at large notwithstanding attempts in the UK to create a 'share-owning' democracy.

2 Accounting-based communications cannot convey many aspects of corporate activity. Financial statements represent the pinnacle of accounting colonization by providing a dominant representation of an organization which eclipses other possibilities.

Another related example concerns the emerging pressures for environmental awareness. Might there not be the possibility of a new accounting to be found here which could reverse the colonizing tendencies described above? Here we feel that much care is needed. The external consequences of organizational activity have been acknowledged for many years and programmes for cost-benefit analysis have sought to quantify the effects of these externalities in economic terms. In effect this requires an extension of the accounting calculus into ever wider domains beyond the organization. In other words, one possible outcome of a programme for environmental accounting could be an *intensification* of the juridification process. The question of the environment could be captured by expert accountants who have merely extended their existing expertise in new directions involving new frontiers of 'asset' recognition, such as fresh air.

In the context of current environmental awareness, this is a possibility that should cause considerable unease. In a broad sense, individualistic forms of economic rationality supported by accounting have been responsible for *creating* the newly perceived crisis. As every game theorist knows, individually rational actions may have, and have had, damaging collective consequences (see Hollis, 1987). To take an extreme example, organizational emphasis on profit obscures the effects of environmental damage because the latter does not appear as a cost to the organization. To internalize such external costs, for example via 'green' taxes, misses the point that it is not sufficient simply for accounting to co-opt the relevant environmental variables and formalize them within a new calculus. What is needed is a *change* of corporate practice, and for this a more substantive rather than a formal regulatory practice is necessary. New conceptions of corporate accountability are required. What may be needed is therefore *less* accounting in its traditional sense and a recovery of the social and subjective dimensions of accountability that Arrington and Puxty (1991) have articulated.

The ecological question is used here for illustrative purposes only but it shows the potential ambiguity of programmes for a 'new' accounting which is non-colonizing and non-distorting. Habermas's

Critical Theory effectively abstains from these substantive first-order issues in favour of a procedural conception of undistorted communication. Although we cannot specify *ex ante* what a 'truly' communicative and enabling accounting would look like, we can identify the risks of colonization.

In other words, it is public forms of discourse which are the ultimate form of steering medium and which must subsume others such as accounting. Accounting threatens to 'delinguistify' the public realm (Arrington and Puxty, 1991) and to absorb and transform public discourse in its own image. Habermas's theory of communication suggests that a juridical intensification of accounting is a distortion and that the traditional functional claims for accounting in facilitating decision-making systematically ignore the prior formation of the key concepts of economic reason at the level of public norms embedded in the lifeworld.

Conclusion

In this chapter we have explored the potential contribution of Habermas's ideas on systems, lifeworld and steering to a Critical Theory of accounting. We suggested that the technical neutrality of accounting practice is illusory and that accounting is a potentially colonizing force which threatens to 'delinguistify' the public realm. The promotion and institutionalization of methods of economic calculation may have powerful and distorting effects where such methods control the definitions of, say, organizational reality. Whether this occurs is of course an empirical question and we have drawn attention to a number of suggestive studies.

It should be clear from what has been said that accounting is very much the vehicle for economic reason in practice. Hence a Critical Theory of accounting cannot be disentangled from that of economic reason in general (see Gorz, 1989). Economic thinking plays such a dominant role in our lives that it becomes difficult to think and act non-economically. The growth of accounting has undoubtedly promoted the capability for economic understandings of ever greater areas of our social world. Recently it appears that environmental concerns are providing a respite from our reverence for economic thinking. We therefore stand on the threshold of a number of possibilities for questioning the colonizing effects of economic reason. Habermas's Critical Theory provides one, and by no means the only, basis for articulating this. It is a programme of much more than theoretical interest and concerns nothing less than the very basis on which we organize our private and public lives; indeed it concerns the constructed nature of this split between the private and the public domains. 'Accountingization' is perhaps an ugly word, but it expresses the sense in which accounting as method may eclipse broader questions of accountability. Critical Theory posits not simply a rejection of accounting practice as such but a limitation of its aspirations and a reflective awareness of the need for a regulative and therefore facilitating practice. We are only likely to achieve this with the help of broader-based transformations of economic reason and calculation.

Notes

A version of this chapter was presented at the Critical Theory and Management Studies Conference in Shrewsbury, UK in April 1990. The authors are grateful to the participants for their many suggestions. Particular thanks are extended to Mats Alvesson, Ed Arrington, Anthony Hopwood, Kalle Lyytinen, Peter Miller, John Mingers, Tony Puxty and Hugh Willmott.

1 An important by-product of this image is that it entitles us to make *prima facie* comparisons between accounting systems and regimes of different organizations and different countries. The image suggests that we know in advance what will count as accounting in these different settings and only minor technical differences will emerge from such a study. In other words, if accounting is mere technique, then context is irrelevant to our understanding of it. This decontextualized image of accounting has been extensively criticized by Burchell et al. (1980).

2 The academic literature in this area is concerned with the efficiency or otherwise of capital markets, and various theories exist and compete (see Watts and Zimmerman, 1986). In brief, accounting information is 'novel' if its release has an impact on the share price of the company in question. Extensive empirical research has been undertaken to gauge the information value of accounting in this way. If anything, this literature suggests that the 'official' release of accounting information in financial statements has much less impact than might be imagined. A relatively 'efficient' capital market has already acquired the information before financial accounts are published. It is also worth noting that this question of the 'newness' of information is entirely relative to the analyst population of sophisticated capital markets. It is by no means clear that this is the only possible population relative to which accounting may provide information.

3 Hopwood (1990) has suggested that this debate concerns the respective territorial claims of accounting and the law as much as a technical problem of the determination of criteria by which hidden liabilities 'off balance sheet' can be made visible.

4 It must be remembered that an organization, such as a company, is already a 'juridically' constituted entity. It is in this sense a legal fiction.

References

Accounting Standards Steering Committee (1975) *The Corporate Report*. London: ASSC.
American Accounting Association (1966) *A Statement of Basic Accounting Theory*. Sarasota: AAA.
Ansari, S. and K. J. Euske (1987) 'Rational, rationalising and reifying uses of

accounting data in organizations', *Accounting, Organizations and Society*, 12(6): 549–70.

Armstrong, P. (1987) 'The rise of accounting controls in British capitalist enterprises', *Accounting, Organizations and Society*, 12(5): 415–36.

Arrington, C. E. and Puxty, A. E. (1991) 'Accounting, interests and rationality: a communicative relation', *Critical Perspectives on Accounting*, 2(1): 31–58.

Berry, A. J., Capps, T., Cooper, D., Ferguson, P., Hopper, T. and Lowe, E. A. (1985) 'Management control in an area of the National Coal Board: rationales of accounting practices in a public enterprise', *Accounting, Organizations and Society*, 10(1): 3–28.

Bourn, M. and Ezzamel M. (1986) 'Organisational culture in hospitals in the National Health Service', *Financial Accountability and Management*, 2(3): 203–25.

Bourn, M. and Ezzamel, M. (1987) 'Budgetary devolution in the National Health Service and universities in the United Kingdom', *Financial Accountability and Management*, 3(1): 29–45.

Burchell, S., Clubb, C., Hopwood, A. G., Hughes, H. and Naphapiet, J. (1980) 'The role of accounting in organizations and society', *Accounting, Organizations and Society*, 5(1): 5–27.

Cooper, D. and Sherer, M. (1984) 'The value of corporate accounting reports – arguments for a political economy of accounting', *Accounting, Organizations and Society*, 9(3/4): 207–32.

Dent, J. (1986) 'Accounting and organisational cultures: a field study of the emergence of a new organisational reality', Working paper, London Business School.

Financial Accounting Standards Board (1978) *Statement of Financial Accounting Concepts No. 1 – Objectives of Financial Reporting by Business Enterprises*. Connecticut: FASB.

Gorz, A. (1989) *Critique of Economic Reason*. London: Verso.

Gray, R., Owen, D. and Maunders, K. (1987) *Corporate Social Reporting: Accounting and Accountability*. Englewood Cliffs, NJ: Prentice-Hall.

Habermas, J. (1971) *Towards a Rational Society: Student Protest, Science and Politics*, trans. J. J. Shapiro. London: Heinemann Educational Books.

Habermas, J. (1984) *The Theory of Communicative Action*, Vol. I: *Reason and the Rationalization of Society*, trans. T. McCarthy. Cambridge: Polity Press.

Habermas, J. (1987) *The Theory of Communicative Action*. Vol. II, trans. T. McCarthy. Cambridge: Polity Press.

Hines, R. (1988) 'Financial accounting: in communicating reality we construct reality', *Accounting, Organizations and Society*, 13(3): 251–61.

Hollis, M. (1987) *The Cunning of Reason*. Cambridge: Cambridge University Press.

Hopwood, A. G. (1984) 'Accounting and the pursuit of efficiency', in A. G. Hopwood and C. R. Tomkins (eds), *Issues in Public Sector Accounting*. London: Phillip Allen. pp. 167–87.

Hopwood, A. G. (1987) 'The archaeology of accounting systems', *Accounting, Organizations and Society*, 12(3): 207–34.

Hopwood, A. G. (1990) 'Ambiguity, knowledge and territorial claims: some observations on the doctrine of substance over form', *British Accounting Review*, 22(1): 79–87.

Kaplan, R. S. (1983) 'Measuring manufacturing performance: a new challenge for managerial accounting research', *The Accounting Review*, 58(4): 686–705.

Knights, D. and Collinson, D. (1987) 'Disciplining the shop floor: a comparison of the disciplinary effects of managerial psychology and financial accounting', *Accounting, Organizations and Society*, 12(5): 457–77.

Lasch, C. (1978) *The Culture of Narcissism*. New York: Basic Books.

Laughlin, R. C. (1987) 'Accounting systems in organisational contexts: a case for critical theory', *Accounting, Organizations and Society*, 12(5): 479–502.

Laughlin, R. C. (1988) 'Accounting in its social context: an analysis of the accounting systems of the Church of England', *Accounting, Auditing and Accountability Journal*, 1(2): 19–42.

Luhmann, N. (1982) *The Differentiation of Society*. New York: Columbia University Press.

March, J. G. (1987) 'Ambiguity and accounting: the elusive link between information and decision making', *Accounting, Organizations and Society*, 12(2): 153–68.

Marcuse, H. (1986) *One-dimensional Man*. London: Ark.

Miller, P. and O'Leary, T. (1987) 'Accounting and the construction of the governable person', *Accounting, Organizations and Society*, 12(3): 235–66.

Miller, P. and Power, M. (1992) 'Accounting, law and economic calculation', in M. Bromwich and A. G. Hopwood (eds), *Accounting and the Law*. London: Prentice Hall/ICAEW. pp. 230–53.

Napier, C. and Noke, C. (1992) 'Accounting and the law: an historical overview of an uneasy relationship', in M. Bromwich and A. G. Hopwood (eds), *Accounting and the Law*. London: Prentice Hall/ICAEW. pp. 30–54.

Otley, D. T. (1980) 'The contingency theory of management accounting: achievement and prognosis', *Accounting, Organizations and Society*, 5(4): 413–28.

Preston, A. M. (1989) 'The taxman cometh: some observations on the interrelation between accounting and Inland Revenue practice', *Accounting, Organizations and Society*, 14(5/6): 389–414.

Preston, A., Cooper, D. and Coombs, R. (1990) 'Fabricating budgets: a case study of the production of management budgeting in the National Health Service', Discussion Paper, Boston University.

Roberts, J. and Scapens, R. (1990) 'Accounting as discipline', in D. Cooper and T. Hopper (eds), *Critical Accounts*. London: Macmillan. pp. 107–25.

Solomons, D. (1986) *Making Accounting Policy*. Oxford: Oxford University Press.

Tinker, A. and Neimark, M. (1987) 'The role of annual reports in gender and class contradictions at General Motors: 1917–1976', *Accounting, Organizations and Society*, 12(1): 71–88.

Watts, R. L. and Zimmerman, J. L. (1986) *Positive Accounting Theory*. New York: Prentice-Hall International.

Weber, M. (1978) *Economy and Society*. Berkeley: University of California Press.

Willmott, H. (1983) 'Paradigms for accounting research: critical reflections on Tomkins and Groves' "Everyday Accountant and Researching his Reality"', *Accounting, Organizations and Society*, 8(4): 389–405.

Winch, P. (1964) 'Understanding a primitive society', *American Philosophical Quarterly*, 1: 307–24.

Zeff, S. (1978) 'The rise of economic consequences', *Journal of Accountancy*, Dec.: 56–63.

7

Marketing Discourse and Practice: Towards a Critical Analysis

Glenn Morgan

In the world of business in the 1990s, the idea of marketing has central importance. In the contemporary discourse of self-understanding which is promoted by managers, politicians, academics and the media, the modern business enterprise is about much more than the production of goods and services. It is about serving the customer's needs through the production of appropriate commodities. This in turn requires informing the customer about what is on offer and, in the process, articulating and shaping needs. Thus the modern business enterprise is engaged in a process of constructing the means through which consumers themselves produce their own identity. For the marketing profession this is a neutral, harmless task, a simple case of the circulation of information. The company researches the marketplace, produces the appropriate product, markets it through the most efficient channels and informs the public of its merits through advertising. The market itself remains a realm of freedom, in which choice and the sovereignty of the individual consumer remain paramount. For Critical Theory, however, the myth of market freedom and with it the myth of marketing itself need to be unpacked. In this chapter I aim to do that by showing how the discourses and practices of marketing are productive of, as well as constituted by, a particular sort of society. Marketing is not a neutral way of looking at the world; it has distinctive power effects for organizations, managers, consumers and society as a whole. A critical approach to marketing will seek to uncover those effects that exist beneath the level of everyday consciousness. It will seek to reveal the conditions of possibility for marketing as a way of thinking about and doing particular social relations. In this way, it will link the critique of marketing to the critique of society.

The importance of developing a critique of marketing has been recognized before. For example Firat et al. in their introduction to one of the few collections of critical material on marketing argue that

Today, marketing needs a thorough deconstruction. . . . For a healthy process of criticism and deconstruction, we must not be afraid to pose as questions what we assumed were answers, and we must not pull back from being radical in every sense. . . . We must go to the very roots of existence of the knowledge enterprise we call marketing and question those roots, asking questions that will enable a thorough and robust understanding of those roots. We must be radical in seeking novel and revolutionary alternatives to our set ways. (Firat et al. 1987: xvii–xviii)

In this chapter I seek to build on these ideas and to mount a critique that engages with marketing both at the level of managerial discourses and practices *and* at the level of society as a whole.

My argument is that marketing is best understood as a set of practices and discourses which help to constitute and shape social relations in modern Western societies. A world in which 'marketing' as a profession, as a discipline, as a managerial practice, as a way of looking at the world, has such high importance is a very distinctive world. It is the world of twentieth-century Western industrialized societies in which mass consumption is the cultural norm, if not the material reality, for most of the population (the argument here is informed particularly by Bauman, 1988). It is a world in which the production of commodities and services is no longer the central problem; the gravity has shifted to consumption, to persuading people to buy the things that are produced. It is a world in which individual and social identity are more than ever bound up with the consumption of goods and services. What has not yet been sufficiently clearly recognized in critical analysis is that marketing stands at the centre of these social processes. It is the discourse through which actors, organizations and consumers understand and seek to control these processes. What the discourse cannot do, however, is to articulate its own conditions of possibility, i.e. why marketing has become so significant. It cannot effectively understand itself and its social construction except in terms of a naive scientism which assumes the progressive, unproblematic unfolding of ever more accurate knowledge. To provide a proper analysis of the emergence, reproduction and power effects of marketing it is necessary to draw on the resources of Critical Theory. Such a project will therefore be simultaneously a critique of a particular type of society, one in which commodification and materialism have become the predominant modes of life, as well as a critique of marketing per se.

The chapter consists of two sections, which seek to elaborate this argument. In the first section I focus on the way in which marketing has been constructed in orthodox marketing literature. This leads into a discussion of the underpinnings of this literature and how it constructs a particular view of human beings and society. In this section I attempt to establish an overall framework for looking at marketing in societies. In the second section I draw upon different critical traditions to examine ways in which the critique of marketing can be further extended into empirical research. The goal of the chapter as a whole is to provide the reader with a sense of the possibilities inherent in a critical study of marketing. I am attempting to construct a series of signposts rather than a coherent, unified critical theory of marketing.

Marketing: The Orthodox Approach

Let us first consider the framework within which marketing as a way of understanding organizations and acting upon organizations and consumers has been constructed. I start by simply describing some of the common terms of marketing discourse which to practitioners and others would be the basic tools of their trade. These so-called tools, however, raise wider issues that some of the more reflective of marketing academics have gone on to consider. By examining these authors, in particular Drucker and Kotler, it is possible to reveal more clearly the nature of the marketing enterprise and how it is socially constructed. In the second section I will consider alternative ways of developing critical research on marketing.

In the commonsense understanding of participants in the marketing process (whether managers or academics), marketing is perceived as all those practices concerned with the interface between the customer and the organization at the level of products and services. This categorization is further broken down into two aspects: 'marketing knowledge' and 'marketing management'. The former refers to the general framework of knowledge that has been developed in academic marketing; the latter concerns the exploration of the issues of how to apply this knowledge in particular organizational contexts. There is clearly no rigid divide between these two phenomena and the distinction is mainly for heuristic purposes (for a textbook approach see Kotler, 1985a). The orthodox approach posits that 'marketing knowledge' provides the basis for particular organizational practices that through effective 'marketing management' deliver organizational success.

Marketing knowledge concerns the relationship between the customer and the organization. It focuses on the following features:

The Customer Marketing is concerned to generate knowledge about potential and actual customers. This knowledge mainly derives from statistical analyses of the demographic (age, gender, occupations etc.), attitudinal and behavioural characteristics of the population involved. It seeks to generate predictive and explanatory models of the sorts of people who will buy particular products or services and how they can be persuaded to do so.

The Marketing Channels This refers to knowledge concerning the impact of different channels on sales and marketing. It seeks to generate knowledge of the relative efficiency (sometimes theorized as 'transaction costs') of different channels, e.g. the role of direct marketing, the nature of retail outlets, and so on, as well as the impact of different variables on the efficiency of outlets in particular types of channel, e.g. the impact of 'athmospherics' such as colour, design or sound on retail buying behaviour.

Competition in the Market Marketing is concerned to generate knowledge of the 'objective features' of the competitive environment in which organizations operate. Competitor analysis, linked to market segmentation theory, generates models of the environment in which organizations can locate their own particular competitive advantage.

This marketing knowledge becomes the basis for marketing management in particular organizational contexts. In general terms, marketing management concerns applying marketing knowledge to create the optimum 'marketing mix' for particular organizations. The marketing mix is often simply referred to as the 'four Ps' – product, place, price and promotion. How does the organization ensure that it has the right product at the right price selling in the right place and supported by the right promotion? Marketing locates these decisions in the wider framework of the overall profitability of the organization as affected by phenomena such as product life-cycles and product portfolio planning.

In theory, marketing knowledge provides the framework through which marketing management is practically accomplished. Utilizing marketing knowledge in this way is seen as a crucial ingredient in organizational success.

Marketing Discourse: Some Preliminary Considerations on its Conditions of Possibility

Thus far I have simply presented in a very abbreviated form the basic framework that constitutes marketing. This framework is subject to variation and elaboration in textbooks, courses and business practices. Nevertheless, it is possible to identify certain key features. First, the model is firmly based on a positivistic view of the world. It conceives of a world independent of the observer, which is predictable, stable and knowable. Marketing claims scientific status in so far as it uses scientific methodologies to gain knowledge of that part of the world which it defines as 'marketing' (see especially Hunt, 1990 and Dholakia and Arndt, 1985; also attempts to articulate alternatives in Anderson, 1983; Arndt, 1985; Muncy and Fisk, 1987). It embodies a view of the linear progress of 'scientific theories' in which the development of ever more sophisticated techniques of measurement and analysis leads to improvements in understanding. In such a view, improvements in understanding lead to improved 'marketing', which in turn is believed to be causally linked to organizational success.

Based on a technical-rational view of knowledge, the dominant model of marketing assumes a parallelism between the natural and social world. In the same way that natural scientific understanding is seen to give rise to technologies which can control and direct phenomena in the outside world, so this view of marketing assumes that there is equivalent knowledge of social phenomena that can provide for successful manipulation and control. Thus consumers are knowable, limited entities, the characteristics of which can be captured in the same way as can the characteristics of natural phenomena. Marketing generates 'technologies of governance' (particularly associated with market research based on large-scale quantitative data) which assume that social relations and social identities are fixed and constrained.

It is axiomatic to attempts to develop a critical understanding of management in general that the elision of differences between the natural and the social worlds in positivistic approaches is totally unsatisfactory. However, this elision of differences between the natural and social worlds in positivistic has a paradoxical effect because it generates much of the dynamism of the discipline. For example, in marketing, there can be no end to marketing surveys, not because techniques to uncover attitudes and behaviour have not yet been perfected but because consumers are self-conscious and self-aware. Surveys and the qualitative interviews and group sessions which are now emerging as alternative methodologies can only capture a particular moment within a particular context. For any particular company, they can never provide sufficient information to guarantee success. On the contrary, a dialectic is set up between the attempt to know the customer and the attempt to sell to the customer. This incessant dialectic is a black hole into which marketing expertise is poured with variable effects. So in this context the gap between positivism and its attempts at manipulation on the one side, and the complex nature of social relations on the other side, becomes colonized by marketing management, offering a range of solutions to why things have not worked as expected. Positivistic approaches, then, are not undermined but reproduced within a framework where social relations are ignored or treated as 'objective variables'.

Marketing is not alone amongst the management sciences in drawing upon this positivist discourse. On the contrary, this has been the predominant mode of self-understanding in management. Authors such as Habermas (1971) have traced this to the nature of capitalist society and the way in which exploitation of human labour has been part of the same process as the exploitation of the natural world. The positivistic orientation enables people to be treated as things; it allows the construction of a framework of exploitation in which specifically human characteristics, particularly related to communication, understanding and self-development, are ignored and debased in the interests of material production and the creation of surplus value. Marketing is by no means peculiar in its positivistic orientation; what is different is how in the current era this has been developed. It is here that marketing reveals its role in a wider process of social transformation, towards the ever greater dominance of the market over social life. It is to this that I now turn.

At one level marketing presents itself as a limited number of scientifically rigorous theories (understood in a positivistic sense), and its relevance is strictly limited to particular areas of business and management. Such an approach, however, would be seen as naive not just by Critical Theorists interested in the role which marketing takes in the reproduction of wider social relations. Some more self-reflective theorists within marketing itself would also reject this narrow definition of marketing. If we examine this in more detail, we can begin to see how the self-understanding of marketing goes beyond a narrow technicist view towards a vision of society as a whole.

Take, for example, the work of Peter Drucker, one of the gurus of American management, who has sought to bridge the gap between academic and management discourse and in the process has sold many books to practising managers. He has stated that:

> Marketing is the distinguishing unique function of the business. . . . Marketing is so basic that it cannot be considered a separate function on a par with others such as manufacturing or personnel. It is first a central dimension of the entire business. It is the whole business seen from the point of view of its final result, that is, from the customers' point of view. Concern and responsibility for marketing must, therefore, permeate all areas of the enterprise. (quoted in Doyle, 1987: 122)

In this perspective, marketing becomes the essential part of the whole organization. Implicit in this argument is the idea that there has been a fundamental change in business. At the turn of the century the essential element in 'scientific management' was production, as exemplified in Taylorism. However, as production problems were resolved, the key issue became that of selling products in competition with other producers. In this phase of development, marketing takes on central importance and, according to Drucker, the organization should now revolve around marketing, not production.

The centrality of marketing is further reflected upon by Kotler, who has sought to establish marketing concepts as central to the analysis of human behaviour per se. He distinguishes three levels of marketing consciousness. The first is where marketing is defined in terms of market transactions, i.e. the subject matter of marketing is that class of situation where buyers and sellers meet to exchange goods. The second is where two parties meet to exchange things which are of value to them. Kotler refers to this as organization–clients transactions, thereby enabling him to incorporate transactions between political parties and voters, voluntary organizations and their clients, non-business organizations of all sorts and their 'customers'. In this view, every organization (whether it is market-based or not) should be conceived of as producing something for a client or customer. Therefore, all organizations can be said to be centrally involved in 'marketing'. At this level, all the tools and techniques of studying and serving the market are of relevance. Kotler, however, wants to go even further than this and argues that there is a higher state of 'marketing consciousness' in which 'marketing applies to an organization's attempts to relate to all of its publics, not just its consuming public' (Kotler, 1985b: 55). At this level it is not so much exchange which defines the sphere of marketing, as a transaction per se. 'Marketing is specifically concerned with how transactions are created, stimulated, facilitated and valued. This is the generic concept of marketing' (Kotler, 1985b: 56). This in turn allows Kotler to argue that marketing can be viewed as a 'category of human action indistinguishable from other categories of human action such as voting, loving, consuming'! Kotler argues that

> It is tempting to think that the three levels of marketing move from market transactions to exchange to influence. . . . The concept of influence undeniably plays an important role in marketing thought. . . . The marketer is a specialist at understanding human wants and values and knows what it takes for someone to act. (Kotler, 1985b: 62)

According to Kotler, all relationships between people can be seen in marketing terms. So what begins as a positivistic approach to a limited range of phenomena becomes generalized to human relationships *in toto*. Kotler presents this 'innovation' in humanistic terms. It is a 'beneficent' technology that helps voluntary organizations, public bodies and political parties to achieve what they wanted to do anyway. In other words, to return to the previous discussion, marketing is a neutral tool; it is a lens which reveals to the viewer in clearer detail what was already there and therefore allows action to be taken on the basis of firmer knowledge.

Once again, however, it is necessary from the point of view of Critical Theory to reject this neutrality. Marketing is by no means neutral. On the contrary, it is a particular way of seeing and 'doing' human relationships. The very discourse of a 'market' implies something specific about human relationships. In particular it implies that they are essentially concerned with exchange, bargaining, influence and negotiation. Whilst at one level this is a discourse of freedom – the freedom to choose that is characteristic of the market – it is also a discourse that conceals underlying inequalities of power which are produced and reproduced both inside and outside the market transaction, for example inequalities between capital and labour, men and women, black and white. It opens up the promise of a world of equal choice for all but, beneath that promise, inequalities of power and wealth remain and are reproduced.

Drucker and Kotler present marketing as a neutral tool. What they neglect to consider is that the discourse of marketing itself constitutes social relations as it becomes applied; it does not stand aloof from them. It actively participates in the self-constitution of subjects through commodities. It projects images of self, of fulfilment and of happiness through the purchase of goods and services. It links these images to the vision of a rational society, one in which, in contrast to non-market societies such as the old Eastern European states, efficient production flows from companies striving to meet the wishes of the consumer. It produces a consumer of goods and services wrapped up in them as part of self-image. The self is voided of moral character, and appearance becomes everything. Furthermore, marketing, efficiency and consumer satisfaction become entwined with attempts to import a new discourse into voluntary or state organizations, transforming them at their roots into structures that fit more easily with the dominant market and marketing ethos of the society. For example, in the British health service the rhetoric of marketing as a liberating force for the consumer is employed liberally to cover over a transformation which is reconstructing, if not deconstructing, the citizen's right to health care.

Kotler presents marketing discourse as an aid to more efficient organizations in the public and voluntary sectors. But what this means is the transformation of social relations in those locations. It means a progressive introduction of positivist ways of looking at people in these contexts. It means a continuous resort to market mechanisms in order to monitor and evaluate social relations. It means, in particular, a monetization and commodification of social relations. In this world, marketing can tell us the 'price of everything, but the value of nothing'! Anything can be marketed. It does not have to be the more obvious goods and services; it can be 'good causes', 'political parties', 'ideas'. The whole world is a market and we are consumers in a gigantic candy-store. Just sit back and enjoy it!

But at what cost? What is happening to a society in which value is synonymous with price? What specifically human values can stand out against this contamination? What happens to those people and countries who are outside the candy-store? What happens when human relationships are monetized, when human identity is constructed out of the possession of commodities? In Critical Theory, these questions must come to the fore (see Bauman, 1988 for a particularly insightful exploration of these issues). In the critical analysis of marketing, they have a specific urgency and relevance. Marketing's self-understanding is illusory; it brackets off its wider social responsibility and presents itself as neutral, whereas in fact it is centrally involved in constituting this particular type of society. It is crucial to find ways to dig into that self-understanding, to undermine it, to provoke it, to resist it. In the next section I consider four approaches that can be the basis of such a critique.

Marketing and Critical Analysis

This section explores four different ways of developing a critical approach to marketing, sketching out possible directions in which further empirical research could proceed that could contribute to the task of understanding the role that marketing plays in the constitution of modern societies. I have chosen four approaches which are well known in the area of management studies and which have already made important contributions; they are associated with Burrell and Morgan (1979), Habermas (1971), Braverman (1974) and Foucault (1979, 1981). I indicate how they might be fruitfully developed in relation to marketing.

Paradigmatic Pluralism and Critical Theory
Burrell and Morgan (1979) have argued that underlying social theories in general and theories of management in particular are assumptions about the nature of the social world and the nature of social reality. The social world, they argue, can be seen in terms of order or conflict, whilst knowledge of the social world can be conceived of as being objective or subjective. Combining these dimensions, Burrell and Morgan have created a classificatory system in which social and organizational theories can be located. The

authors argue that management and organization theory have been dominated by one particular set of assumptions – that the social world is an objective reality and that social order is its predominant characteristic. They argue that this is not the only way of looking at things and that there are other approaches, which can be explored with equal validity.

In marketing, Burrell and Morgan's thesis has been adopted and applied by Arndt (1985), who argues that marketing research is dominated by the structural-functionalist approach. He contrasts this with other possible approaches – the 'subjective world paradigm' which he associates with 'motivational research', 'interpretive studies' and symbolic interactionism, the sociopolitical paradigm (Arndt avoids concepts such as 'structural Marxism', which Burrell and Morgan use) and the 'radical subjectivist approach', renamed by Arndt the 'liberating paradigm' in which he lumps both 'action research' and 'critical research'.

Other than Arndt's work, there appears to be little material in marketing which specifically tries to develop the notion of alternative paradigms. However, it is significant that, without explicit reference to Burrell and Morgan, there has developed over the last decade a strong research tradition utilizing an interpretive framework to consider consumer behaviour. For example, in a recent issue of the *Journal of Consumer Research*, the main US journal in this area, the editor wrote that;

> The positivist paradigm that has dominated consumer research over the past three decades is being challenged by a new paradigm that is variously labeled post-positivist, naturalistic, interpretive and post-modern. Whichever of these labels one accepts the challenge to 'business-as-usual' or 'normal science' in Kuhnian terminology is both clear and funda-mental. The very foundations of the research enterprise are at issue, as the new paradigm questions the ontological, axiological and epistemo-logical assumptions that have been implicit in consumer research as typically practiced. (Lutz, 1989)

This approach now has a considerable following within the study of consumer behaviour (see, e.g., Belk et al., 1988, 1989; Hirschmann, 1985, 1988, 1990; Holbrook, 1987a). It rejects the technical-rational view of marketing as a science that must have a useful outcome for management. Firat et al. say of this research:

> [It] generates knowledge that pertains to the consumption experience of individuals, households, and communities, regardless of the direct consequences of such experiences for market exchange or buying-selling processes. . . . They are questioning the validity of research done solely for consulting purposes for the marketing organizations. They are further

arguing that marketing management implications of their research should not be a criterion of evaluation of their work. (Firat et al., 1987: xv)

This interpretive approach is of increasing importance and will be considered further in the next section. Its comparative strength, however, reflects the distinct weakness of other paradigms. For example, there is little that could be seen as radical structuralist or radical humanist, to use Burrell and Morgan's terms.

Whether it would be worth developing this model further depends upon how one evaluates this approach as a whole. In particular, the approach is relativistic and offers no guidance on how to choose between different theories. Associated with this is the problem that the theories are abstracted from their social and historical context, thus further undermining any potential critique (see Reed, 1985, 1990 for developments of this argument). Similarly, Arndt's argument is merely a call for paradigmatic pluralism; it generates no criteria for evaluating different theories; there is no historical perspective on the construction of theories; there is no theory of emancipation or resistance through theoretical or practical challenge. Arndt is content to advocate paradigmatic pluralism as an end in itself:

> By limiting itself to the empiricist orientation and logical empiricist paradigms such as instrumental man, marketing has remained essentially a one-dimensional science concerned with technology and problem-solving. The subjective world and liberating paradigms challenge the assumptions of empiricism by generating questions resulting in quite different research questions. While no paradigm or metaphor is more than a partial and incomplete truth, the *notion* of paradigms should be viewed as an argument for paradigmatic tolerance and pluralism. The yin and yang of progress in marketing include both the logic, rigor and objectivity of logical empiricism and the socio-political paradigm and speculations, visions and consciousness of the subjective world and liberating paradigms. (Arndt, 1985: 21–2)

Thus Arndt ends up supporting the positivistic paradigm as just as valid as the other paradigms – a conclusion that hardly seems set to challenge the dominant orthodoxy in a serious way. Furthermore, this is characteristic of the way in which the paradigm approach tends to end up in endless discussions of suppositions and metaphors (e.g. Gareth Morgan, 1980, 1986) without either evaluating the different metaphors or considering how they relate to the development of particular social and organizational settings. Whilst the paradigm framework in marketing may help researchers confront their underlying presuppositions, it is limited in its role in analysing marketing as a set of discourses and practices.

Habermas and Critical Theory
The second strand of Critical Theory which I wish to consider derives from Habermas (1971, 1979), whose voluminous work can be drawn on in many ways. This section concentrates on the significance of the distinction he draws between technical rationality, hermeneutic understanding and Critical Theory. As has already been argued, the idea that management is a scientifically rational and efficient application of neutral knowledge, on a par with the natural sciences, has always faced the problem that the people who are the subjects of the knowledge can choose to act differently. They have consciousness and understanding, which affects their actions and their responses to managerial controls. Thus, there has been a dialectic in a number of management specialisms between approaches which treat people as objects to be manipulated in accordance with scientific laws (i.e. technical-rational approaches) and approaches which treat them as subjects (the hermeneutic approach). In the hermeneutic approach the idea of management science is abandoned. Instead emphasis is placed on understanding how people come to share meanings. At first sight this may appear to have little relevance to managers, but recently there has been an increased interest in the area of actors' meanings, and in particular in the generation of consent (e.g. 'soft systems approaches' in operational research, human relations in personnel, 'managing culture' in strategic management).

In marketing, the rise of the interpretive school has been highly significant. It has sought to place the issue of meaning and the constitution of meaning within marketing settings firmly on the research agenda. It has drawn inspiration from the hermeneutic tradition, particularly as developed in social anthropology. In its challenge to the predominant positivist paradigm the interpretive approach has also sought to distance itself from managerialism, though whether it can continue to do that may be considered doubtful, particularly if we use Habermas's framework to consider further its claims to offer a radical alternative.

Habermas argues that it is necessary to go further than simply uncovering meanings. He argues that it is necessary to understand how meanings are constituted and, in particular, how power is implicated in that process. Habermas distinguishes between the 'ideal speech situation' and the 'distorted communication'. In an ideal speech situation, people are able to communicate freely and reach consensus on the basis of their shared understandings. In systematically distorted communication, power and influence are being used to generate a 'false consensus'. So it is not sufficient simply to understand how people see the world and reach consensus. One must also be able to understand how certain forms of meaning have been generated through manipulation of power. Hermeneutic analysis must be placed in the context of Critical Theory, i.e. understanding how particular ways of seeing represent certain power and class interests.

This argument is particularly important in making sense of the interpretive approach to marketing. This can be illustrated by considering a recent debate regarding the role and significance of advertising. Pollay (1986) argues that advertising is increasingly a 'distorting mirror', which generates materialism and individualism. Holbrook (1987b), on the other hand, as an adherent of the interpretive paradigm, presents a view of advertising as part of a social process of meaning construction which occurs at a variety of levels – institutional, group, individual. Social actors are not the passive recipients of manipulatory messages created by advertising agencies monolithically subverting 'decent' values and replacing them with corrupted and degraded materialism. To Pollay's (admittedly under-theorized) social criticism, Holbrook counterposes the hermeneutic view that the meanings of individual actors must be taken seriously and, equally, that no one set of values is inherently superior to any other. This leaves Holbrook with no way of understanding how these meanings become constructed, or how they might be different. He thereby comes close to implicitly endorsing all advertising practice, thus losing any critical edge either to his analysis of advertising or to the analysis of mass consumption more generally.

From Habermas's position (and it is one shared with other authors in the Frankfurt critical tradition; see, e.g., Jay, 1973: ch. 6; Held, 1980: ch. 3 for a discussion of this wider tradition, which includes authors such as Marcuse, 1964 and Fromm, 1974), there has to be the possibility that advertising is not 'pure communication', but 'systematically distorted'. In this context, people can misunderstand their situation through the manipulation of communication. Thus advertising is treated as one area of the 'critique of ideology' and modern culture more generally (see Ewen, 1976, 1988; Ewen and Ewen, 1982; Thompson, 1990). Habermas and the Frankfurt School seek to retain a position from which the mass consumption ethic of modern culture can be criticized. In this view it is not sufficient to accept the meanings that people hold; it is also necessary to question why they hold them and to see that mass consumption as a way of life is open to critical analysis. This directs attention, in particular, to the material underpinnings of capitalist production and the role of marketing and advertising in reproducing that system. Thus the presentation of interpretive approaches as the 'radical' alternative to marketing orthodoxy needs to be challenged. Hermeneutic analysis is certainly

a progressive step in the analysis of marketing in so fa
with the problematic of positivism and the endorse
terialism, but in itself it is not sufficient. It is neces:
ground the way in which meanings are socially constitu
requires an appreciation of the transformation of soc
and the role of marketing in that process. Habermas's work provides considerable resources for such an analysis.

Braverman and Marxist Approaches

Another potentially productive area to draw on for critical studies
derives from Braverman (1974). Braverman presented his arguments as complementary to those of Baran and Sweezy (1966) in
their analysis of the economic development of monopoly capitalism.
In particular, Baran and Sweezy argued that the postwar Western
economies had moved into a cycle of 'over-production'. The central
problem for these economies was to sell their products at a profit.
Baran and Sweezy argued that 'false needs' had to be created
amongst people. They had to be made to believe that they 'really'
wanted commodities such as cars, televisions, clothes, and so on,
which could be produced and sold at a profit, even though these
commodities contributed both to the despoliation and pollution of
the environment and to the privatization of social life. Meanwhile,
public services such as education, health and public transport, which
capitalists could not run at a profit but which were crucial to a
decent standard of life, would be left to decline. In this view,
marketing and advertising are explained as 'functionally' necessary
to advanced capitalist economies because they are the means
whereby people are persuaded to buy what they do not 'really
need'.

Braverman adapts this approach in his own work, arguing that
scientific management as a whole is developed in the interests of
capitalists. This sort of approach assumes that there is one course of
action which is clearly in the 'interests of capital as a whole' and that
this is the course which is followed. Thus the nature of marketing
flows unproblematically from its 'function' in the reproduction of
capitalist relations. However, the way in which managerial actions
are constituted is much more complex than this unidimensional
model allows. Definitions of what is in the interests of capital and/or
management are socially constructed and cannot be assumed by
reference to an inner 'essence' that implies a clear and unfailing
logic which actors somehow follow (these arguments are reviewed
in a number of places: e.g. Morgan, 1990: ch. 1; Knights and Willmott, 1990). What marketing is, how it has been defined and
enacted, also differs in particular social settings. To neglect these

differences and reduce management to the agent of the unseen hand of capitalism is highly problematic.

One author who has tried to take serious account of this argument whilst maintaining the overall Marxist framework is Peter Armstrong. Armstrong has written on a number of management groups, particularly personnel, engineering and accountancy, and has sought to show how in the framework of capitalist accumulation there is a struggle within management between various groups for a central role in defining the 'interests of capital' (Armstrong, 1984, 1987a, 1987b). Rather than seeing this purely as a political process of inter-group competition (e.g. as in Pettigrew, 1973), Armstrong relates this process to the conditions of ownership and control in enterprises and the way in which professional groups articulate their interests through constructing them as in the interests of capital as a whole. He emphasizes the differences that occur between societies on the basis of complex antecedent conditions, which structure the conditions under which managerial specialisms develop.

Although Armstrong himself has not sought to apply this framework to marketing, it clearly has potential application. For example, one of the central questions which Armstrong considers is how the domination of certain groups, in particular accountants, impacts on the overall way in which British industry has developed. Armstrong argues that the relatively poor performance of British industry can be explained by the dominance of financial criteria in managerial decisions. He contrasts this to the role which engineering and design play in other countries. A similar issue has been taken up within marketing itself, though without Armstrong's theoretical framework. For example, a number of authors have contrasted the dominance of accounting with the relatively low prestige and status of marketing. They have blamed the problems of British industry on the lack of marketing skills in its higher echelons, a point also made by the National Economic Development Office, which in 1981 reported that its 'sector committees continue to identify the lack of commitment to marketing as the single most important constraint in UK and overseas market shares' (reported in Doyle, 1985: 89; see also Baker et al., 1986; Wong et al., 1988; Doyle, 1987; Day and Wensley, 1983; Piercy, 1986).

Potentially, then, there is a point of connection between the approach of Armstrong and those of the authors cited. The relations between management specialisms and the impact of this on economic performance is a common interest and addresses an important question. Yet there remains the problematic link between these issues and the development of capitalism. For Armstrong, who follows Braverman in this, there is a strong and direct link. In the

end, any management specialism must be analysed by i
this overriding structural context. For the authors cited (Dc
Baker et al., 1986; Wong et al., 1988; Doyle, 1987; Day and \
1983; Piercy, 1986), this issue is not examined. They imply t.
struggle between management specialisms is an ineradicable p.
organizational politics which can be understood in its own r.ght
without reference to the wider context. In my view, this is inadequate
and the issue they address cannot be considered outside an understanding of the wider social context.

As has already been stated, there are some serious problems with
this type of Marxist approach. However, there are three elements
that do appear worth retaining for the critical analysis of marketing.

1 How is marketing as a discourse and set of practices linked to
   phases of capital accumulation?
2 How does marketing as a management specialism constitute itself
   as central to the interests of capitalism?
3 How does marketing as a particular management specialism relate
   to other such specialisms within the overall management division
   of labour?

Foucault, Power and Knowledge
The main elements of Foucauldian analysis which have been taken up
in the study of management concern the idea that the modern world is
characterized by emerging discourses of power and knowledge (see,
e.g., Rose, 1990; Hopwood, 1987; Miller and O'Leary, 1987).
Knowledge is a way of constructing the world, of differentiating it
into various elements and through this process taking control over
the elements and disciplining the self and social institutions. Knowledge cannot be traced to an inner essence, i.e. to its social origins in
the interests of one class or other. The way knowledges emerge is
contingent and complex. The search for origins is an irrelevance;
instead, the analyst should focus on what the knowledge does – on its
'power effects'. Thus discourses of knowledge are always embedded
in social practices – ways of 'doing the world' that flow out of
'knowing the world' in a particular way.

It is important to note that in this view power is not simply
repressive, i.e. how one social group or class constrains another.
Instead, one of the main power effects of discourses concerns the way
in which they help people understand their own selves (e.g. as
consumers) in a particular way. By knowing oneself as a particular
sort of subject one begins to take actions in a particular way; one
becomes empowered within the terms of the discourse (Rose, 1990).

Why should Foucauldian analysis be particularly relevant to

marketing? The answer to this cannot be given in the abstract. Foucauldian analysis involves the understanding of specific social practices and discourses; it focuses on the micro-power effects of these practices and discourses. What is it that marketing as a discourse actually does to the way in which people live their lives? How are its power effects as a discourse constructed?

The constitution of marketing as a discourse and set of practices is the key issue in Foucauldian analysis. At one level, this task is associated with the wider problem of the constitution of management knowledge and the role of management education. Here, marketing as a particular form of management knowledge was constructed first of all within American business schools in the early twentieth century; as an academic discipline and later as a form of management practice it has been crucially shaped by that context. In particular, the significance of the dominance of American management education styles in the English-speaking countries has been the basis for a particular construction of marketing (on the US business schools and the relationship between the different emerging knowledge areas see Sass, 1982; Sedlak and Williamson, 1983; Locke, 1984; Bartels, 1962; Jones and Monieson, 1990). At present there is very little work that considers how marketing as an academic discourse has constituted its object of analysis and its methods of inquiry within specific institutional settings.

This relates to the second aspect of the discourse, which concerns the interrelationship of the academic development of the discipline and its incorporation in organizations. The American Marketing Association (AMA) Task Force (1988) was crucially concerned with this interface and the feeling amongst practising managers that the academic discipline was not 'delivering', yet there is no systematic research on these interconnections. As an example of the importance of this one can consider the fact that marketing as an academic discipline developed earliest in Midwestern American universities, where it was particularly concerned with the problems of farmers in selling their produce. The problem was that merchants tended to control marketing opportunities and force low prices on farmers. Academics within the emerging business schools of the Midwest at the turn of the twentieth century shared in the progressive ideology of many of their intellectual contemporaries and were concerned to improve the power position of the farmers *vis-à-vis* the merchants. Thus as consultants and experts, the first university appointees in marketing tended to be radicals concerned to empower the farming community. If that was the origin of marketing, what has happened since to bring it into closer alliance with big business?

This in turn raises the importance of considering how marketing as knowledge and practice has developed over time and in different societies. The conditions of possibility for marketing in Britain were considerably different to those of the USA, partly because traditional attitudes to management were much more entrenched. In Britain, marketing has frequently come into organizations as a way of clearing away what have been construed as outdated attitudes – for example the role of marketing in the changing nature of the financial services industry (see the studies in Morgan and Murray, forthcoming).

From Foucault's perspective, these issues are of more than historical interest. They involve a 'genealogical' approach to the past, which considers the complex conditions of possibility of various forms of knowledge and practice. This involves a 'history of the present', not as the expression of a hidden rationality – the so-called Whig Interpretation of History[1] – but as a contingent construction of particular social practices. Viewing the present in this light undermines the attempt of practitioners to claim that existing arrangements embody objective, rational 'truth'. The reason why history and genealogy are important is that they allow us to understand more clearly how particular institutional arrangements were set up and empowered such that they now appear 'normal'. A proper genealogy of marketing therefore holds out considerable potential as a tool of critique.

Such an analysis also helps us to consider how marketing has become embedded in the construction of social subjects and thus in the transformation of capitalist societies as a whole. Marketing discourse seeks to constitute the subjectivities of consumers and managers within organizations. At one level this is an issue about advertising. Returning to the debate discussed earlier, Holbrook argues that the consumer must not be treated as a cultural dope and that advertising itself should be seen as a social process (see Slater, 1989 for one of the few studies of how advertising agencies actually work; also Leiss et al., 1990). There is a need for studies of how advertisers constitute consumers and modes of addressing consumers. At another level, there is the issue of how consumers incorporate these messages and internalize them as part of their identity (see the discussion of the products of the life insurance industry in Knights and Morgan, 1991c). Once again, it is important to avoid the trap of seeing the consumer as a cultural dope. There is considerable evidence of the way in which the messages of marketers are the basis for further 'signification work' by consumers (see the review in Morgan and Knights, 1990). Similarly, there are issues concerned with how managers within organizations come to see themselves in terms of marketing. What difference does this make to their way of working? What difference does it make to their sense of identity? (See Knights and Morgan, 1991a, 1991b, 1991c; Morgan and Knights, 1991 for a discussion of a number of these issues).

The Foucauldian approach raises important issues about how marketing is constituted and the power effects it has on subjects, both consumers and managers. It raises these questions in the context of an analysis of social transformation that is complex and still subject to debate (see e.g. Poulantzas, 1978 and Minson, 1985 on the conservative implications of Foucault's view of power; also Gordon, 1987 and O'Neill, 1986 on the parallels between Foucault and Weber and their views on society as a whole). By undermining the taken-for-granted status of discourses and practices, Foucault can contribute strongly to the critique of marketing and its role in contemporary Western societies.

Conclusions

Marketing is a substantial and powerful discourse which is currently dominated by a highly positivistic and normative approach to knowledge. This is causing dissatisfaction even within the realms of its own practitioners. It is necessary to turn outside of marketing to critical theories developed in other areas for alternative perspectives. Overall, it is important to see marketing as part of the process whereby a particular form of society is constructed, one in which human beings are treated as things, where identity is reduced to the ownership of commodities and all social relations are conceived in market terms. In understanding how marketing contributes to these processes it is necessary to develop a critique of existing social arrangements as much as a critique of marketing itself. These elements of critique are combined in various ways in the approaches I have considered in the second part of this chapter. Four alternatives were identified and considered. All four provided useful tools of critique, though clearly each has its own particular strengths and weaknesses. Whereas some management specialisms (such as accounting and personnel) already have their alternative approaches well developed and evaluated, marketing, which is just as important as these two specialisms in contemporary organizations, has as yet no significant forum for critical debate, nor well-developed alternative perspectives. What is needed at this stage is an initial recognition that marketing can be subjected to critical analysis, followed by relevant research to show how such an approach can be put into practice. This chapter has aimed to provide certain signposts for the direction which such research could take.

Note

1 See, for example, the way in which the history of marketing is treated in some of the papers in Nevett and Fullerton, 1988; Nevett and Hollander, 1987; the work of Fullerton, 1987a, 1987b, 1988a, 1988b, appears to be the main exception to this.

References

American Marketing Association (AMA) Task Force on the Development of Marketing Thought (1988) 'Developing, disseminating and utilizing marketing knowledge', *Journal of Marketing*, 52 (Oct.): 1–25.

Anderson, P. F. (1983) 'Marketing, scientific progress and scientific method', *Journal of Marketing*, 47 (Fall): 18–31.

Armstrong, P. (1984) 'Competition between the organized professions and the evolution of management control strategies', in K. Thompson (ed.), *Work, Employment and Unemployment*. Milton Keynes: Open University Press.

Armstrong, P. (1987a) 'Engineers, managers and trust', *Work, Employment and Society*, 1 (4).

Armstrong, P. (1987b) 'The rise of accounting controls in British capitalist enterprises', *Accounting, Organizations and Society*, 12 (5).

Arndt, J. (1985) 'The tyranny of paradigms: the case for paradigmatic pluralism in marketing', in Dhoklakia and Arndt (1985).

Baker, M. J., Hart, S., Black, C. and Abdel-Mohsen, T. M. (1986) 'The contribution of marketing to competitive success: a literature review', *Journal of Marketing Management*, 2 (1): 39–61.

Baran, P. and Sweezy, P. (1966) *Monopoly Capitalism*. Harmondsworth: Penguin.

Bartels, R. (1962) *The Development of Marketing Thought*. Homewood, Illinois: Richard D. Irwin.

Bauman, Z. (1988) *Legislators and Interpreters*. Cambridge: Polity Press.

Belk, R. W., Wallendorf, M. and Sherry, J. F. (1988) 'A naturalistic enquiry into buyer and seller behavior at a swap meet', *Journal of Consumer Research*, 14 (March): 449–70.

Belk, R. W., Wallendorf, M. and Sherry, J. F. (1989) 'The sacred and the profane in consumer behavior: theodicy on the odyssey', *Journal of Consumer Research*, 16 (June): 1–38.

Braverman, H. (1974) *Labor and Monopoly Capital*. New York: Monthly Review Press.

Burrell, G. and Morgan, G. (1979) *Sociological Paradigms and Organizational Analysis*. London: Heinemann.

Day, G. S. and Wensley, R. (1983) 'Marketing theory with a strategic orientation', *Journal of Marketing*, 47 (Fall): 79–89.

Dholakia, N. and Arndt, J. (eds) (1985) *Changing the Course of Marketing: Alternative Paradigms for Widening Marketing Theory* (Research in Marketing, Supplement 2). Greenwich, CT: JAI Press.

Doyle, P. (1985) 'Marketing and the competitive performance of British industry', *Journal of Market Management*, 1: 87–98.

Doyle, P. (1987) 'Marketing and the British chief executive', *Journal of Marketing Management*, 3 (2): 121–32.

Ewen, S. (1976) *Captains of Consciousness*. New York: McGraw Hill.

Ewen, S. (1988) *All Consuming Images*. New York: Basic Books.

Ewen, S. and Ewen, E. (1982) *Channels of Desire*. New York: McGraw Hill.
Firat, A. F., Dholakia, N. and Bagozzi, R. P. (eds) (1987) *Philosophical and Radical Thought in Marketing*. Lexington, MA: D. C. Heath.
Foucault, M. (1979) *Discipline and Punish*. Harmondsworth: Penguin.
Foucault, M. (1981) *History of Sexuality Vol. I*. Harmondsworth: Penguin.
Fromm, E. (1974) *The Anatomy of Human Destructiveness*. London: Cape.
Fullerton, R. A. (1987a) 'The poverty of ahistorical analysis: present weakness and future cure in US marketing thought', in Firat et al. (1987).
Fullerton, R. A. (1987b) 'Marketing action and the transformation of western consciousness', in Nevett and Hollander (1987).
Fullerton, R. A. (1988a) 'How modern is modern marketing? Marketing's evolution and the myth of the "production era"', *Journal of Marketing*, 52 (Jan.): 108–25.
Fullerton, R. A. (1988b) 'Modern western marketing as a historical phenomenon: theory and illustration', in Nevett and Fullerton (1988).
Gordon, C. (1987) 'The soul of the citizen: Max Weber and Michel Foucault on rationality and government', in S. Whimster and S. Lash (eds), *Max Weber, Rationality and Modernity*. London: Allen & Unwin.
Habermas, J. (1971) *Towards a Rational Society*. London: Heinemann.
Habermas, J. (1976) *Communication and the Evolution of Society*. London: Heinemann.
Held, D. (1980) *Introduction to Critical Theory*. London: Hutchinson.
Hirschmann, E. (1985) 'Primitive aspects of consumption in modern American society', *Journal of Consumer Research*, 12 (Sept.): 142–54.
Hirschmann, E. (1988) 'Upper class WASPS as consumers: a humanist inquiry', *Research in Consumer Behavior*, 3: 115–47.
Hirschmann, E. (1990) 'Secular immortality and the American ideology of affluence', *Journal of Consumer Research*, 17 (June): 31–42.
Holbrook, M. B. (1987a) 'O, consumer, how you've changed: some radical reflections on the roots of consumption', in Firat et al. (1987).
Holbrook, M. B. (1987b) 'Mirror, mirror, on the wall, what's unfair in the reflections on advertising?', *Journal of Marketing*, July: 95–103.
Hopwood, A. (1987) 'The archaeology of accounting systems', *Accounting, Organizations and Society*, 12 (3): 207–34.
Hunt, S. D. (1990) 'Truth in marketing theory and research', *Journal of Marketing*, 54 (July): 1–15.
Jay, M. (1973) *The Dialectical Imagination*. London: Heinemann.
Jones, D. G. B. and Monieson, D. D. (1990) 'Early development of the philosophy of marketing thought', *Journal of Marketing*, 54 (Jan.): 102–13.
Knights, D. and Morgan, Glenn (1991a) 'Corporate strategy, organizations and subjectivity', *Organization Studies*, 12 (2): 251–73.
Knights, D. and Morgan, Glenn (1991b) 'Selling oneself: subjectivity and the labour process in the sale of life insurance', in C. Smith, D. Knights and H. Willmott (eds), *White-Collar Work: The Non-Manual Labour Process*. London: Macmillan.
Knights, D. and Morgan, Glenn (1991c) 'Organization theory, consumption and the service sector', paper presented to conference, 'Towards a New Theory of Organizations', Keele University, April.
Knights, D. and Willmott, H. (eds) (1990) *Labour Process Theory*. London: Macmillan.
Kotler, P. (1985a) *Marketing Management*, 5th edn. Englewood Cliffs, NJ: Prentice-Hall.

Kotler, P. (1985b) 'A generic concept of marketing', in B. M. Enis and K. K. Cox (eds) *Marketing Classics: A Selection of Influential Articles*, 5th edn. Boston: Allyn & Bacon.

Leiss, W., Kline, S. and Jhally, S. (1990) *Social Communication in Advertising*, 2nd edn. London: Routledge.

Locke, R. R. (1984) *The End of the Practical Man: Entrepreneurship and Higher Education in Germany, France and Great Britain 1880–1940*, Greenwich, CT: JAI Press.

Lutz, R. J. (1989) 'Editorial', *Journal of Consumer Research*, 16 (June).

Marcuse, H. (1964) *One-dimensional Man*. London: Sphere.

Miller, P. and O'Leary, T. (1987) 'Accounting and the construction of the governable person', *Accounting, Organizations and Society*, 12 (3).

Minson, J. (1985) 'Strategies for socialists: Foucault's conception of power', in M. Gane (ed.), *Towards a Critique of Foucault*. London: Routledge & Kegan Paul.

Morgan, Gareth (1980) 'Paradigms, metaphors and puzzle solving in organization theory', *Administrative Science Quarterly*, 25.

Morgan, Gareth (1986) *Images of Organization*. Beverley Hills, CA: Sage.

Morgan, Glenn (1990) *Organizations in Society*. London: Macmillan.

Morgan, Glenn and Knights, D. (1990) 'Consumption and the analysis of organizations', paper presented at the World Congress of Sociology, Madrid, Spain, July.

Morgan, Glenn and Knights, D. (1991) 'Gendering jobs: corporate strategy, managerial control and the dynamics of job segregation', *Work, Employment and Society*, 5 (2).

Morgan, Glenn and Murray, F. (forthcoming) *The Dynamics of Organizational Change: Case Studies in the Financial Services Industry*. London: Macmillan.

Muncy, J. A. and Fisk, R. P. (1987) 'Cognitive relativism and the practice of marketing science', *Journal of Marketing*, 51 (Jan.): 20–33.

Nevett, T. and Fullerton, R. A. (1988) *Historical Perspectives in Marketing*. Lexington: D. C. Heath.

Nevett, T. and Hollander, S. C. (eds) (1987) *Marketing in Three Eras*. East Lansing, MI: Michigan State University Press.

O'Neill, J. (1986) 'The disciplinary society: from Weber to Foucault', *British Journal of Sociology*. 37 (1): 42–60.

Pettigrew, A. (1973) *The Politics of Organizational Decision-Making*. London: Tavistock.

Piercy, N. (1986) 'The role and function of the chief marketing executive and the marketing department: a study of medium sized companies in the UK', *Journal of Marketing Management*, 1 (3): 265–89.

Pollay, R. W. (1986) 'The distorted mirror: reflections on the unintended consequences of advertising', *Journal of Marketing*, 50 (April): 18–36.

Poulantzas, N. (1978) *State, Power, Socialism*. London: New Left Books.

Reed, M. (1985) *Redirections in Organizational Analysis*. London: Tavistock.

Reed, M. (1990) 'From paradigms to images: the paradigm warrior turns post-modernist guru', *Personnel Review*, 19 (3): 35–40.

Rose, N. (1990) *Governing the Soul*. London: Routledge.

Sass, S. (1982) *The Pragmatic Imagination: A History of the Wharton School*. Philadelphia: University of Pennsylvania Press.

Sedlak, M. W. and Williamson, H. F. (1983) *The Evolution of Management Education: A History of the Northwestern University J. L. Kellogg Graduate School of Management*. Urbana: University of Illinois Press.

Slater, D. (1989) 'Corridors of power', in J. F. Gubrium and D. Silverman (eds), *The Politics of Field Research*. London: Sage.

Thompson, J. B. (1990) *Ideology and Modern Culture*. Cambridge: Polity Press.

Wong, V., Saunders, J. and Doyle, P. (1988) 'The quality of British marketing: a comparison with US and Japanese multinationals in the UK market', *Journal of Marketing Management*, 4 (2): 107–30.

8

Information Systems and Critical Theory

Kalle Lyytinen

Information Systems (IS) is a young technology-driven field of study spurred by huge advances in computer technology and telecommunications. However, only recently have we seen discussions of research strategies and the theoretical foundations of IS research (see e.g. McFarlan, 1985; Mumford et al., 1985; Cooper, 1988; Orlikowski and Baroudi, 1989), and the field is still dominated by naive realism (see e.g. McFarlan, 1985). No wonder, then, that critical and 'continental' research philosophies, being alien to the 'received view', remain largely unknown. Consequently, the research based on these premises has remained for the larger IS community a mystery, and its results obscure.

However, during the last few years the situation has been slowly changing. Some indicators of this are debates on appropriate research methods (Mumford et al., 1985; Nissen et al., 1990; Orlikowski and Baroudi, 1989), and changes in editorial policies of established journals. Accordingly, there is an obvious need to summarize and evaluate what critical social theory (CST) has contributed to IS research so far. Also to continue research in this area, major research challenges need to be identified. In this chapter I set out to address these tasks. The goal of the chapter is twofold. First, I clarify the basic tenets of Habermas's Critical Theory and their contributions to the field of IS. I also take a critical look at the research outcomes obtained. Secondly I formulate a research agenda for critical IS research.

The chapter is organized as follows. We begin with a short overview of the IS field and research conducted in which the role of IS in organizational activity and management action and issues raised by the introduction of new technologies are discussed. In section 3 the reader is acquainted with the basic notions and ideas of Habermas's Critical Theory as they have been applied in IS. In section 4, I summarize major research results achieved from applying Critical Theory *in* IS. Section 5 outlines a tentative research agenda for Critical-Theory-based Information Systems studies – that is, I try to identify necessary and sufficient conditions for developing a Critical Theory *for* IS.

Information Systems – a Field Associating Technology with Organizations

Information Systems Research – a Short Overview

Information Systems is a young field of study, and consensus on its research goals, methods and theories has yet to emerge with clarity. In this chapter the term 'information system' is used to describe all different sorts of IS from payroll to group-decision support systems. In the discussion that follows I will accept the definition of IS as 'a computer-based organizational information system which provides information support for management activities and functions' (Ives et al., 1980: 910). Thus the definition stresses that IS is an amalgam of technological, organizational and managerial challenges raised by rapid developments in computing technologies. Historically, the field has also grown from the combined efforts of three associated disciplines: computer science, management science and organization theory (Swanson, 1985).

A few aspects in the above definition require comment. First, the notion of 'information support' should be understood broadly to cover storage, transmission, manipulation and delivery of symbolic representations that are relevant to, or shape, organizational action. Secondly, the 'management activities and functions' are assumed to apply to all organizational participants, not merely those called 'managers'. Thirdly, although the field is not bound to any particular technological basis, its focus and problem formulations are always tied up with the idea of *technological change* in IS. Finally, in contrast to some established fields, such as accounting, which deal with specific types of calculating practices (see Power and Laughlin, Chapter 6 in this volume), IS research is more concerned with the generic problems of information processing.

Information systems research can be defined as 'the study of effective design, delivery, and usage of IS in organizations and society' (Keen, 1980: 10). A few observations are relevant here. First, the definition illustrates that IS research has both descriptive and normative purpose, normative because the IS field is primarily a *constructive* activity i.e. the main focus of the research has been upon *how to design and deliver*. In this sense, the research settings have traditionally been very close to the mundane problems of developing and implementing IS. Therefore research into methodological 'prescriptions' for 'effective' design and delivery, and the actual implementations of various tools and applications, has formed the bulk of published research.

An alternative research stream has focused on describing the *actual usage* of IS. Because the actual usage may largely differ from the espoused usage pattern this stream of research has been much more insightful about how computing affects organizations. Many of these studies have relied on established sociological schools to study organizational life (Kling, 1980) and therefore they have been more aware of their research assumptions. However, these studies have had very little, if any, impact on the dominating 'managerial' and 'engineering' studies into computing.

Second, the term 'effective' requires clarification. Traditionally the concept has been interpreted in managerial terms and limited to economic criteria for evaluating IS-related activities. A common way to phrase it is to discuss the 'efficiency', the 'effectiveness', and the 'systemic' impacts of IT-related investments (Mason, 1989; Gurbaxani and Whang, 1991). In this chapter I will interpret the term to mean *any* criteria by which the delivery, design and usage of the IS are judged in human affairs.

Finally, the notion of 'organization' has traditionally meant hierarchical 'bureaucracy', but this is not necessarily so any more. Developments in information technology have permitted new business structures to arise or old business arrangements to be transformed, leading to a richer picture of available organizational designs. A key question in many situations therefore is: given the technological options available, what are the appropriate organizational and managerial designs to produce and deliver something 'effectively'?

Information Systems in Organizations

In order to analyse the potential impact of IS in shaping and mediating organizational action we shall classify organizational roles served by computer-based IS. We can distinguish six major roles of information systems (see also Gurbaxani and Whang, 1991). They:

1 increase economic efficiencies;
2 streamline and shape basic business transactions and change their delivery channels;
3 collect and summarize information relevant to managerial decisions and help rationalization and automation of decision-making;
4 monitor and record performance of employees and organizational units (groups, departments, Strategic Business Units);
5 maintain records of the status and change of organizations' goals, structure, products and environment; and
6 provide a channel for symbolic interaction and establish an attentive symbolic environment for organizational action.

These roles are largely self-evident and most of them existed in organizations long before the introduction of computers. We shall focus on the impact of information technology on each role.

1 IS have a direct impact on the economics of information processing. They are understood to improve the quality and productivity of information processing and reduce labour costs (the ratio between fixed and variable capital changes, in a Marxist wording). These developments have inspired research efforts to criticize IS in serving managerial strategies of deskilling and intensification of 'scientific management' (Braverman, 1974; Kling, 1980; Hirschheim, 1986; Attewell and Rule, 1984). But contradictory results have been obtained from empirical studies when these hypotheses have been tested, leading to a number of new theories of work design (see Ehn, 1988).

2 A large and growing portion of modern organizations depends heavily on IS for execution of basic business transactions. To this end organizations have built large transaction-processing systems – for example seat reservation systems – to streamline and rationalize their business transactions. This has often decreased costs associated with carrying out these transactions (Williamson, 1985) and permitted new types of business arrangement to emerge. It is worth noting that very little, if any, research has been done on the critical ramifications of such developments on consumer rights, consumer protection and the vulnerability of society's services if they are to a larger extent delivered by electronic channels. The impact of large economic coalitions that produce and maintain these systems upon national economies is also severely under-researched.

3 Traditionally IS have been seen to produce the 'fuel' to the organizational decision-making machine (cf. Cooper, 1988). Many studies in IS have been inspired by this role, which was well established in the early writings of Herbert Simon (1977). IS decrease 'the boundness' of decision-making rationality by relaxing the bounds that prohibit informed optimization of the decision problem. Several factors contribute to this: reduced cost to access and manipulate information, a faster decision cycle, which permits more alternatives to be explored, and higher information quality (accuracy, timeliness), which allows for more informed decisions. In this role IS have substantially shaped the prevailing managerial ideology by strengthening the instrumental rationalization of organizations (for criticisms see Björn-Andersen and Eason, 1980; Boland, 1987).

4 IS have an important role in monitoring the performance of individuals and larger organizational units (groups, departments, etc.). This serves several important goals: (1) IS provide a means to direct attention to important aspects of organizational performance;

(2) IS reduce possibilities for covert and insincere actions; and (3) IS provide an explicit contract or implicit rules to evaluate the performance of agents and compensate accordingly. By using IS, management get reliable and 'objective' measures to reward agents and to shape their perceptions and behaviours. Many critical accounts of computing (Rule et al., 1980; Mowshowitz, 1976; Briefs et al., 1983) view IS as a new device to reinforce control and surveillance of the workforce leading to an organizational 'iron cage' with increased alienation.

5   Organizations suffer from unclear, ambiguous and complex co-ordination problems, which require a lot of communication and documentation. There are ample reasons for keeping track of the status and change of various factors in a company's internal and external environment. Some examples will suffice to illustrate the argument: goals, plans and operating procedures must be disseminated to geographically distributed agents in order to ensure their proper co-ordination; knowledge must be kept about various activities that would be lost if people left the company; various tasks and resources must be continually distributed to organizational units through bargaining, and so on. In all these activities IS can support by carrying out complex documentation and communication tasks. Many studies claim that such developments in IS make organizational life more 'transparent', inducing new forms of organizational control such as new forms of peer control. To highlight this trend Bannon et al. (1988) use Bentham's model of a panopticon to reveal the ultimate form of such developments.

6   Finally, IS induce and create a 'new' organizational reality. IS rely on, and necessitate, the development of a 'common' view of the symbolic field in which they operate. Accordingly, IS require carefully designed (negotiated) channels for symbolic interaction that resist evolution and transformation. They have grown into relatively fixed and constant elements that are available to make sense of organizations' mission, environment and operation and thereby shape management attention. In this evolution IS may marginalize more hazardous, spontaneous and intuitive forms of organizational sense-making, leading to a more unified management 'world-view'. This may have disastrous consequences on management action (Hedberg and Jönsson, 1978), and it may also entail a uniform and monolithic 'symbolic universe' needed to explain and understand what the organization is all about, i.e. it may build up a more pervasive managerial ideology (Berger and Luckmann, 1967; Klein and Lyytinen, 1991).

Overall, IS involve many of the classical problems of organizational design and management. In many cases an IS may serve several of the above roles simultaneously, which increases the importance of understanding their organizational and managerial repercussions. IS should therefore not be ignored in critical studies of modern management and organization.

Critical Theory and IS – Common Areas of Concern

Several IS studies and research schools have observed the growing impact of information technology on modern management. Even within the confines of classical management studies new areas are becoming popular due to the larger 'visibility' of the information-processing aspects of organizations: for example the view of organizations as information-processing entities (Galbraith, 1977), the growing interest in transaction cost theory (Williamson, 1985), and its cousin, agency theory (Alchian and Demsetz, 1972).

More 'progressive' accounts of IS development are becoming quite numerous (see Lyytinen, 1987). For example, Bjerknes et al. (1987) concentrate on trade union rights and on the impacts of computerization on the workplace. In particular, they criticize the negative impacts of more pervasive computerization on roles (1), (3) and (4) (see p. 161 above). The primary focus of this 'Scandinavian approach' has been to protect workers' skills and rights and to promote democracy. Criticisms of managerial 'ideology' can be found in several empirical studies of computing (e.g. Kling, 1980; Attewell and Rule, 1984; Hirschheim, 1986). A majority of these studies have focused on roles (1), (3), (4) and (5) of information systems.

A widely applied and discussed instrumental criticism of IS methodologies is Checkland's (1981) work that focuses on underlining symbolic and sense-making aspects of organizational and managerial action (see also Mingers, Chapter 5 in this volume). His work has contributed to an understanding of the critical role (6) of IS in managerial action.

The Critical Social Theory (CST) of Habermas (1972, 1974, 1979, 1984, 1987) has been launched from *two fronts* into the IS field. Both of them express a common connection between CST and IS research: critique of scientism and relationships between theory and practice; and the nature of social action and the type of knowledge it is based on. Therefore most studies in IS inspired by CST stem either from the endemic critique of the reigning positivistic research paradigm, or from attempts to develop more 'socially informed' methods and theories for IS. I will briefly outline the first of these before concentrating on the nature and potential of the second.

The *first front* has been particularly affected by Habermas's early work on knowledge-constitutive interests (Habermas, 1972). His theory has been applied by several authors in discussing and evaluating the dominant research paradigm (Lee, 1990; Lyytinen and Klein, 1985; Klein, 1984; Ehn, 1988; Ngwenyama, 1987). Most of this work has emphasized that *practical interest* in mutual understanding is necessary if one wants to grasp how organizational agents actually use information systems in making sense of their environment (Boland, 1984). These works have discussed emancipation much less. Only Lyytinen and Klein (1985) and Klein (1984) note that the concepts of autonomy and responsibility should also be taken seriously into account in IS research, and that information systems should serve the values of the widest possible audience, and that they should foster criticism and reflection.

The *second front* has applied Habermas's theory of universal pragmatics and communicative rationality and has sought to develop and explain some parts of IS use and IS development with it. The main thrust in this area has been to adopt Habermas's taxonomy of social action to gain a more refined understanding of the nature of social action associated with 'the design, delivery and usage of information systems'. This research stream has emphasized that social action concepts have implications for the research strategy – especially the concern for 'lifeworld' understanding (Habermas, 1984), and the necessity to apply reconstructive theories (Habermas, 1979) in analysing IS use (Goldkuhl and Lyytinen, 1984).

In *The Theory of Communicative Action*, Habermas (1984) outlines primary action types in which an actor might engage during any organizational activity. Among these, four are prominent in IS: *instrumental, strategic, communicative,* and *discursive.*[1] These action types provide a means of Weberian 'idea type analysis' to reconstruct and clarify the essential nature of diverse organizational activities.

Instrumental and strategic are two basic instances of a more general action type which Habermas calls *purposive-rational.* Purposive-rational action is action directed at attaining rational objectives – the 'achieving of success'. Here, the actor attempts to achieve measurable objectives, and measures the success of his actions by how nearly he achieves his objectives and how efficient the deployed means are. Purposive-rational action applies technical rules that have satisfied some empirical test of the efficiency and effectiveness of the means.

Instrumental action is directed towards agents (objects) as though they were inanimate elements in the actor's environment which can be manipulated in ways that serve the actor's needs. Usually our attitude towards nature (in science and engineering) follows assumptions underlying this action type, but several mechanistic models of organizational behaviour are also representatives of this action-type orientation. Most technology-related tasks in IS development such as, for example, decision-oriented models (role 3 above) follow this action orientation.

Strategic action is directed against rational actors (opponents) who may engage in rational counteraction. Accordingly, an actor's chosen strategy must be measured by taking into account the effects of his actions on situations: what benefits one actor may be harmful to another. Thus an actor must cope with co-operative and conflicting interest situations and find the best strategy for pursuing his goals (see Morgan, Chapter 7 in this volume). In industrial economics as in political studies of organizational behaviour (despite their huge difference in terminology and research methods) assumptions of human behaviour are close to the strategic action type. Typical IS-related studies founded on similar assumptions are recent studies on competitive strategies linking information systems to market segments by intensifying customer linkages (Wiseman, 1985; roles 2 and 4 in the above analysis).

An actor may also pursue *communicative action*. In this case the success orientation is replaced by a desire to understand a communicating partner. Communicative action is oriented towards 'consensual norms', which define mutual expectations about how actors in a given situation should behave in terms of communication. This, of course, presupposes the existence of a shared pool of background assumptions and beliefs. Typical research focusing on communicative action includes ethnographic studies guided by the interest in 'organizational culture' and 'symbolic nature of organizational life'. In information systems the last role of information systems – to provide a channel and environment for symbolic interaction – is an example of this type of action orientation.

When an agreement between a group of actors about a shared background can no longer be taken for granted, the actors embark upon *discursive action*. Here various assumptions concerning communication background are subjected to careful analysis and their validity is tested. Discursive action is thus oriented towards the co-operative search for truth, the clarification of unclear message content, the analysis of the intended use of the messages and so forth. Such action is initiated when doubts are raised by actors as to whether a message is sincerely produced, or whether it is understandable, true, correct and appropriate for the situation. Discursive action tries to discover and weigh the arguments proposed for or against a message, in terms of its clarity, truthfulness, correctness and appropriateness (see Forester, Chapter 3 in this volume). These four criteria of clarity, veracity, sincerity and social acceptability define the validity of (*a priori*) communications, in the same manner as effectiveness is used to measure purposive-rational actions (Habermas, 1984).

Discursive action is thus aimed at justifying (redeeming) any or all the four claims, should one become the subject of doubt. This requires that all actors respect certain *ground rules* that are anticipated in the idea of rational justification of claims put in favour of, or against, the raised claims (Habermas, 1979). In short, this situation problematizes the current organizational status quo and requires it to be transformed towards a structure where all actors have a chance to express opinions, to enter or leave the discourse, and to honour what Habermas (1979) calls 'the force of the better argument'. Discursive action is thus self-referential in the sense that it can be used to justify itself, i.e. there is nothing outside presupposed 'ideal speech' that can be used to justify its internal norms. However, Habermas (1979) claims that if we did not presuppose it we would not have any reason to converse seriously at all. So the justification claim does not lead to infinite regress.

Information systems can hardly be said to exemplify an 'ideal speech' situation (Lyytinen and Hirschheim, 1988). Some examples of border cases in IS that improve organizational competence to open democratic and rational debates are taken into consideration in a later section on alternative models of IS development. Clearly, this aspect of social activity deals mainly with roles (3), (5) and (6) of information systems. However, in most cases it goes beyond the current main roles of IS.

Critical Theory in Information Systems

It is easy to find studies that share some underlying assumptions with Habermas's action typology. For example, in implementation studies (Robey, 1984; Franz and Robey, 1984) instrumental and strategic action orientations have been applied to understand the same implementation process. Similarly, when analysing the development process and the requirements specification process (e.g. Boland, 1978, 1979), instrumental and communicative orientations have been confronted. Nissen's work (1989) in responsible uses of IS, based on Toulmin's (1958) work on 'uses of argument', recognizes communicative and discursive elements of IS use.

Yet, despite its obvious applicability CST has, as yet, had a very modest impact on IS research. A major focus in studies so far has been in observing imperfections in the existing research by applying basic elements of Critical Theory in IS. In more specific terms, we can divide the applications of Critical Theory in IS into the following three categories:

1 criticism of the underlying instrumental rationality bias in information systems, and their 'management ideology';
2 criticism of the dominating research canons and the imperfections of the 'scientistic' programme; and
3 classification and criticism of existing 'technology-driven' development models and the exploration of alternative approaches to develop and use information systems.

Each of these areas will now be discussed in more detail.

Criticism of Instrumental Reason and Management Ideology
Because of the pervasive nature of instrumental rationality in the IS field, this research area has received most attention. It includes two 'classics' in the computing literature: Weizenbaum's (1976) criticism of the assumptions of Artificial Intelligence, and Winograd's and Flores's (1986) analysis of decision-making and language theories applied in the design of computer artefacts. Both works have received wide recognition, probably because they are criticisms launched by 'enlightened', widely known computer scientists. The scholarly ties of Habermas's Critical Theory in these works are modest. Weizenbaum turns his attention to classics of the Frankfurt School, especially Marcuse's *One-dimensional Man*. Winograd and Flores deal primarily with the phenomenology of design, and rely on Heidegger and Gadamer as their source of inspiration (Winograd and Flores, 1986: 9), though their conclusions of the necessity of practical understanding in designing for social domains are similar to those of Habermas (1972). They also use some of Habermas's ideas when discussing the nature of language, and see Habermas's ideal speech situation as a valuable metaphor, though lacking a useful structure to handle issues related to a speech act's validity. Similar types of criticisms of instrumental reason are found in Bryant (1988), Klein and Hirschheim (1987), Mowshowitz (1976), Björn-Andersen and Eason (1980), Ngwenyama (1987), and Ehn (1988).

Criticism of Scientistic Research Canons
Most of this genre of research uses the inadequacies of scientism, as outlined in Habermas's work (1972, 1974), as a starting point in analysing and evaluating current IS research (Klein and Lyytinen, 1985; Nissen, 1985; Lyytinen, 1986; Lee, 1990). The papers reiterate in the context of IS research the key arguments of recent discussions on scientism (Habermas, 1972, 1974; McCarthy, 1978; Bernstein,

1976). Their value is that they show the abstract philosophical discussions directly apply to IS research. These works have advanced metascientific debate in IS research and pointed out that IS research cannot evade problems of scientism. Here too, reputable 'insiders' have pointed out that research methodology goes beyond teaching experimentation and statistical analysis techniques; issues pertaining to ontology, epistemology and the nature of human action need to be discussed and debated in the research community (Lee, 1990; Lyytinen and Klein, 1985; Nissen, 1985).

Criticism of and Suggestions for Alternative Models of IS Development

As noted in the section discussing the nature of IS, most of the IS research literature has concentrated on developing prescriptions (methods) to organize and guide IS development work. In this situation an important concern is: what are the underlying assumptions of knowledge, information, organization and human behaviour that inform these prescriptions? In addition, what are valid grounds to assess and criticize these prescriptions?

In this area, the major contribution has been Lyytinen's (1986) classification of development approaches into a framework based on their epistemological and ontological foundations. Lyytinen bases his effort on Habermas's interest theory and theory of communicative action and shows that a majority of approaches in the field share an interest in technical control -- despite the fact that IS development affects three realms of human activity: technology, symbols and organization. Most IS development approaches, he argues, treat all three realms similarly and presuppose that knowledge of these domains can be acquired and evaluated using the same means. It is claimed that this is an important reason for the high level of IS failure rates and endemic problems in systems development, i.e. it is one example of 'the colonization' of the lifeworld (see Power and Laughlin, Chapter 6 in this volume). In Lyytinen et al. (1991) this analysis is extended to cover criteria by which systems development is evaluated (see also Ciborra and Lanzara, 1989).

Based on these insights several researchers have employed CST to develop alternative approaches to designing IS (Ngwenyama, 1987; Winograd and Flores, 1986; Lyytinen and Hirschheim, 1988; Klein and Hirschheim, 1985; Hirschheim and Klein, 1989; Ehn, 1988). As the distance from the abstract reconstructions of Critical Theory to the mundane concerns of IS development is large, these approaches have largely been hypothetical, eclectic, and in most cases untried.

Ngwenyama (1987) points out that approaches to knowledge 'engineering' cannot ignore concepts of social system and lifeworld which are crucial in orienting human action that is supposed to be supported by the expert system. He also points out that human action is dependent on several knowledge types and several of them defy the description and formalization required by the expert systems. However, this type of knowledge should not be ignored during the development of the expert system (Dreyfus and Dreyfus, 1986).

Klein and Hirschheim (1985) discuss the weaknesses of trying to 'predict' (using the idea of technical control) the consequences of computer applications. This, they argue, is in doubt because human beings create, change and enact their environments. As a solution, they propose a hermeneutic forecasting method based on role-playing and scenarios. Klein (1986) also uses Habermas's action theory to understand and analyse office activity and explains its short-term and long-term effects (such as consensus deficit and colonization of the office work, legitimation crisis, etc.). However, he offers no concrete prescriptions for dealing with these issues.

In recent work, Hirschheim and Klein (1989) draw upon Burrell and Morgan (1979) to compare neo-humanist (CST)-based IS development with the functionalistic, the relativistic paradigm (approaches focusing on sense-making and symbolic interchange), and the radical structuralist paradigm (approaches focusing on class conflict and false ideology). The study deploys 'key stories' to shed light on differences, and to articulate the consequences of privileging different paradigms on IS. Due to the shortage of empirical studies founded on neo-humanism, their analysis of Critical-Theory-based IS development is largely hypothetical, though it primarily provides insights into the key targets and goals of IS development and how it could be harnessed to human emancipation.

Lyytinen and Hirschheim (1988) discuss the possibilities of using IS in supporting the ideal speech situation. They observe two situations where this could happen: IS as a means to generate a discourse, and IS as an input to discourse. In the first case, due to IS's role in mediating and making things happen, the possibility of expanding IS usage to cover discursive elements is limited. Examples of changes in this direction are (1) networking that may overcome limitations of time and space; (2) enhanced inference capabilities that may improve and enlarge the validity of arguments; (3) conferencing, which could motivate people to raise agendas for discursive activity; (4) security controls that could strengthen anonymity and thereby motivate people to communicate criticisms and submit radical change proposals.

Summary
The literature on the Critical Theory in IS, though growing in quantity and depth, has mainly adopted Critical Theory as it is 'received'

in the philosophical literature. Moreover, many of the works are fragmentary (Ehn, 1988; Lee, 1990; Flensburg, 1985). Unfortunately, some of the writers even show insufficient reading of Critical Theory (Flensburg, 1985).

Even more substantial works within IS use Critical Theory in a rather mechanistic way by reiterating the key arguments of Habermas's thinking. In these cases, Critical Theory has mainly offered a classificatory scheme (i.e. the three interests, or Habermas's action typology) to organize and evaluate research. In these cases the taxonomies have served as a means of raising researchers' awareness of the ontological, epistemological and ethical dimensions of IS research. Although they are illuminating, they have hardly made any major contribution to the further development of Critical Theory, or to the development of more specific theories of IS.

Critical IS research with a sufficiently broad view of the 'effective design, delivery and usage of IS', but at the same time with a sufficiently specific and accessible focus on IS, is yet to emerge. Minor steps in the right direction have been made in some recent works (see Lyytinen and Hirschheim, 1988; Hirschheim and Klein, 1989). For Critical Theory to penetrate the IS community as a viable research approach two aspects have to be developed: (1) the research must become systematic i.e. focused research programmes are needed; and (2) the field must educate researchers who are capable of carrying out systematic investigations in the area. In the next section the first aspect is discussed in more detail. For the second see for example, Klein and Lyytinen (1985) for some proposals.

Elements of a Research Strategy

In order to move from fragmentary critical IS research to systematic 'praxis'-oriented research, future studies should change their goals and research content. The inquiry needs to shift from critique into more concrete and problem-focused studies of the implications of Critical Theory for IS. The studies should incorporate several dimensions into the analysis of computing in organizations: totality/concrete situation; lifeworld/system structure; current status and evolution/history etc., associated with an understanding of, and focus on, ideology criticism (for example detailed description of instrumental reason) and emancipation. In other words the research should step from elevated critique into the practical research mode: what Burrell (1990) has called 'entryism'. In this research model, critical inquiry is concerned with the improvement of the human condition through IS, criticism of alienated and distorted practices, development of alternative IS forms and organizations, and with finding and enclaving an arena for emancipatory IS activity. In this shift two research challenges look most demanding:

1 development, refinement and criticism of Habermas's theory of communicative rationality; and
2 development of methodology that consolidates insights from critical theory into organizational action.

Both these challenges flow directly from the conclusions above. The first is suggested by the fact that, to date, research has been almost exclusively philosophical. The second theme is closely related to the first, but is more far-reaching – it is necessary to make CST in IS more practical. This can only be done by developing methodologies that recognize and support reflective development practices.

Refinement of Habermas's Action Theory
One current hindrance in making Critical Theory a more credible research area is the lack of empirical studies. Habermas's own concern was never to develop an operational and 'testable' theory for social action or cognition, though he claims from time to time that his constructs are empirically testable. In this sense, a direct translation of Habermas's action types into concrete events in a social domain is a difficult research task. The task is difficult because it involves great problems in selecting a correct level of analysis (what are actions?), a high level of ambiguity (what are the real orientations?), and an ambiguous level of aggregation (who are the actors?). Forester (1989, and Chapter 3 in this volume) comes furthest in this direction in his rich analysis of the nature of planning as an attention-shaping practice.

Despite these caveats, I think that some fragments of social activity in IS could be fruitful for applying Habermas's typology in understanding real-world episodes. IS is a fruitful area because it unites technological, symbolic and organizational (such as power, authority, decision-making) issues in a challenging and interesting way. Such studies might provide a plausible starting point for developing and refining Habermas's theory so as to render it more useful for empirical research. Similar studies have been carried out (Hirschheim et al., 1987; Boland, 1984) by applying similar frameworks, which ignore the discursive elements in human action. In all these cases interesting results have emerged. In carrying out such an empirical research programme several problems emerge (see Mingers, Chapter 5 in this volume):

1 how to apply and 'read' the action typology in concrete settings;
2 how to analyse larger action complexes such as sequencing of activity and their institutionalized features;

3 how to illuminate 'discursive activity' in real settings and how to solve the practical problems in bringing it about;[2]

4 how to analyse in concrete situations modes that make possible the testing of validity claims and how to identify categories which are rich enough to describe the variety and contents of such claims;

5 the extent to which modes of communicative rationality are dependent on the specific field.

In response to this challenge Forester (Chapter 3 in this volume) has applied Habermas's typology in the critical ethnographic analysis of planning practice. The problems in IS development should be largely similar, though the level of analysis should focus rather on types of actions than on specific instances of actions. In finding out various orientations, specific instruments such as Kelly's repertoire grid technique (Gutierrez, 1987) or in-depth interviews could be applied. These approaches are, however, quite limited as they focus on individuals' 'cognitive maps' and 'individual phenomenology' and thus are blind to higher levels of social activity and to institutional and structural constraints.

Patterning of action sequences into larger action complexes and examination of how these patterns become institutionalized seem to suggest a fruitful way of understanding what goes on in the social domain and how it is 'constructed'. Habermas barely touches this issue and he is never clear about what features in the action environment trigger changes in action orientations, and to what extent these become routinized and institutionally produced, for example what makes people react to some issue in discursive terms instead of initiating a strategic move. In the IS field these studies could illuminate how different types of information and knowledge are incorporated into action, how this takes place, and what roles IS can play in shaping action orientations.

To this end a research setting needs to be established where such problems can be meaningfully posed. Here studies that unify analysis and clarification of validity claims raised against ongoing communications during IS development would be of great value. In these settings the barriers that prevent people raising validity claims should be identified and the study should include a critical evaluation of how these could be relaxed. In this way we could also study the scope and process of *participation* in a new light. Most discussions on participation (Mumford, 1983) have focused on the positive functional outcomes (such as job satisfaction, increased productivity) related to participation. Critical Theory could offer a new agenda to using the idea of 'ideal speech' as a model of participation. The potential to harness and structure emerging IS applications such as group-decision systems and electronic meeting systems (Vogel and Nunamaker, 1990; Lyytinen, 1992) to increase argument should also be explored.

Another relevant direction for research would be to explore different speech act taxonomies and what means they offer to raise and analyse validity claims. Habermas (1984) classifies various speech acts based on the validity claims that are inherent in them – for example constatives raise the issue of veracity and so on. Lyytinen and Hirschheim (1988) follow another road to show how validity claims can be as easily connected with Searle's typology. This analysis connects several types of validity claims with each speech act. This research area could contribute in developing more varied and differentiated speech act classifications that could serve various research needs.

Finally, such studies should take into account larger wholes, i.e. conversations and conversation domains (for example the strategic planning of IS could constitute one such domain, and a process of planning one conversation). Habermas offers a flat view of communication spaces by distinguishing only speech acts and discourses that are needed to redeem various validity claims. However, speech acts combine into rich and multi-faceted conversations on a social domain that relate to one or several conversation domains (such as strategic planning, monitoring of performance, customer relations etc.). These larger arenas are not just parts of the background – i.e. 'lifeworld' – they also evolve in a fairly structured and analysable way. How these larger arenas should be taken into account in a critical analysis of action is still an open question. Power and Laughlin (Chapter 6 in this volume) offer some insights into how one can use Habermas's system/lifeworld dichotomy in this type of research task. Obviously, in this way a richer understanding of social structures that prevent and/or mobilize actors when participating in different action complexes could be advanced.

Methodology Research on IS Development
Methodology research is needed to link the descriptive and theoretical studies with a constructive view of IS research on 'how to design and deliver effectively'. In this area several research areas are in need of examination:

1 integration of proposed methodologies with Habermas's social action framework;
2 critical methodology development;
3 detailed studies of methodical practices.

IS development initiates a large-scale organizational change that intertwines technological change with organizational problem-solving (and problem formulation), sense-making and power. Unfortunately, all these changes are usually studied as separate and independent dimensions. For example, open systems metaphors and social psychology (Mumford, 1983) offer a way to analyse problem-solving, while adaptation to change, political bargaining and resource allocation models (Kling, 1987) focus on power. Ethnomethodological studies of IS change concentrate on sense-making and culture (Bjerknes and Bratteteig, 1987). Each of these dimensions of change is supported with some methodological guidelines: sociotechnical methods (Mumford, 1983) support system adaptation and problem-solving capacity, web (Kling, 1987) and network models (Aaen, 1990) facilitate direct bargaining, and soft-systems methods (Checkland, 1981) foster sense-making. However, few attempts have been made to unify and correlate these dimensions in a systematic manner (see e.g. Wood-Harper et al., 1985). Habermas's action theory suggests an integrating mechanism to describe these change processes in a unified manner. This research area requires that some basic ideas of Habermas's theory be formulated in mundane and concrete terms that prescribe how organizational change can be initiated in each of these dimensions.

The critical methodology of IS development, however, does not stop here. An emancipatory view of society and associated understanding of coercion, power and distortion must be conjoined with an innovative methodological framework. Here insights from planning theory and OR methodology (Ulrich, 1983, 1988; Mingers, Chapter 5 in this volume) can provide a starting point for elaborating a critical methodology of IS development. The general idea of planning and change is similar – only the specific instances and types of change are different. In more specific terms, critical IS methodology could benefit from Habermas's universal pragmatics – each IS design should pass the criteria of comprehensibility, veracity, sincerity and appropriateness (see Forester, Chapter 3 in this volume). In more specific terms, each stakeholder should ask: (1) am I in a position to understand what the change is all about; (2) is the change proposal technically sound and valid, and are all aspects taken into account; (3) has the proposal been developed with good intentions (what are the hidden agendas?); and (4) is the change appropriate in terms of values and norms that are acceptable for the widest possible audience in the design situation?

Finally, critical IS methodology research should be enriched with more detailed and explicit critical studies of IS development practices, i.e. how methodologies constitute and sustain these IS development practices and how they affect their change (Willmott et al., 1990). By focusing on this area, I believe, the gap between abstract prescriptions and concrete practices can be diminished. On this level we can treat the material, concrete practices that depend on, and generate, power relations, and describe their linkages with knowledge. Here, the Habermasian programme probably needs to be supplemented and refined with the works of other 'Critical Theorists' such as Foucault (cf. Dreyfus and Rabinow, 1982; Mingers, Chapter 5 in this volume), and Giddens (Giddens, 1984; see e.g. Orlikowski, 1989) whose work is more helpful for analysing concrete local practices, their structuring into networks of resources, skills and power, and their historical evolution.

Notes

The paper has greatly benefited from the detailed and constructive criticisms of Heinz Klein, John Mingers and Hugh Willmott.

1 Habermas himself does not use the term discursive, but it could easily be added into his analysis (in fact it is mentioned in What is universal pragmatics? (Habermas, 1979: 209, notes)).

2 Habermas's own contributions in addressing this problem are modest. As Mingers (Chapter 5 in this volume) amongst others has pointed out, there is a lack of discussion of power in Habermas's writings and his view of emancipation from power and distortions is a cognitivist one – radical change is primarily a matter of transforming attitudes and understanding.

References

Aaen, I. (1990) 'Mellem Skylla og Kharybdis inom Systemudvikling', PhD dissertation, Department of Electrical Engineering, Aalborg University (in Danish).
Alchian, A. and Demsetz, H. (1972) 'Production, information costs and economic organization', *American Economic Review*, 62(5): 777–95.
Attewell, P. and Rule, J. (1984) 'Computing and organizations: what we know and what we don't know', *Communications of the ACM*, 27(12): 1184–92.
Bannon, L., Björn-Andersen, N. and Due-Thomsen, B. (1988) 'Computer support for cooperative work: an appraisal and critique', in H-J. Bullinger (ed.), *Information Technology for Organizational Systems*. Brussels: North-Holland.
Berger, P. and Luckmann, P. (1967) *The Social Construction of Reality*. Harmondsworth: Penguin.
Bernstein, R. (1976) *Restructuring of Social and Political Theory*. Oxford: Basil Blackwell.
Bjerknes, G. and Bratteteig, T. (1987) 'Florence in Wonderland: systems development with nurses', in Bjerknes et al. (eds), *Computers and Democracy*. Aldershot: Avebury. pp. 279–96.
Bjerknes, G., Ehn, P. and Kyng, M. (eds) (1987) *Computers and Democracy*. Aldershot: Avebury.
Björn-Andersen, N. and Eason, K. (1980) 'Myths and realities of information systems

contributing to organizational rationality', in A. Mowshowithz (ed.), *Human Choice and Computers*. Amsterdam: North-Holland.

Boland, R. (1978) 'The process and product of systems design', *Management Science*, 24(7): 887–98.

Boland, R. (1979) 'Control, causality and information system requirements', *Accounting, Organizations and Society*, 4(5): 279–94.

Boland, R. (1984) 'Sense-making of accounting data as a technique of organizational diagnosis', *Management Science*, 30(7): 868–82.

Boland, R. (1987) 'The in-formation of information systems', in R. Boland and R. Hirschheim (eds), *Critical Issues in Information Systems Research*. Chichester: Wiley.

Braverman, H. (1974) *Labor and Monopoly Capital – The Degradation of Work in the Twentieth Century*. New York: Monthly Review Press.

Briefs, U., Ciborra, C. and Schneider, I. (eds) (1983) *Systems Design for, with, and by the Users*. Amsterdam: North-Holland.

Bryant, A. (1988) 'The information society: computopia, dystopia, myopia', *Prometheus*, 3(4): 61–77.

Burrell, G. (1990) 'Oral comment on Deetz's paper', at Shrewsbury Workshop on Critical Theory and Management Studies, 3 April.

Burrell, G. and Morgan, G. (1979) *Sociological Paradigms and Organizational Analysis*. London: Heinemann.

Checkland, P. (1981) *Systems Thinking – Systems Practice*. Chichester: Wiley.

Ciborra, C. and Lanzara, G.-F. (1989) 'Change and formative contexts in information systems development', in H. Klein and K. Kumar (eds), *Systems Development for Human Progress*. Amsterdam: North-Holland. pp. 21–40.

Cooper, R. B. (1988) 'Review of management information systems research: a management support emphasis', *Information Processing & Management*, 24(1): 73–102.

Dreyfus, H. and Dreyfus, S. (1986) *Mind over Machine – The Power of Human Intuition and Expertise in the Era of the Computer*. Oxford: Basil Blackwell.

Dreyfus, H. and Rabinow, P. (1982) *Michel Foucault: Beyond Structuralism and Hermeneutics*. Chicago: University of Chicago Press.

Ehn, P. (1988) 'Work-centred design of computer artifacts', PhD dissertation, Umeå University Department of Information Processing, Arbetslivscentrum.

Flensburg, F. (1985) 'Two research methodologies for studying user development of data systems', in E. Mumford et al. (eds), *Research Methods in Information Systems*. Amsterdam: North-Holland. pp. 281–98.

Forester, J. (1989) *Planning in the Face of Power*. Berkeley: University of California Press.

Franz, D. and Robey, D. (1984) 'An investigation of user-led system design – rational and political perspectives', *Communications of the ACM*, 27(12): 1202–9.

Galbraith, J. (1977) *Organization Design*. Cambridge: Addison-Wesley.

Giddens, A. (1984) *The Constitution of Society*. Cambridge: Polity Press.

Goldkuhl, G. and Lyytinen, K. (1984) 'Information system specification as rule reconstruction', in T. Bemelmans (ed.), *Beyond Productivity – Information Systems for Organizational Effectiveness*. Amsterdam: North-Holland. pp. 79–95.

Gurbaxani, V. and Whang, S. (1991) 'The impact of information systems on organizations and markets: an economic perspective', *Communications of the ACM*, 34(1): 59–73.

Gutierrez, O. (1987) 'Some aspects of information requirements analysis using a repertory grid technique', in R. Galliers (ed.), *Information Analysis – Selected Readings*. Sydney: Addison-Wesley. pp. 347–64.

Habermas, J. (1972) *Knowledge and Human Interests*. London: Heinemann.

Habermas, J. (1974) *Theory and Practice*. London: Heinemann.

Habermas, J. (1979) *Communication and the Evolution of Society*. Boston: Beacon Press.

Habermas, J. (1984) *The Theory of Communicative Action. Vol. I: Reason and the Rationalization of Society*, trans. T. McCarthy. Boston: Beacon Press.

Habermas, J. (1987) *The Theory of Communicative Action. Vol. II: Lifeworld and System*, trans. T. McCarthy. Boston: Beacon Press.

Hedberg, B. and Jönsson, S. (1978) 'The design of semi-confusing information systems for organizations in changing environments', *Accounting, Organizations and Society*, 3 (1): 47–64.

Hirschheim, R. (1986) 'The effect of a-priori views on the social implications of computing: the case of office automation', *ACM Computing Surveys*, 18 (2): 165–95.

Hirschheim, R. and Klein, H. (1989) 'Four paradigms of information systems development', *Communications of the ACM*, 27 (11): 1199–216.

Hirschheim, R., Klein, K. and Newman, M. (1987) 'A social action perspective of information systems development', in J. DeGross and C. Kriebel (eds), *Proceedings of the 8th International Conference on Information Systems*, Pittsburgh. pp. 45–56.

Ingram, D. (1987) *Habermas and the Dialectic of Reason*. New Haven, CT: Yale University Press.

Ives, B., Hamilton, S. and Davis, G. (1980) 'A framework for research in computer based management information systems', *Management Science*, 26 (9): 910–34.

Keen, P. G. W. (1980) 'MIS research: reference disciplines and a cumulative tradition', in E. McLean and W. McFarlan (eds), *Proceedings of the 1st International Conference on Information Systems*, Philadelphia. pp. 9–18.

Klein, H. (1984) 'Which epistemologies for future information systems research?', in M. Sääksjärvi (ed.), *The Report of the Seventh Scandinavian Research Seminar on Systemeering, Vol. I*, Publication of the Helsinki Business School. B-74. pp. 60–91.

Klein, H. (1986) 'Organizational implications of office systems: toward a critical social action perspective', in A. Verrijn-Stuart and R. Hirschheim (eds) *Office Information Systems*. Amsterdam: North-Holland.

Klein, H. and Hirschheim, R. (1985) 'Fundamental issues of decision support systems: a consequentalist perspective', *Decision Support Systems*, 1 (1): 5–24.

Klein, H. and Hirschheim, R. (1987) 'Social change and the future of information systems development', in R. J. Boland and R. A. Hirschheim (eds), *Critical Issues in Information Systems Research*. Chichester: Wiley. pp. 275–306.

Klein, H. and Lyytinen, K. (1985) 'The poverty of scientism in information systems', in E. Mumford, R. Hirschheim, G. Fitzgerald and A. T. Wood-Harper (eds), *Research Methods in Information Systems*. Amsterdam: North-Holland. pp. 131–62.

Klein, H. and Lyytinen, K. (1991) 'Towards a new understanding of data modelling', in C. Floyd, H. Zullighoven, R. Budde and H. Keil-Slavik (eds), *Software Development and Reality Construction*. Berlin: Springer-Verlag.

Kling, R. (1980) 'Social analyses of computing: theoretical perspectives in recent empirical research', *Computing Surveys*, 12 (1): 61–110.

Kling, R. (1987) 'Defining boundaries of computing across complex organizations', in R. Boland and R. Hirschheim (eds), *Critical Issues in Information Systems Research*. Chichester: Wiley. pp. 307–62.

Lee, A. S. (1990) 'Architecture as a reference discipline for MIS', in H.-E. Nissen, H. K. Klein and R. Hirschheim (eds), *Information Systems Research: Contemporary Approaches and Emergent Traditions*, Amsterdam: North-Holland.

Lyytinen, K. (1986) 'Information systems development as social action – framework and critical implications', PhD dissertation, Department of Computer Science, University of Jyväskylä, Finland.

Lyytinen, K. (1987) 'Different perspectives on information systems: problems and solutions', *Computing Surveys*, 19(1): 5–42.

Lyytinen, K. (1992) 'Computer supported cooperative work (CSCW): issues and challenges – a structurational analysis', Department of Computer Science, University of Jyväskylä.

Lyytinen, K. and Hirschheim, R. (1988) 'Information systems as rational discourse: an application of Habermas's theory of communicative action', *Scandinavian Journal of Management Studies*, 4(1/2): 19–30.

Lyytinen, K. and Klein, H. (1985) 'The critical theory of Jürgen Habermas as a basis for a theory of information systems', in E. Mumford et al. (eds), *Research Methods in Information Systems*. Amsterdam: North-Holland. pp. 219–36.

Lyytinen, K., Hirschheim, R. and Klein, H. (1991) 'The effectiveness of office information systems – a social action perspective', *Journal of Information Systems*, 1(1): 41–60.

McCarthy, T. (1978) *The Critical Theory of Jürgen Habermas*. Boston: Beacon Press.

McFarlan, F. W. (ed.) (1985) *The Information Systems Research Challenge*. Cambridge, MA: Harvard Business School Press.

Marcuse, H. (1964) *One-dimensional Man*. London: Abacus.

Mason, R. O. (1989) 'Information systems in systemic era', Lecture given at the Information Technology 1989 Conference, Jyväskylä, Finland, 16–18 May.

Mowshowitz, A. (1976) *The Conquest of Will – Information Processing in Human Affairs*. Reading, MA: Addison-Wesley.

Mumford, E. (1983) *Designing Human Systems for New Technology – the ETHICS Method*. Manchester: Manchester Business School.

Mumford, E., Hirschheim, R., Fitzgerald, G. and Wood-Harper, A. T. (eds) (1985) *Research Methods in Information Systems*. Amsterdam: North-Holland.

Ngwenyama, O. K. (1987) 'Fundamental issues in knowledge acquisition: towards a human action perspective of knowledge systems', PhD dissertation, School of Management, SUNY Binghamton, New York.

Nissen, H.-E. (1985) 'Acquiring knowledge of information systems – Research in a methodological quagmire', in E. Mumford et al. (eds), *Research Methods in Information Systems*. Amsterdam: North-Holland. pp. 39–51.

Nissen, H.-E. (1989) 'Information systems development for responsible action', in H. Klein and K. Kumar (eds), *Systems Development for Human Progress*. Amsterdam: North-Holland. pp. 91–113.

Nissen, H.-E., Klein, H., and Hirschheim, R. (eds) (1990) *The Information Systems Research Arena of the 90s*, Proceedings of the IFIP WG. 8.2. Working Conference, Copenhagen 14–16 December.

Orlikowski, W. (1989) 'The duality of technology – rethinking the concept of technology in organizations', unpublished working paper, Sloan School of Management, MIT.

Orlikowski, W. and Baroudi, J. (1989) 'IS research paradigms: method versus substance', Sloan working paper 3028–89–MS, Sloan School of Management, MIT.

Robey, D. (1984) 'Conflict models of implementation research', in R. L. Schutz (ed.), *Management Science Implementation*. New York: Elsevier.

Rule, J. et al. (1980) *The Politics of Privacy*. New York: New American Library.

Simon, H. A. (1977) *The New Science of Management Decision*. Englewood Cliffs, NJ: Prentice-Hall.

Swanson, B. (1985) 'Information systems: necessary foundations', Information Systems working paper 6–85, UCLA-Graduate School of Management, Los Angeles.

Toulmin, S. (1958) *The Uses of Argument*. Cambridge: Cambridge University Press.

Ulrich, W. (1983) *Critical Heuristics of Social Planning*. Berne: Werner-Haupt.

Ulrich, W. (1988) 'Systems thinking, system practice, and practical philosophy: a program of research', *Systems Practice*, 1 (2): 137–63.

Vogel, D. and Nunamaker, J. (1990) 'Group decision support system impact: a multimethodological exploration', *Information & Management*, 18 (1): 15–28.

Weizenbaum, J. (1976) *Computer Power and Human Reason – from Judgement to Calculation*. New York: Freeman.

Williamson, O. (1985) *The Economic Institutions of Capitalism*. New York: Free Press.

Willmott, H. C., Mouritsen, J., Flensburg, P. and Elkjaer, B. (1990) 'Systems developers: preoccupations, knowledge and power', *Proceedings of the 11th International Conference on Information Systems*, Copenhagen, December.

Winograd, T. and Flores, F. (1986) *Computers and Cognition: a New Foundation for Computer System Design*. Norwood, NJ: Ablex.

Wiseman, C. (1985) *Strategic Information Systems*. Illinois: Irwin.

Wood-Harper, A., Antill, L. and Avison, D. (1985) *Information Systems Definition – The Multiview Approach*. Oxford: Basil Blackwell.

9
Personnel/Organizational Psychology: A Critique of the Discipline

Brian D. Steffy and Andrew J. Grimes

Personnel/organizational psychology and its relationship to and impact upon organizational practice is evaluated in this chapter. Personnel/organizational psychology (POP) is a generic category meant to subsume two fields of study: human resource management (HRM) and organizational psychology. Both of these fields share common roots in scientific management and human engineering concepts developed in the first quarter of this century, though during the last four decades HRM and organizational psychology have diverged in the subject matter they address and in some of the presuppositions they make in conducting their 'science'.[1] HRM has addressed the strategic and tactical actions undertaken by organizations to manage its employees. HRM strategy focuses on the role of personnel policies in enhancing and strengthening productivity and corporate culture. Perhaps to a greater extent, it focuses on the concrete personnel practices that most medium to large organizations invest in: job analysis, human resource planning, recruitment, external selection, internal selection, training, performance appraisal, compensation and labour relations (Mahoney and Deckop, 1990). These activities comprise what labour economists and industrial sociologists refer to as 'internal labour markets' (Doeringer and Piore, 1971): the policies, procedures and practices undertaken by management to regulate the mobility, rewards and working conditions of employees. These practices are designed and implemented with the expectation that they will lead to a more stable, satisfied and productive workforce, facilitate the socialization, training and evaluation of incumbents, and sustain an equitable, or fair, system for allocating pay and mobility opportunities. Generally, it can be stated that the study of HRM is not based on some overarching theoretical framework; instead, analysis is eclectic, addressing issues as they emerge in the practices of the human resource function. HRM, as a discipline, is one of the most applied of the organizational sciences.

In contrast, organizational psychology has not been driven as much by practice, and there is really no corresponding organizational role

(Mahoney and Deckop, 1990). Organizational psychology more closely resembles the traditional empirical-analytic social sciences, which view their mission as the construction and validation of theories from which we can explain and predict organizational behaviour. Practitioners may or may not choose to employ their knowledge products. While the domain of its analysis overlaps partially with HRM, it confines its study, not to the functional practices of personnel administrators, but to more abstract topics such as leadership, work motivation, decision-making, organizational culture, stress, group dynamics, communication, and job characteristics/design (Szilagi and Wallace, 1990).

HRM and organizational psychology, nevertheless, are similar in a number of respects, and it is these similarities that this chapter will address. First, many HRM applications are at least partially justified by theories set forth by organizational psychologists. For example, compensation practices may be rooted in any of a number of work motivation theories (Milkovich and Newman, 1987). Performance appraisal practices drawn from decision theory, and training practices are strongly influenced by motivation and learning theory. Both largely subscribe to the individual as their unit, or level, of analysis. But HRM and organizational psychology are similar in an even more fundamental respect. Theory construction in organizational psychology and the design of HRM practices are based upon a highly empirical-analytic form of science that is rooted in the natural sciences (Cook and Campbell, 1979). In this chapter we outline the basic principles of this approach, as well as the presuppositions underlying that analysis. Within space limitations we develop the following points. First, personnel/organizational psychology, like all disciplines, is an area of study that possesses a self-regulating code of discourse, a set of rules that reflect its ontological content, epistemological strategy and methodological tactics. Secondly, the character of POP's discourse, the theories it produces and the practices it legitimizes, when applied to organizations, shape the policies and practices that regulate human resource activities. We argue that dominant forms of POP possess the potential to systematically restrict workplace democracy and participation. Thirdly we focus on the validation (truth-seeking) procedures employed by POP and argue that validation procedures must be more broadly reflective and 'critical' if a more emancipatory and empowering POP is desired.

The critical analysis we outline borrows primarily from the works of Jürgen Habermas and Michel Foucault. We recognize that Habermas, Foucault and other Critical Theorists discussed below differ on fundamental philosophical and methodological issues. Nevertheless, we draw from various sources to inform us on the presuppositions and behaviour of knowledge-producing disciplines, the style of theory produced by a POP characterized as neo-positivist, the dynamic relationship between theory and its application to organizational practice, and the subsequent influence of these practices on work as it is experienced by employees. Implicit in the work of Habermas and Foucault is the pursuit of an analytical framework that stresses the potential for transgression of or resistance to dominant objectifying practices and discourses. In the context of work organizations these objectifying practices consist of the behavioural technologies, measurement systems and governing policies instituted by management and legitimized by a neo-positivist POP.

A Neo-positivist Personnel/Organizational Psychology

Psychology in general and POP in particular have not witnessed the schisms and debates that characterize other organizational and social sciences (i.e. macro-organizational theory, sociology, political science). Schisms often take the form of alternative competing paradigms for conducting analysis in the discipline (Burrell and Morgan, 1979). But agreement among scholars within POP cannot be attributed to the discipline's relative success in uncovering explanatory laws. In fact, few stable, enduring and generalizable laws that go beyond common sense have been uncovered (Gergen, 1982; Sack, 1980; Steffy and Grimes, 1986; Veldsman, 1990). The seemingly close adherence to a common paradigm and its unwillingness to self-reflect and critique itself may be due to psychology's close links to biology and, therefore, its continued faith that it will uncover explanatory laws by seeking functional relationships between sets of variables, extending the natural science paradigm to the study of behavioural and social phenomena. Also, a sociological perspective may suggest that POP, as a discipline of study, is generated within a community of scholars and practitioners, a community governed by paradigmatic rules that possesses the means of neutralizing potential threats to its hegemony.

The paradigm governing POP is defined as neo-positivist (see Cook and Campbell, 1979). Neo-positivism is deeply rooted in logical positivism, a philosophy of science that dominated logicism, mathematics and the natural sciences in the early twentieth century. For the logical positivist the principal function of science is the confirmation of generalizable laws and theories governing the relationships among and between classes of observable variables (Gergen, 1982). The scientist, by employing objective, standardized and uniform methods of observation, or 'methodology', can uncover these relationships that are assumed to exist, or be 'out there'. The analysis presupposes that the objective, neutral analyst can reliably and accurately observe isolatable and hermeneutically sealed facts to verify that empirical reality corroborates hypothesized laws and theories. Laws and theories are themselves formulated through a highly abstract, mathematical language, also assumed to be hermeneutically sealed. If a correspondence between the abstractly coded language and empirical fact is found, then the law, or hypothesized relationship, is assumed to be confirmed and true. There is little critical reflection in conducting such a science. Ontological and epistemological questions are largely assumed to be irrelevant. Inquiry is confined only to those propositions that are empirically testable, or observable (Geuss, 1981). Criticism is confined to questions of whether the internal rules of method are followed. As pointed out by Habermas (1973), in a positivistic science, epistemological critique, endemic to philosophy and social theory, is reduced to a normative epistemology, or the narrow rules prescribing methodology.

Of course the assumptions underlying logical positivism have long been recognized as insufficient for the social sciences (Cook and Campbell, 1979). Neo-positivism is a modification of the logical positivism agenda. It is similar to logical positivism in its adherence to the goals of explanation and prediction, as well as its emphasis on testing hypothesized relationships and causal propositions using formal, objective measures. It is dissimilar in two respects. First it rejects the presupposition that social/behavioural laws and theories can be directly confirmed (Popper, 1972), but supports a deductive process by which alternative competing theories of explanation are gradually falsified or supported by evaluating whether the hypothesized relationships that comprise the theory are corroborated by empirical facts, or validated. Each theory represents an abstract model of empirical reality; a conceptual framework that can be broken down into its isolatable constituent variables and the hypothesized relationships between them (Bacharach, 1989). Variables are abstract representations of 'things' or events that are assumed to be out there. They are operationalized through formal measurement procedures such as questionnaires and interviews (Naylor et al., 1980). Statistical analysis is then employed to test the probability that hypothesized relationships are significant, or there. As a given theory gains less support under varying conditions and samples, the theory is dropped by the scientific community and alternative theories come to the forefront (Cook and Campbell, 1979).

Secondly, neo-positivism interjects more reflective critique into its analysis than does logical positivism, though we later argue that this critique is still too narrow in scope. Neo-positivism recognizes that observed facts, the observer (scientist) and also the process of observation, or method, are infused with subjectivity, or value-laden and socially constructed (Hear, 1980). Researchers possess limited perceptual skills, are culturally conditioned and have intentional or unintentional aims. Critical reflection is necessary in POP, since so many of the variables and relationships it analyses, as well as the procedures it employs, are subjective and substantially less than perfectly reliable and accurate. The value-ladenness of POP research cannot be assumed away, but must be reflected upon. However, as will be discussed, neo-positivism's capacity for self-reflection is limited, since it still largely confines its critique to whether the normative rules of 'method' have been followed, specifically, in the case of POP, whether proper validation procedures have been used.

Validation, Critical Reflection and the Production of Knowledge

The cornerstone of a neo-positivist POP is the validation of knowledge statements. Validation refers to the formal scientific procedures discussed above to validate, or attest to the truth of, (1) hypothesized relationships between variables; and (2) personnel decisions based on some practice, policy or procedure. Implicit in validation procedures is the assumption that once an explanation or theory is validated it can be communicated to society at large and 'enlighten the profession of management' (Van de Ven, 1989: 486). Validation is pivotal not only to theorists, but also to the practitioners who apply knowledge. POP bears the burden of proving that recommended practices and policies are effective, or have economic 'utility' (Steffy and Maurer, 1987). Effectiveness and utility are defined in terms of a practice's validity: does a practice do what it is supposed to do? Does the selection test or interview lead to the hiring of better performers? Does the performance appraisal programme lead to correct promotion and reward decisions? Does the training programme improve work performance? Does a motivation or leadership theory explain the organization's problems? Does a theory of job stress help the organization understand why its members are in distress?

Scope and Source of Reflection

But what are the practical implications of POP's validation procedures? How reflective are POP's scientists and how does POP's capacity for critical reflection shape knowledge production and the discipline's impact on practice? To understand this, we need first to appreciate the *scope and source* of validation in POP.

The scope of reflection in POP is confined to the critique of internal validity, external validity and construct validity (Cook and Campbell, 1979). Internal validity questions focus on whether the measures used to operationalize variables are reliable and whether statistical relationships (i.e. correlation) between sets of variables exist. Internal validity is hampered when the assumptions underlying statistical analysis do not hold, measures are unreliable, adequate controls on the sample and experimental parameters cannot be obtained, and it is not possible to determine the direction of causal inference. External validity refers to the generalizability of any specific validity study. That is, if a theoretical relationship is found in one study or situation, would those same findings be obtained in other contexts or places, at other times, and with different groups of employees? If all validation checks are specific to time, place and sample analysed, then the basic mission of POP cannot be met. Findings must be assumed to generalize to other situations if the work of the critical rationalist is to be fruitful. If not, then we must assume that POP is essentially a hermeneutic science. External validity is adversely affected when the characteristics of the sample analysed (i.e. homogeneous in race, gender, age) do not resemble the heterogeneous characteristics of the population that the researcher wants to generalize to, the situation of the test (i.e. laboratory study) does not resemble the organizational world, or the test or theory is time-specific and findings do not generalize beyond the present historical moment.

Another critical concern, sometimes subsumed under external validity concerns (Cook and Campbell, 1979), is construct validity. The construct validity issue necessarily arises in most validation procedures. Construct validation procedures inform us of whether the variables and measures employed in hypothesis testing actually have an empirical referent; that is, whether there is a real-world counterpart to conceptual things and events. This is an important concern since POP deals, not so much with concrete, manifest things like physical properties, but with abstract traits that may be more social constructions of POP than real variables. For example, when we measure intelligence, leadership style, motivation or cognitive style, do these constructs have a real ontological grounding, or are they merely social constructions? To what degree are such constructs infused with the values and political aims of the designer of the concepts, variables and measures?

A potential danger exists in POP when a construct with question-able ontological status gains an inappropriate reified status. Its variable name is integrated into the public's language, and measures, or tests, of the variable gain a commodity status. For example, we can critically question the existence of constructs recently popular among personnel selection specialists, for example honesty/integrity, intelligence and cognitive style. Variable definitions and their measures may be deficient and contaminated in that the analyst and even the process of analysis, or methods and procedures, impose their definition on the construct, respective of empirical reality. Construct validation, therefore, should be prior to any other validation step. Surprisingly, personnel/organizational psychologists may not 'construct validate' their terms. It is difficult to do so and statistical procedures give us only a crude approximation of a construct's ontological status. Caution should be taken to ensure that questionable traits do not, over time, gain an inappropriate real-world status. Yet a decision to construct validate every variable may constitute an assault on the legacy of accepted terms (e.g. intelligence, satisfaction) and practices (e.g. selection tests). Even a rigid adherence to its own normative epistemology could alter the knowledge production and knowledge products of POP.

A Critical Theory of Personnel/Organizational Psychology

There has emerged in recent years criticism of a POP dominated by the neo-positivist paradigm. Some working within the discipline (see Alvesson, 1987; Burrell and Morgan, 1979; Clegg, 1989; Mumby, 1988; Steffy and Grimes, 1986; Veldsman, 1990) suggest that: (1) there exists a wide gap between theory content and what practitioners are interested in; (2) few theories other than the most banal and commonsense have been consistently supported; (3) the bulk of research focuses on static, regulative issues and not important, dynamic issues such as organizational power, conflict, politics and ideology; and (4) the methodological rigour of an empirical-analytic POP leads to fragmented and specific explanations of organizational phenomena, but does little to increase our understanding of the real complexities of organizational life. Responding to sceptics, POP scholars call for a return to traditional research values and encourage greater methodological rigour. They claim that the advancement of knowledge is served best by their paradigm, where criticism is largely confined to whether theory construction and validation procedures comply with methodological rules (see Bacharach, 1989; Van de Ven, 1989).

While POP splits and delineates between observer and observed, fact and method, theory and practice, and knowledge and power, Critical Theorists point to the artificiality of these distinctions.

Together, Foucault and Habermas create a reflective 'space' for dismantling POP and then reconstructing it. Foucault's analysis is employed to appreciate the character of disciplines, the rules and regulations that limit and define the boundaries of the discipline, the way these self-imposed limits on knowledge production affect knowledge products, and how these knowledge products shape the experience of work. Habermas's Critical Theory includes a reflective analysis of the dynamic interplay of theory and practice, as well as the relationship between 'praxis', the subjective and self-willed actions of organizational members, and decision rules and behavioural technologies legitimized by a neo-positivist POP. For Habermas, the social sciences, in opting for a non-participatory and non-obtrusive research methodology, become increasingly impotent in changing organizational practice. He suggests that the scholar should become a more active change agent who, through reflexive analysis, seeks a theory that empowers greater autonomy and responsibility.

POP's Epistemological Tactics
Using Foucault's framework we can begin to explore the discursive practices of any discipline, specifically the consequences of (1) a discipline grounding itself in a single level of analysis; and (2) a discipline that severs its relationship with other human/social science disciplines. Foucault (1970, 1972) suggests that the epistemological strategies and tactics regulating knowledge production define the parameters, shape and function of knowledge products. This is obvious. Foucault, however, further suggests that these knowledge products will support organizational practices that reflect the naive assumptions underlying epistemological strategies and tactics and, hence, adversely delimit the self at work. This is explored below.

Level of Analysis   A discipline's level of analysis reflects whether its primary analytical unit or focus is, for example, the individual, organization, market, or national social culture. A broader categorization found in many of the social sciences is the distinction between 'micro' and 'macro'. Micro-analysis, including POP, largely focuses on the individual or actor, while macro-analysis (organizational theory) focuses on the structures that administer and control individuals. A rigid adherence to the micro–macro distinction has been accused of discounting large components of real-world phenomena which are not the primary focus of either subdiscipline (Giddens, 1984; Sack, 1980). POP, for instance, largely focuses on the individual. Structural constraints (e.g. role load, unemployment threat, type of administrative controls) are entered into analysis, but primarily as a secondary tactic, injected *post hoc* to better explain the circumstances and behaviours of the subjective agent. POP's epistemological *strategy* does not make a serious attempt to integrate micro and macro perspectives. Analytical dualism is assumed and no substantive correct steps are undertaken. Consequently, the level of analysis problem results in a narrowing of POP's definition of its ontological domain. Explanations are at best partial and, given that entire spheres of organizational reality are ignored, knowledge products could be biased in favour of behaviourally oriented theories and practices that de-emphasize structural constraints, collective action and issues endemic to the analysis of collectives such as conflict, class, politics and power.

Subject-Matter Domain By the beginning of the twentieth century the human/social sciences could be delineated into three broad 'epistemological regions' (Foucault, 1972; Gutting, 1989), though, since then, we have seen within each of these regions further differentiation into subdisciplines and fields of study. The three broad regions are biology, to which psychology (POP is a subfield) is linked, economics, to which sociology and all of its subfields are linked, and philology, which includes the study of language, symbols, culture, and so on. According to Foucault (1972), any modern discipline is necessarily linked to one of these three epistemological regions, though it is bonded to and should account for the level of analysis and subject-matter domain of the other two regions. Assuming this, since POP confines its analyses principally to individual attitudes and behaviours, researchers should critique how well POP has incorporated material from the economic/sociological and philological sciences. To the extent that POP omits and assumes away the subject matter of the other regions, it is ontologically biased. Its categories, variable/construct names and definitions increasingly represent the delimited character of its socially constructed world-view. Knowledge products reflect the epistemological tactics employed in knowledge production.

Co-dependence of Knowledge Production and
Organization Practice
Foucault (1978, 1979) addresses the dynamic linkage between rigid, fixed rules for knowledge production, the implementation of knowledge products in social institutions and the potential adverse impact of knowledge products on the workplace. He ties together his argument with his conceptualization of 'power'. For Foucault, power cannot be defined only in terms of hierarchical social structures where dominant groups hold power over non-dominant ones, and where the dominant groups are seeking to substantiate and legitimize

their dominant position through ideology and control. Certainly we cannot deny that such asymmetrical social relationships exist, but Foucault decentres the self, takes the agent out of his analysis, and offers a broader analysis of power. Power has its basis in the increasing rationalization of social conduct, a rationalization that objectifies the subjective self. Members at all levels of social institutions, whether they are managers, professionals or non-managers, are objectified as a result of this increasing rationalization. Social institutions are both hierarchically and horizontally differentiated and if we perceive power as a scarce resource, dominant groups certainly seem to have greater control of and access to the tools of rationalization. Still, for the subjective actor – regardless of one's role within the social structure, whether one designs the tools of subjugation or is subject to their use – the individual is objectified.

Increasing 'rationalization' has its foundation in the increased proliferation and acceptance of epistemological strategies (a neo-positivist POP) and tactics (validation procedures) that inform the design and implementation of administrative structures and systems that govern social institutions, in this case, work organizations. We are not claiming that all administrative practices have their roots in POP, but arguing that its impact is on the rise. For instance, in the US, equal employment opportunity legislation and subsequent court decisions, influenced by industrial/organizational psychologists, has substantially legitimized and expanded the use of POP's knowledge products, especially its validation procedures. The influence of POP on practice is further strengthened through other avenues as well. Researchers substantiate their products on the basis not only that they lead to fair employment decisions (Steffy and Ledvinka, 1989), but that decisions based on their knowledge products will be more effective, or economically productive (Steffy and Maurer, 1987), and improve the quality of work-life. These claims, it should be noted, are suspect and have been challenged (see Alvesson, 1987; Steffy and Grimes, 1986; Steffy and Ledvinka, 1989; Steffy and Maurer, 1987). Another explanation for the increasing influence of POP is the role of consultants. Because POP is an applied social science, consultants, often knowledge producers themselves who market the practical application of their products, mediate between the world of 'knowledge' and practice. They facilitate the application of theory to practice. In the US the consultant and practitioner are typically trained as neo-positivists, the former in a PhD-granting institution and the latter in an MBA programme. These two examples illustrate the unique linkage of organization science and organization practice.

But how does POP influence practice and the workplace? What are the 'mechanics' of this linkage? Foucault's analysis of this linkage is vague, but we draw from the above discussion and extend his analysis to our concerns here. Below we propose the avenues of impact.

Subjectivity is Constituted at Work by Objectifying Knowledge Products Generally, for Foucault, power over the employee is enacted through the surveillance, gaze and documentation enabled by the knowledge products of POP. POP's epistemological strategy requires the following tactics: objective reliable and accurate measurement systems to measure individual differences on variables of interest; simplistic, reductionist analytical models to evaluate relationships between individual and job variables; and an intensive programme of data collection and data storage. These tactics, in turn, influence organization practice. For instance, individuals are presented as numerical objects that can be observed, held over time, retrieved, analysed and shared by interested parties. Information not measured, often information depicting the employee as unique, dynamic and ever-changing, may be largely discounted and ignored. Thus, to the extent that administrative decisions are informed by narrow and delimiting analytical models, the organization is objectifying the self.

Foucault might argue that objectification is increasing as a result of methodological and epistemological problems inherent in a neo-positivist POP. Over time, POP, in reaction to problems inherent in its strategy and tactics, has further differentiated by creating subfields and focus areas in an effort to construct theories more effectively. These efforts typically require a renewed and more rigorous emphasis on data collection, as well as the development of more sophisticated measurement procedures and analytical models. Further differentiation and fragmentation of POP's efforts and attention does nothing to broaden its epistemological strategy or expand its analysis to more analytical levels and disciplines, but adds to its provincialism. Its 'ontological potential' is further restricted (Cohen, 1989). As old issues are explored, new issues and problems emerge that are endemic to the new measurement tactics, or the supposed tactical solutions. Is all this effort contributing to the evolution of knowledge, or is POP engaged in a playful 'infinite regress'?

What remain are the tools of disciplinary power: more refined measurement procedures and increasingly narrow theories that, when carried over into practice, ignore the real-world complexities of organization life and magnify and focus the organization's gaze and surveillance. They also necessitate and legitimize further data acquisition and storage. This can be seen in many areas of human resource management. For instance, in efforts to resolve problems associated with what are perceived as unreliable and inaccurate performance appraisal systems, new techniques are suggested that measure only specific, observable and measurable behaviours inferred to be related to successful job performance. Supervisors are encouraged to keep a detailed diary on subordinate behaviours that are to be appraised. Surveillance and documentation are increased. Of course, such a parental system may be regarded as an improvement on one based upon the whims and biases of supervisors, but it does illustrate the connection between validation tactics, the issues that emerge, and how more sophisticated measurement procedures, surveillance and documentation are required to solve the problem. Perhaps solutions may be found, not in more refined measurement systems employed by managers to observe and document the behaviours of non-managers, but by replacing behaviourally based measurement procedures with participatory techniques emphasizing mutually established social contracts, for example management by objectives (Daft and Steers, 1986).

POP Spatially and Temporally Contours the Body at Work   Many of POP's knowledge products contribute to bureaucratic structures (e.g. bureaucratic monarchies) that gaze at, scrutinize, classify and count individual characteristics and behaviours. Collected data are analysed and stored, ensuring that an individual's legacy, good and bad, is not forgotten. This surveillance and documentation contributes to what Foucault (1979) refers to as a subtle coercion of the human body; movement and location are co-ordinated in space and time. The 'anatomy' of behaviour, cognition and movement is prescribed and subjected to probes and measures. For example, the human body is assigned to a particular spatial position within the organization's vertical and horizontal structure. A person's spatial position is influenced by the level of organizational technology, job design and the intradepartmental and interdepartmental flow of work (Daft and Steers, 1986).

On a more subtle level, the employee is controlled by being perpetually positioned within a queue. The purpose of external selection and internal staffing (e.g. performance appraisal) practices and policies is to test, grade and rank-order candidates in a common queue according to predicted work performance. The validity of a test or appraisal system can be defined according to estimates of how correct the ranking in the queue is. Employees and potential employees are thus always forced into competing with one another for scarce opportunities in the queue, and as organizations refine their measurement (diagnostic) systems, the queue becomes more salient, potentially increasing the competitiveness between individuals who are seeking to improve their positions. The queue, even if perfectly correct (valid), is not a vehicle for collective action teamwork, or co-operation. It is not a vehicle for group praxis and it may hinder organizational democracy. In practical terms, if the work requires team effort and collective responsibility, selection practices, especially internal selection practices, could have an adverse impact on productivity as individuals' concerns for queue position outweigh collective concerns and goals.

Other personnel practices facilitate the control of the body. Given that the task requirements of a person's job are analysed and described, rewards in the form of pay increments and promotions are offered to those whose motions, energies and thought processes (cognitive style, emotions) are consistent with task requirements. 'Hard work', though it leads to psychological and physiological stress, burnout, and so on, is rewarded. Going beyond what is expected is a virtue. Type A behaviour, defined here as trying to accomplish more in shorter periods of time, is thought to contribute to heart disease, yet it is consistently found to predict career success (Steffy et al., 1989). This illustrates the potential conflict between work and self, and how personnel practices may contribute to this conflict by forcing the self to adjust itself to the work, and not vice versa.

Knowledge Products May Only Be Fruitful for Managing Employees En Masse   An empirical-analytic, neo-positivist POP leads to the construction of general, vague theories that inform employees, not on how to interact with each other on a one-to-one basis, or clinically, but how to manage others *en masse*. Knowledge products are in the form of general prescriptive rules that provide broad explanations, but typically do not help the employee to understand the intricacies of interacting with others at work. This is the consequence of a biologically oriented POP. Biology deals largely with manifest, concrete variables that are functionally related. POP, on the other hand, works with abstract constructs with questionable ontological status. This means that relationships between these quasi-variables can only be described probabilistically. We can only define the norms of samples, the deviation around those norms, and the probability that a relationship between normalized variables exists. Decision-makers who apply the results of such research have, at best, general technical rules to inform them. The theory that would be practised is simplistic and assumes away the rich detail of real life. To the extent that decision-makers rely exclusively on empirically validated propo-sitions and practices, decisions will be deficiently informed and, if enacted, will have a homogenizing effect on employees' behaviour

(Rouse, 1987). Clinical action, made possible through the free exchange of socially constructed meanings, would be displaced by purposive-rational action dictated by empirically validated technical rules.

Provincial Epistemological Strategies Lead to Substandard Knowledge Products   The ontological curriculum that shapes the discourse of POP shapes personnel practice. As suggested earlier, POP's strategy is limited to the degree that it confines its work to: (1) a single level of analysis; (2) a narrow corner of a single epistemological region; (3) a theoretical language governed primarily, if not exclusively, by analytical, statistical models; (4) measurement tactics that emulate those of the natural sciences and that seek unachievable goals; and (5) a tendency not to broaden its strategy and tactics, but to further differentiate and fragment its energies in the hope that more careful 'study' will reveal solutions to tactical issues and problems, as well as counter the discipline's general impotence, at least as compared to its cousins in the natural sciences. In sum, POP's knowledge products are often deficient, the consequence of analyses which give the individual privilege over collectives, an ignorance of subject matter from other epistemological regions and a reliance on underspecified and simplistic analytical models. Therefore, organizational practices based on these knowledge products will bear the mark of POP's provincial analyses. Space provisions do not permit detailed illustrations of this point. Suffice it to say that POP's conceptualization and measurement of important practical concerns such as fairness, productivity and organizational culture is narrow. A bias towards empirical-analytic procedures, along with a bias towards an individual level of analysis and a propositional language that ignores large segments of subject matter from labour economics, sociology and anthropology, results in very limited definitions of these concepts (Alvesson, 1987; Steffy and Maurer, 1987).

Implications of Habermas's Critical Theory

Foucault's Critical Social Theory evaluates the parochial discourse of the human and social sciences and the ways that bodies of knowledge produced by these disciplines are 'inextricably interwoven with techniques of social control' (Gutting, 1989: 6). Habermas's Critical Theory is most succinctly defined as an empirical philosophy of social institutions (McCarthy, 1979). Critical Theory may retain an empirical-analytic component, but does not give it epistemological privilege (Rouse, 1987). Instead, a broad reflective theory is promoted where descriptive epistemology is introduced to encourage the social scientist to give a full account of the aim and limits of

analysis. The scope of reflection must include an explicit cr
ontological, epistemological and methodological presuppos
well as the impact of various forms of analysis on organizauun
practice and the experience of the self at work. Like the neo-
positivist, for Habermas, critical reflection is enacted through
validation procedures, but the source, or agent, of validation should
be the product of not only the empirical-analytic work of the scientific
community, but the practical concerns of individuals and groups
potentially affected by knowledge products. These practical concerns
are expressed through social discourse. By expanding the scope and
source of reflection the explicit aim of Critical Theory may be met:
the empowerment of the individual and the infusion of democratic
action into social institutions.

For Habermas (1979) communicative action is a condition for
empowerment and democracy. Communicative action facilitates the
building of consensus among social actors reached through the free
social exchange of subject agents. Conversely, communicative action
may be displaced by technical rules and systems validated by an
empirical-analytic social science when the validation of knowledge is
taken away from social actors and assigned to social scientists and
specialists who validate statements and practices according to
methodological standards, or epistemological tactics. In such cases
practical questions are transformed into technical ones. Technical
reasoning may become a normative force that displaces the purposeful discourse between subjective selves.

But if organizational processes are increasingly governed by
objectifying technical rationality at the expense of intersubjective,
communicative action, how do organizations attain and sustain
consensus among their members? Under the negative conditions
outlined above, we might expect employees, unless coerced, to be
quite deviant. Critical Theory, however, contends that, as a whole,
organizational actors are not aware of their objectification. According to Critical Theory, ideology refers to a distorted perception held
by employees that is sponsored by dominant groups to stabilize and
legitimize their control and domination (Habermas, 1975). Ideology
possesses two necessary traits that characterize it as a distorted
perception. First, it is self-imposed. Secondly, members falsely
interpret these self-imposed behaviours as self-determined, or their
own (Geuss, 1981). In other words, members impose distorted forms
of rationality upon themselves by continually reproducing the
normative, objectifying structures that distort communication and
constrain praxis. These self-imposed objectifying organizational
processes are perceived as legitimate and even self-willed because
ideology is itself built upon distorted communication. Therefore, if

organizational communication is structured in a way which sustains ideology (Mumby, 1988), since members are unaware of their state, they have few opportunities to realize their delusion and change. In this sense, power is rooted in distorted communication.

Critical Theory requires that POP critique its own ideological component and extend such analysis to the presence of ideology in the organization. Organizational facts reflect a particular self-masking ideology which should be exposed. In fact, such an approach becomes an 'inquiry of change' (Geuss, 1981), because in conducting a hermeneutical evaluation of the historical and ideological dimension of organizational facts, the researcher has the professed aim of establishing conditions to:

1 engage in discourse concerning the delusions and illusions that characterize ideologies and that legitimize ineffective normative structures;
2 restore group consensus through open communication;
3 validate knowledge through practical discourse; and
4 reassign objectifying behavioural and decision technologies to their neutral and passive status (Habermas, 1973).

Critical Theory pursues this aim, not by recommending a normative theory, but by encouraging a public critique of ideology. The discipline of POP and practising organizations must be perceived as engaged in a reciprocal communicative interaction. Research is a 'speech act' possessing cognitive intent and bearing practical consequences. Assuming this, the researcher, with organizational members, reflects upon the impact of research on organizational actors. Research is thus a form of discourse that should not deny practical intent, but make it explicitly known. How this may be accomplished is outlined below.

Solutions: An Expanded Agenda for Validation

This chapter has largely confined its evaluation to the adverse effects of a POP that abides by narrow validation procedures governed by its epistemological strategy. We have suggested the current validity concepts and validation procedures may be insufficient if we desire human resource management practices that emancipate the self at work such that work is designed to conform to bodily, cognitive and emotional needs, and not vice versa. In sum, a neo-positivist POP may socially construct a 'Theory X' workplace. Certainly it may constrain and sabotage a 'Theory Y' culture. A change in validation concepts and procedures, however, is a precondition for changing practices when practices are extensions of delimiting knowledge products. Such a change requires that analysts do not regress by strengthening their allegiance to positivist strategies and tactics, but that they expand the *scope* and *source* of validation. In light of the Critical Theory outlined above, critical reflection might be broadened so that it touches upon the philosophical presuppositions of POP, the behaviour of the discourse community, and the linkage of theory and practice. Some validity concepts that require broader reflection will now be briefly discussed.

Domain Validity
To what extent has analysis veered from the ideal of including all relevant subject matter and analytical levels? We create the term 'domain validity' to reflect upon whether knowledge production considers relevant material from all epistemological regions and integrates subject material from all relevant analytical levels. To the extent that relevant analytical sources are ignored, knowledge products should be viewed suspiciously. Attached to this concern are traditional construct validity notions. No longer can POP ignore this issue. POP bears the responsibility for evaluating the 'ontological status' of its constructs and ensuring that knowledge products are not at least partially normative, sociopolitical constructions. It requires that the training of social scientists and management students be multi-disciplinary, perhaps at the expense of specialization.

Consensus Validity
Habermas suggests that empirical verification should not be the final arbitrator of truth. In an applied science such as POP the final arbitrator of truth is whether consensus of a plurality of parties can be attained. Validity claims are not tested according to whether empirical evidence supports stated hypotheses. Instead, the criterion of truth lies in the acceptance of knowledge statements by organization members informed by empirical evidence. The final verdict of truth lies in the perceived practicality of knowledge as indicated by social consensus, its 'performative power' (Rorty, 1982). When validity claims are subjected to rational social debate, technical reasoning is subordinated to social and individual praxis.

Genuine consensus, however, can be attained only under conditions of undistorted communication; when an 'ideal speech situation' exists. The implications of this criterion for POP are particularly significant. No longer can the analyst, or scientist, produce knowledge statements and assume that they bear no responsibility for knowledge products. Discourse on the linkage of theory and practice should be documented. Knowledge producers, knowledge users and knowledge recipients must communicate.

Knowledge products are not ahistorical and aimless, but possess latent sociopolitical characteristics that surface and activate when implemented in practice. The critical question then becomes: what are the responsibilities and duties of the scientist in ensuring that knowledge production and knowledge products are enabling and empowering? Will employees, or the unions that represent them, become actively involved in validation procedures? We cannot make this assumption. As suggested, ideology and distorted communication, as well as more obvious constraints such as fear of unemployment, all work against attaining consensus via an ideal-speech community. Habermas does not extend his analyses far enough to offer us a job description of the applied psychologist. Nevertheless, in the spirit of his Critical Theory, we propose the following. First, the analyst should reflect upon the 'interests' of the knowledge product, or its potential consequences if put into use. Given that validation tactics may legitimize questionable knowledge products (e.g. genetic screening for hiring, polygraphs, appraisal via video), a multi-method tactic may be undertaken that includes a hermeneutical analysis of the historical and cultural conditions of these practices and policies and a critical evaluation of their impact upon the self at work. Such information should then be shared with managers and non-managers. The analyst can no longer be assumed to be a passive and neutral bystander.

Secondly, analysts cannot distance themselves from the subject matter they observe or analyse. This may seem a surprising suggestion, but the organizational scientist might copy the tactics of the organizational consultant, minus the pecuniary incentive and the pro-managerial bias. That is, the scientist should gather data and analyse them as a social participant and not as an aloof being from a monastic-life community. The analyst must ensure that data analysed are not hermeneutically sealed, but that the historical, situational and cultural conditions underlying what is observed are clearly appreciated and explicitly reported when results of analyses are communicated to the general public. This requirement suggests that the analyst must presuppose that the process of observation, or the process of procuring data from organizational subjects, is a speech act, and that procured data are contaminated by ideology. Therefore, the scientist bears some responsibility to critique ideology in an attempt to facilitate the development of an 'ideal speech' situation. Of course, once the analyst engages in a critique of ideology he or she becomes an agent of change. Also, the possibility of a positivist POP that produces generalizable (external validity) knowledge statements no longer exists. The observer, observed and process of observation become intertwined. Yet such an intertwining is necessary if the scientist intends to conduct research that is empowering and enables democratic processes.

Finally, resources for research must be made available so that all members of the organization, regardless of hierarchical status, can sponsor studies that address their concerns. A disappointment with most POP research to date is that it seems devoted to the interests of management (Alvesson, 1987). Management possess the resources to subsidize and reward work on topics that may legitimize their concerns, policies and practices. Non-managers do not possess such resources and may be unable systematically to influence knowledge production. Related to this issue is the training of researchers themselves. If new researchers are trained according to a neo-positivist curriculum, and if that curriculum tends to substantiate management's interests, attention needs to be given to other analytical approaches (analytical pluralism) that may also serve other interests (see Burrell and Morgan, 1979).

In sum, these recommendations for expanding the scope and source of validation shift some of the burden for change and empowerment to the scientific community. The required changes constitute a paradigm shift and future work might outline alternative roles for academic departments, business educators and consultants. The discourse within POP would be radically altered, as would its training procedures and perhaps its reward practices. We do not intend to suggest that it is only through altering validation procedures that positive organization change will be effected. Organizational members and regulatory agencies also enable or impede organizational change. Our purpose here has been to provide a framework for exploring the relationship between those who produce knowledge and those whose work is influenced by knowledge products. Implicit in our discussion is the idea that greater reflexiveness in knowledge production will contribute to greater empowerment of individuals at work.

Note

1 In some cases the definition of a term used here may vary from country to country. In this chapter definitions are based upon their usage by US scholars in personnel/ organizational psychology (see Daft and Steers 1986; Mahoney and Deckop, 1990; Szilagyi & Wallace, 1990).

References

Alvesson, M. (1987) *Organization Theory and Technocratic Consciousness*. Berlin/ New York: Walter de Gruyter.

Bacharach, S. (1989) 'Organizational theories: some criteria for evaluation', *Academy of Management Review*, 14: 496–515.
Burrell, G. and Morgan, G. (1979) *Sociological Paradigms and Organizational Analysis*. London: Heinemann.
Clegg, S. (1989) *Frameworks of Power*. London: Sage.
Cohen, I. J. (1989) *Structuration Theory*. London: Macmilllan.
Cook, T. and Campbell, D. (1979) *Quasi-Experimentation*. Chicago: Rand-McNally.
Daft, R. L. and Steers, R. M. (1986) *Organizations: A Micro/Macro Approach*. Glenview, IL: Scott, Foresman.
Doeringer, P. and Piore, M. (1971) *Internal Labor Markets and Manpower Analysis*. Lexington, MA: D. C. Heath.
Foucault, M. (1970) *The Order of Things: An Archaeology of the Human Sciences*. New York: Random House.
Foucault, M. (1972) *The Archaeology of Knowledge*. New York: Pantheon.
Foucault, M. (1978) *The History of Sexuality*. New York: Pantheon.
Foucault, M. (1979) *Discipline and Punish: The Birth of the Prison*. New York: Vintage.
Gergen, R. (1982) *Toward Transformation in Social Knowledge*. New York: Springer-Verlag.
Geuss, R. (1981) *The Idea of a Critical Theory*. Cambridge: Cambridge University Press.
Giddens, A. (1984) *The Constitution of Society*. Berkeley: University of California Press.
Gutting, G. (1989) *Michel Foucault's Archaeology of Scientific Reason*. Cambridge: Cambridge University Press.
Habermas, J. (1973) *Theory and Practice*. Boston: Beacon Press.
Habermas, J. (1975) *Legitimization Crisis*. Boston: Beacon Press.
Habermas, J. (1979) *Communication and the Evolution of Society*. Boston: Beacon Press.
Hear, A. (1980) *Karl Popper*. Boston: Routledge & Kegan Paul.
McCarthy, T. (1979) *The Critical Theory of Jürgen Habermas*. Boston: MIT Press.
Mahoney, T. A. and Deckop, J. R. (1990) 'Evolution of concept and practice in personnel administration/HRM', in T. Peterson (ed.), *Human Resource Management*. Boston: Houghton Mifflin.
Milkovich, G. and Newman, G. (1987) *Compensation*. Dallas: Business Publications.
Mumby, D. K. (1988) *Communication and Power in Organizations: Discourse, Ideology and Domination*. Norwood, NJ: Ablex.
Naylor, J., Pritchard, R. and Ilgen, D. (1980) *A Theory of Behavior in Organizations*. New York: Academic Press.
Popper, K. (1972) *The Poverty of Historicism*. New York: Harper Torchbooks.
Rorty, R. (1982) *Consequences of Pragmatism*. Minneapolis: University of Minnesota Press.
Rouse, J. (1987) *Knowledge and Power: Toward a Political Philosophy of Science*. Ithaca, NY: Cornell University Press.
Sack, R. D. (1980) *Conceptions of Space in Social Thought*. Minneapolis: University of Minnesota Press.
Steffy, B. and Grimes, A. (1986) 'A critical theory of organizational science', *Academy of Management Review*, 11: 322–36.
Steffy, B. and Ledvinka, J. (1989) 'The long-range impact of five definitions of "fair" employee selection on black employment and employee productivity', *Organizational Behavior and Human Decision Processes*, 44: 297–324.

Steffy, B. and Maurer, S. (1987) 'The dollar-productivity value of the human resource function', *Academy of Management Review*, 12: 335–51.

Steffy, B. D., Shaw, K. and Noe, A. W. (1989) 'Antecedents and consequences of job search behaviors', *Journal of Vocational Behavior*, 35: 254–69.

Szilagyi, A. D. and Wallace, M. J. (1990) *Organizational Behavior and Performance.* Glenview, IL: Scott, Foresman.

Van de Ven, A. (1989) 'Nothing is quite so practical as a good theory', *Academy of Management Review*, 14: 486–9.

Veldsman, T. H. (1990) 'Fish without water? Subject philosophy as study of the water within which industrial/organizational psychologists swim', *Human Relations*, 43: 349–68.

10

Critical Social Science for Managers?
Promising and Perverse Possibilities

Walter R. Nord and John M. Jermier

In early Critical Theory (CT), all human beings were viewed as candidates for enlightenment and emancipation (Horkheimer and Adorno, 1972). Typically, however, when social scientists appropriated CT in developing Critical Social Science (CSS), they concentrated on emancipating only some fraction of humanity – a group that a particular writer felt was especially oppressed. In fact, Fay (1987: 82–3) went so far as to suggest that feeling oppressed by others is necessary for one to be a fit subject for CSS:

> Critical social science arises out of, and speaks to, situations of social unhappiness, a situation which it interprets as the result of the ignorance of those experiencing these feelings and their domination by others. It is this experience of unhappiness which is the wedge a critical theory uses to justify its entrance into the lives of those it seeks to enlighten and emancipate. . . . If they are happy before it [CSS] approaches them, they are not fit subjects for a critical theory.

While Fay captured the most usual use of CSS, his statement is overly restrictive. There is no inherent reason why any field of knowledge cannot benefit almost everyone, at least to some degree. With respect to CSS, for example, nothing prohibits elite groups from appropriating it (or portions of it) for their own use, which might include the further domination of others. Such a possibility raises some serious questions about the general emancipatory potential of CSS. In this chapter we examine the value of CSS for one relatively elite group – managers – and explore the implications of this use for the emancipatory project.

The editors of this volume triggered our interest in this topic by asking us to consider the implications of CT for management practitioners and other elites. Since, like most students of CSS, we previously drew on these ideas hoping to promote the liberation of oppressed groups (Nord, 1974, 1977, 1978; Nord and Stablein, 1985; Jermier, 1981, 1983, 1985, 1988), the editors' request placed us in a new role, forcing us to view CSS from a vantage-point rarely used.

From this perspective, new possibilities for CSS appeared. Some are quite consistent with the emancipatory agenda, whereas others contradict it.

CSS might be employed by elites in several ways. First, CSS can enlighten members of elite groups in much the same way that it can anyone, by giving them insights into unrecognized sources of domination. Secondly, since some members of elites are dominated by other members of their group, CSS might help them in a manner analogous to how it would help any oppressed group. Thirdly, CSS (or at least portions of it) could be employed by elites to further oppress the oppressed. Finally, CSS could be used by elites in struggles with other elites outside their group.

Our analysis stems from two sources of information about CSS: academic treatments and our efforts to teach it to managers.[1] It is presented in five sections. First, major themes in CSS are reviewed. Secondly, ways that CSS can enlighten elites are explored. Thirdly, variations in managers' interests and identities and the nature of their work are described to show how CSS can be used in intra-elite conflicts (e.g. competition between groups of managers). Fourthly, ways that CSS might serve managers in their traditional roles (in contrast to how it might help them work in more liberating ways) are considered. This discussion reveals the perverse potential of CSS to increase domination. Finally we treat the value of CSS in inter-elite struggles, including struggles that may involve critical social scientists.

Major Themes in Critical Social Science

Broadly conceived, CSS offers an intellectual framework for resisting domination by traditional science and technology, institutionally distorted communication, owners of capital, and patriarchal forces. In the organizational context, these themes highlight a number of otherwise neglected issues by advancing a partisan theory of organization for the exploited (cf. Morgan, 1986; Jermier, 1991). Since CSS can mean many different things to different people, it is necessary to state briefly what we take to be its major themes. CSS, as we will use it here, is based on three intellectual traditions. First, it includes the perspectives of the Frankfurt School and other European Critical Theorists (see Tar, 1977; Bronner and Kellner, 1989). Secondly it draws on Marx's theory of capitalism. Thirdly CSS includes the evolving socialist-feminist critique of capitalist patriarchy.

Informed by all three traditions, CSS sensitizes us to the political

:ontent of scientific work; the ways that positivistic and hermeneutical studies can facilitate oppression instead of emancipation; the need to demystify language through the analysis of discourse; and the material and psychic injuries resulting from class struggle and the gender structuring of society.[2] CSS provides an emancipatory path for both scientific inquiry and social affairs to deal with these problems.

Themes from the Frankfurt School

With respect to scientific inquiry, as Alvesson and Willmott put it,

> Critical Theory (CT) exposes the indissoluble connection between politics, values and knowledge and, thereby, stimulates deeper reflection upon the *politics* and *values* which underpin and legitimize the authority of 'scientific' knowledge. [CT] . . . is concerned to problematize . . . the socially constructed nature of their 'objects' of investigation and the historical and cultural understandings which inform practical reasoning. (1988: 2)

Through helping to demystify language, CT offers a similar promise of emancipation in social affairs. As Forester observed:

> Mediated by language and communication, organizationally structured ideological distortions block citizens' basic abilities to make sense of the situations they face. These practical distortions are disabling, obscuring what is the case, subverting cooperative and reciprocal social relations, claiming legitimacy for the illegitimate, deceiving actors about the truth of events no less than about the truth of what they may do, or may become. Because critical theory provides a means of examining how such systematic *institutional* distortions of communication may undermine and threaten our most ordinary sense of what seems to be the case, it provides a provocative, politically and morally illuminating structural phenomenology for examining the nature and consequences of various modes of human organization. (1983: 244)

Themes from Marx

The emancipatory framework CSS offers is enhanced by incorporating Marx's theory of capitalism. Marx's analysis is valuable because it stimulates analysis of sources of oppression that arise from the political economy. In his early writings Marx contrasted the fully free, creative human producer with the alienated labourer under capitalism. In his later writings Marx specified the dynamics of exploitation and domination of labourers at the point of production. Under capitalism, direct producers sell their labour power to employers. The employers extract surplus value – wealth created by labour but appropriated by employers – and pay labour only a subsistence wage. In this way owners of capital live off the labour of others. Despite his sarcastic comments, Marx viewed owners of capital less as totally malicious exploiters than as pitiful agents of history, fulfilling a mission that would lead to the revolutionary transformation of capitalist society.

Marx expected the capitalist system to create and perpetuate two primary classes with deep-seated antagonisms. Even though the generation of wealth and material comfort in advanced capitalist economies has been associated with less economic misery than Marx expected, members of the capitalist class claim a disproportionate share of the benefits of production. At the same time, the human costs of production seem to be disproportionately assumed by the working class. Working men and women are exposed to substantially higher risks of injury in the form of physical and mental health problems; drug and alcohol dependency; illiteracy; family disintegration; infant mortality; exposure to violent crimes; induction into military service and war; degraded leisure activities, and so on.

We emphasize Marx's analysis here, since many Critical Theorists give only limited attention to the sources of oppression rooted in the 'real' conditions of political economy. This lacuna is a serious constraint on the emancipatory potential of CSS. Accordingly, combining the analysis of ideology and distorted communication advanced by CT with the type of inquiry stimulated by Marx yields a more comprehensive framework. The synthesis of these two traditions forms the core of what we refer to as CSS.

Themes from Feminist Analysis
Traditionally, Marxist analysis of class has downplayed the role of gender in domination (Gottfried and Fasenfest, 1984). Gender has been also neglected in CT.[3] Recent feminist writings (e.g. Collinson and Knights, 1986) provide a basis for correcting these omissions. It is well known that women are paid significantly less than men doing comparable work. Equally disturbing is the fact that women routinely experience discrimination in job recruiting and selection, 'ghettoization' in secondary labour markets, and structural and social-psychological barriers to career advancement. They find little relief in trade unions and other occupational associations in which men usually occupy leadership positions and control access to benefits and opportunities in a fashion similar to gender structuring in the workplace. In this connection it is important to note that to the degree that labour is divided along lines of gender, it constitutes a potential barrier to effective collective action.

In short, CSS has substantial potential to contribute to human emancipation. To us, the appropriate conception is a synthesis of several themes in critical scholarship. This includes analysis of language and discourse, consideration of the 'real' conditions of political economy, and problems associated with the gender structuring of society. These themes constitute the view of CSS we have presented to a variety of managers. Their reactions stimulated many of the following ideas.

Success of CSS in Enlightening Managers

Overall, managers differ greatly in their readiness to consider CSS ideas. Some seem to be totally unwilling to do so, but in our experience this number is surprisingly small. Most seem willing to discuss the ideas in reasoned fashion. They readily recognize that, to some extent, everyone is imprisoned by ideologies and distorted linguistic processes. They see that, regardless of one's specific purposes, everyone has something to gain from recognition of the fundamental distortions that afflict human communication.

Many managers are especially intrigued by discovering the obfuscation inherent in certain terms from everyday business discourse, such as efficiency. Generally, people will agree that efficiency is defined as output divided by input. When one raises the question about what outputs are to be included (pollution, job-related illness, and so on), it is clear that the normal indices represent a particular set of interests and that the word efficiency is loaded with political content. This example seems very useful in communicating the spirit of CSS. It helps managers understand how language serves interests.

With this recognition, managers can readily see how various bodies of knowledge entail fundamental interests. This makes it easy to realize that economics as well as humanistic theories must be considered in context – a context that is historical and political. Thus the interests that theories serve, their origins, their assumptions, and so on must all be considered. Similarly, many readily see the fallacy of assuming that existing forms of organization and types of technology are inevitable. In addition, potential biases that particular interests can introduce into thought and discourse concerning diverse sets of subjects, such as economics and radical job and organizational redesign (e.g. Quality of Work Life), all become open to inquiry and question. Further, arguments such as the possibility that the work ethic could have served as a source of domination or to paper over contradictions in American society (Rodgers, 1974) become more easily appreciated.

Making managers aware of the influence of history on organizations seems to be particularly productive. The history of personnel administration, when presented in a political economic context (see Watson, 1977; Jacoby, 1985), provokes particularly interesting reactions. When exposed to these ideas, some managers commented that though they had studied human resources management for years they were never asked to consider its history, and were amazed at what they learned when they did.

Managers also recognize the similarity of some aspects of CSS (e.g. ideal speech) to what they have learned in the past that may be useful in the pursuit of technically effective organizations. For example, many managers recognize that introducing change successfully is often aided by undistorted communication. In this sense, discourse approaching realization of Habermas's (1984) four validity claims – truth, rightness, truthfulness and comprehensibility – is apt to further the interests of all involved. Moreover, to the degree that managers make decisions about how to use people, distorted communication is a source of misinformation that can lead to some poor choices, with 'poor' defined in terms of traditional managerial criteria.

In dealing with these matters, the use of CSS by managers appears likely to resemble the use they have made of the work of psychologists such as Carl Rogers and well-known students of management such as Chris Argyris. However, as we will discuss in more depth below, this parallel is troubling, because the use that has been made of such work – despite the emancipatory spirit of its proponents – has, in our view, often been far from emancipating.

CSS also helps managers gain insight into sources of bias in science. While managers vary in their exposure to scientific research methodology, most tend to adopt implicitly the value-neutral, natural science model of inquiry. In this context, using CSS to explore values supporting traditional organizational and other social research is often illuminating. When it is proposed that much scientific work related to management is implicitly biased in favour of owners of capital, top managers and other elites, the question of how one might conduct research and develop theory to serve broader interests arises. Some even seek to become actively involved in producing CSS.

In this regard, we have occasionally found that managers invite us to conduct CSS research in their organization. Recently, one of us (Jermier) introduced MBA students taking a class in organizational behaviour to the counter-positivist notion of critical epistemology. The next semester, Vicki Marsee, Director of Nursing at the region's Cancer Hospital and Research Institute, invited and sponsored a study of worker health and safety issues. She expressed an interest in co-authoring articles from the research as well as dealing with practical problems that were identified.

In another instance, one of us (Nord) introduced a few CSS ideas to executive MBA students taking a mainstream organizational behaviour course. Some time later, John Clancy, one of the more sophisticated thinkers in the class, approached Nord to direct his master's thesis, which was published subsequently as a book entitled *The Invisible Powers* (1989). The book explores the role of metaphors in the language of business over the centuries. Clancy would probably have written something like this without the brief exposure to CSS in the class and his book is only loosely linked to CSS. The point is that some management practitioners have the intellectual capability to contribute to CSS.

With respect to material and psychic injuries resulting from life in class-structured contexts, most managers seem to share an interest in learning how Marx's theory of capitalism relates to their circumstances. In some way, all managers experience the pressures associated with capital accumulation and efficiency imperatives. Usually, they have not thought systematically or deeply about how capitalism works. They have never been invited to read and discuss Marx or other critics of capitalist systems. As a result, following some relatively trivial discussion about the failure of totalitarian communism, the myth of mobility and equal opportunity in advanced capitalist societies, and the real value of expanded material growth, it becomes possible to examine capitalism critically.

In this context, many basic questions can be treated productively. What historical forces elevated the rights of capital owners to a position of ascendancy over the rights of employees? Is resistance to management control by workers inevitable? Is resistance to capital control by managers inevitable? Questions of this nature can increase managers' awareness of a number of taken-for-granted assumptions. Often they develop a good conceptual understanding of the primary causes of labour unrest and the pressures in their own jobs. Our impression is that few engage in the soul-searching that could result from thinking critically about the deeper meanings of humanistic management, but it is not uncommon to hear them wonder about the extent to which they are victimized by capitalist dynamics.

Some of the more lively discussions have been stimulated by Marxist-feminist perspectives that detail the injuries resulting from gender-structured work. Most managers we have encountered express an interest in equality of the sexes, although many are sceptical that gender bias is significant. After data are presented on the pay gap between men and women in comparable jobs, on the distribution of child care and household duties in dual-career couples, and on the incidence of sexual harassment at work, most are prepared to examine frameworks that attempt to explain the nature of dual labour markets and other barriers to advancement encountered by women. Once gender bigotry is presented as an example of intra-class stratification, it becomes possible to link this with broader patterns of 'class busting' that undermine development of a sense of community at work. Our impression is that few, if any, change their ways of life or work behaviour radically as a result of thinking systematically about gender and work, but it does become clear to most how capital elites may benefit from the gender structuring of work.

In sum, CSS can be a source of enlightenment and intellectual stimulation to a wide spectrum of managers. Many are receptive to trying to explore CSS and the general human condition. Many of these benefits (e.g. awareness of the controlling aspects of language, the dangers of reifying existing social arrangements) are those that advocates of CSS would expect their ideas to yield for almost anyone who studied them seriously.

CSS and Intra-elite Conflicts

Critical writers, especially those who are Marxist inspired, seem to postulate two general groups (capitalists and workers or elites and non-elites) and treat both groups as homogeneous entities. Conceptualizations such as this, by obscuring conflicts within the groups and the social dynamics these differences may stimulate, can be very misleading. For example, sometimes no distinction is made between owners (capitalists) and managers. Likewise, conflicts among managers themselves, such as those among various specialists (Wardell, 1990), are overlooked. Discussions of CSS with managers demonstrate the importance of keeping these differences in mind, particularly because they reveal the potential value of CSS for elites engaged in intra-elite struggles.

Managers differ widely on a number of dimensions. Considerable variation is introduced by individual differences in values and in demographic characteristics. Other diversity is spawned by specialization within managerial work and differences in hierarchical standing.

Recently, several writers have observed how managers vary on important values. For example, Deetz and Mumby (1990) distinguished between profit-centred and career-centred managers, observing that the latter are increasingly common and have substantially different interests to the former. LaNuez and Jermier (1993) elaborated on Wright's (1985) analysis of the heterogeneous, contradictory class locations of managers. By focusing on social and political dimensions, they described five distinct orientations (corporate, public welfare, collegial/professional, extra-work, and worker). Each orientation represents a unique set of interests and identities. For example, managers holding a corporate orientation identify closely with capital elites and are totally committed to the firm and its profitability, whereas those with a public welfare orientation embrace the firm's social responsibilities.

Other personal characteristics introduce further diversity among managers. Some of the most salient are age (and career stage), gender and race. The existence of these divisions and the tensions they introduce are obvious from even a cursory reading of managerial periodicals (see Frost et al., 1986). Likewise, disparate educational achievements (e.g. MBAs vs non-MBAs) are often associated with tensions among managers.

Organization structures themselves are sources of diversity in managerial interests. Wardell (1990) observed competing interests among managers who specialize in different control techniques (e.g. accounting, engineering, human resources). Moreover, Laurent (1978) argued, every manager is both an autonomous leader and a dependent follower, depending on the angle from which we look at her or him. This point is helpful as we review research on the supervisory authority and organizational power of managers (Melin, 1989). There is wide variation in the channels through which managers participate in decision-making (e.g. number of staff hired, product or service quality, resource allocation, organizational budget). Equally wide variation exists in supervisory authority concerning tasks (work methods, pace of work) and in supervisory authority concerning sanctions (discipline, warnings, dismissals).

Taken together, these differences are a source of goal conflict and competition for scarce resources among managers. At any given time, some individuals or groups are apt to be more successful than others in influencing organizational goals and allocation of resources. These less influential managers might be referred to as oppressed managers. We suspect that they are likely to find CSS appealing for many of the same reasons as other oppressed groups might.

Among managers we have worked with, those who embrace CSS most enthusiastically are those who hold more or less radical counter-ideological beliefs and/or are frustrated with their current organization and their position in it and seem to be challenging the received views about organizational life. Following LaNuez and Jermier's (1993) framework, many of these managers seem to hold a worker orientation, identifying closely with workers and labour unions. Others appear to hold an extra-work orientation, having withdrawn, at least temporarily, from their present work context. The remainder of this group seem to hold a public welfare orientation. They are in conflict with received views of corporate conduct and are driven by social ideals. Members of each of these groups tend to be alienated in some way from dominant elites and narrow corporatist interests and orientations.

This reaction is more typical of those in the so-called 'soft areas', such as human resources and public relations. These managers have much to gain by showing that the current emphasis on 'hard criteria' is in large measure a product of the institutionalization of interest-driven ways of thinking. Human resource specialists, frustrated with their inability to get others to see the longer-run perspective and the conflicts between how organizations manage their human resources and what they hope to get from them, feel strongly supported by the spirit of CSS. Moreover, they come to see the limitations in their training as human resource specialists stemming from the decontextualized ahistorical manner in which they have been taught.

In some sense, human resource specialists seem more apt to include the emancipatory interest in what they take away from CSS. After all, the rhetoric, if not the spirit, of a great deal of applied behavioural science on which human resource professionals have drawn so heavily, has much of this spirit. Further, we suspect that many human resource professionals were attracted to their field because of this connection. Still, some of the attraction of CSS to them seems to stem from the advantages they might gain in competition with those emphasizing corporatist interests in their own organizations.

This type of reaction is also typical of those managers who seem to be denied upward mobility and influence in decision-making. While most of these people are employed at lower managerial levels, position in the hierarchy is not the only relevant factor. According to Melin, about 70 per cent of US managers can be categorized as 'lower level' (1989: 226). Many in this group appear to have more in common with workers than with elites. They constitute the majority of oppressed managers in the broader population, but tend to be under-represented in our experiences with graduate learners.

Many oppressed managers have returned to school because they have experienced the downside of corporate mobility tournaments, 'right-sizing' schemes, coalition wars or discrimination. Some have held (or still hold) relatively elite positions in their organizations, but have become disenchanted with corporate careers. Many women and minorities in graduate programmes who have experienced discrimination in employment or are aligned with social and political movements challenging white male domination are especially receptive to CSS.

Of course, these individuals (as well as many others) are likely to be selective in the portion of CSS that attracts them. Like the human resource specialists, they are interested in changing the way that people are treated by organizations. They perceive themselves to be victims of what Schiemann and Morgan (1983) called the hierarchy gap, which results from the perception of organizational participants that top management is insensitive to their views and that they are unable to communicate with higher-level managers. Consequently, they are apt to be highly interested in emancipatory themes.

Finding ways to increase the congruence between one's central values and one's job is a possible form emancipation in the workplace may take. In general, oppressed managers may be attracted to CSS because they are actively seeking such congruence or what Culbert and McDonough (1985) termed successful alignment. According to Culbert and McDonough alignment is the process 'an individual goes through in attempting to relate his or her subjective and self-centered interests to what he or she perceives as the objective requirements of the job' (1985: 124). Alignment can be improved by changing how one's efforts are perceived and/or by changing the 'reality' of the organization. By speaking to both courses of action, CSS offers oppressed managers ways of understanding their plight and ways to do something about it.

In sum, recently published work and our own experiences converge in suggesting the importance of recognizing diversity within the management group. This recognition directs attention to struggle within this group. It appears that those who are less successful in the contest, the ones we termed oppressed managers, are understandably attracted to CSS. Moreover, since they are oppressed, CSS seems capable of operating in the way suggested by Fay (1987). Clearly, then, CSS, with its emancipatory interest, has some value for many managers.

However, what about managers who are more successful members of the elite group? Do they have anything to gain from CSS? In the next two sections we show that they do and that this possibility suggests some constraints on the emancipatory contribution of CSS.

CSS – Some Raw Materials for More Effective Domination?

We have seen how aspects of CSS might serve the interests of a broad constituency of management practitioners without contradicting the moral purpose of this perspective – emancipating the oppressed. Presentations of CSS that emphasize broad victimization of all employees and the destruction of a sense of community (because of distorted communication, elite-biased science, and class and gender structuring) can appeal to managers' humanistic interests. In some respects, the value of CSS is universal – it benefits all humans potentially and hence differences among managers are not important.

On the other hand, given the world as it is now, people often have incentives to pursue particular rather than universal objectives. More specifically, elites have incentives to oppress non-elites even further and the more powerful members of elite groups have incentives to press their interests against less powerful members. Any given body of knowledge or technology, regardless of its substance, is potentially a source of advantage.

Throughout history, ideas and technologies promoted as vehicles to improve the human condition – regardless of the philosophies on which they rest, the goals their developers envisioned, or substance – have been used by some people to dominate others. Marxism, psychoanalysis, *laissez-faire* economics and Christianity are a few of the long list of possible examples. (It is interesting to note that in many ways the first three of these are explicit in their objective of promoting human freedom.) Why should CSS be less susceptible to such usage?

An adequate answer to this question would require in-depth exploration of how such ideas have been 'misused'. Such a history of ideas is beyond the scope of this chapter, but we can speculate about a few characteristics of these bodies of thought that have contributed to their 'misuse'.

First, they often allow considerable latitude to define what the ideas call for operationally. Frequently, latitude arises from what a theory omits. For example, as Gouldner (1980) noted, it was the lack of a theory of change that allowed Marx's ideas to be used by Lenin as a basis for establishing a dictatorship. The abstract nature of ideas can also widen latitude of acceptable interpretations – the greater the abstraction, the more difficult it is to know when the ideas are being used as they were intended.

Secondly, there is no law that says that one must use the entire set of ideas. Consequently, people may appropriate subsets that are especially conducive to their own interests and ignore others. For example, spokespersons for firms in oligopolistic industries can ward off government intervention by championing the merits of free markets, without speaking about the importance of price competition as a force that makes free markets contribute to economic welfare.

Thirdly, the complexity of ideas plays a role. If a set of ideas is complex enough, certain people can claim privileged understanding. For example, people who have gone through extensive training in psychoanalysis, and have themselves been analysed, may be viewed as the only ones able to use it. Such privileged positions are, of course, conducive to the development of an elite. Further, the more complex the ideas the less likely they are to be generally accessible and therefore the more likely they are to be accessible only by some elite group.

How do the characteristics of CSS stand on these dimensions? In our view, CSS ranks highly on all of these problematic characteristics. It is abstract, subject to partial utilization, and complex. Consequently, those who advance CSS as an emancipatory vehicle must show that it is not subject to such 'misappropriation'.[4] In any case, if circumstances make it useful, there is good reason to expect it could be used by elites for their own particular purposes. Do such circumstances exist in the contemporary management context?

In our view, they do. Many management theorists and corporate leaders are enamoured of topics of culture and the social construction of meaning as tools in the long quest for Barnard's (1938) promise of harmonious co-operation. The analysis of language and meaning embodied in CT may be extremely productive in enhancing their understandings. Further, in comparison to previous times, managers are well educated – most have college and even graduate degrees. In comparison to more thoroughly oppressed groups, members of the managerial elites are better prepared to access the ideas of CSS. Moreover, they have the resources to hire others to help them distil the complexity into forms they can use for their particular ends. In the past we have seen the complex ideas that underlie seemingly humanistic approaches (e.g. transactional analysis, organization development) distilled into techniques and schemata that serve to perpetuate oppression in the name of overcoming it. Clearly, there is potential for managerial elites to have the complex ideas of CSS partially distilled in ways that suit their objectives. Unless these ends are consistent with emancipating others, there is no reason to expect that these efforts will lead to more general emancipation. To illustrate, consider how ascendant managers with corporate orientations might use CSS.

Managers currently in charge of organizations have an interest in preserving current hierarchical relations. As they learn more about how discourse acts as a source of control, their abilities to distort communication to legitimize and advance their own advantages within organizations are apt to be increased. In fact, CSS may be especially helpful in this regard.

Writers in the critical tradition view one of their major contributions as making capital and labour aware of the fact that they both misunderstand the creation of surplus value and how the superstructure operates to perpetuate this misunderstanding (Deetz and Mumby, 1990). What will members of a dominant elite and others with corporate orientations do with such information? It is hard to know, but they certainly have incentives to use this perspective to strengthen the very forces that perpetuate their own advantage. They may discover, for instance, that less surplus value comes from technology and more from human capital than they thought. Further they may learn that their control over human capital is aided by continued obfuscation of the creation of surplus value. Consequently they will realize that, at least in the short run, they have reasons to perpetuate the old distortions and buttress them with new ones. They may even derive a few pointers from CT on how to do this better.[5]

Similarly, if capital's elites learn that fragmentation within the workforce (and the working class more generally) enhances the tractability of labour, what incentives exist to move them to transform segmented labour markets? Systematic analysis of the costs to minorities, women and workers in general may do no more than solidify their basic belief that these have been effective tactics in minimizing and controlling working-class resistance. Similarly, improved ways of controlling the alienated managers and other less powerful members of the elite may be forthcoming.

In sum, there is good reason to expect that members of elite groups have incentives to control other members of their group and to control other more oppressed groups more fully than they now do. Further, there is little reason to assume that CSS will be used *in toto*. If CSS does provide insights into the process of domination, members of elite groups have incentives to appropriate these parts to enhance their own position. They may totally disregard the moral critique of domination provided by CSS using the ideas in an instrumentally rational manner. Further oppression rather than widespread emancipation certainly could result.

Despite the perverse outcomes they might facilitate, we have continued to use CSS ideas in educating elites, for one obvious reason: at a minimum, these ideas have emancipatory *potential*. We choose to emphasize CSS because we believe that most conventional organization and management studies texts lack emancipatory potential. So, while there is no guarantee that dominating elites will be inspired by CSS ideas to more enlightened and humanistic thought and practice, the possibility does exist. We are not aware of another set of ideas that is as comprehensive and bold in emancipatory content.

CSS and Inter-elite Struggles

Elites often compete with other elites. This fact suggests one final use that CSS may have for elites in general and managers in particular.

CSS may make elites aware that their own long-term vulnerability is apt to be most threatened by the failure of their discourse to keep pace with social change. For example, Gouldner (1979) observed that one reason the 'Old Class' (i.e. the moneyed class) is threatened by the 'New Class' (technical intelligentsia and intellectuals) is that the language of the New Class makes that of the old class ineffective in cultural discourse. To illustrate: if the notion of social ecology with its emphasis on collaborative relations and total ecosystem development (Boulding, 1981; Astley 1984) becomes a dominant paradigm, the arguments based in the pursuit of individual economic interests through competitive tactics become difficult to sustain. One lesson for elites from CSS is to invest continually in reinventing and updating their discourse to sustain advantage.

In addition to this proactive implication, CSS may make elites more sensitive to messages they might otherwise communicate that would ultimately undermine their own positions. For example, US corporations are major sponsors of television shows that help shape how people view organizations (see Vande Berg and Trujillo, 1989). These corporations have much to lose if business is portrayed in unfavourable terms. Among other things, they will be more vulnerable to political elites that have incentives to control business. CSS may increase the sponsors' awareness of how meaning is constructed and hence their potential for constructing meanings that advance class-wide interests.

Further, enhanced awareness of the domination inherent in communication can increase the effectiveness with which elites use media to sustain their advantage. To illustrate, CT provides great understanding about how meanings are constructed. For example, using CT, Gouldner (1976) advanced some provocative insights concerning the workings of modern media. He noted that modern media (newspapers, radio, television) function in ways that communicate single events in decontextualized fashion. Assuming such media shape the deep structure of society, such an insight, if true, could have substantial implications for elites seeking to exercise control. If elites use their resources to stage a number of events that send a certain message, they could exercise considerable control without dealing explicitly with ideology. The basic ideology need not be communicated – it can be constructed in one's interests if enough of the 'right' individual events can be communicated.[6]

In addition, when one considers the nature of the competition among modern elites, there is the intriguing prospect that CSS may play a very special role. Our awareness of this possibility stems from Gouldner's (1979) thoughts concerning the competition between the Old and New Classes. The special importance of CSS is derived from the centrality of the culture of critical discourse (CCD). To

Gouldner, the culture of critical discourse (CCD) was 'an historically evolved set of rules, a grammar of discourse. . . . This grammar is the deep structure of the common ideology shared by the New Class. *The shared ideology of the intellectuals and intelligentsia is thus an ideology about discourse.*' (1979: 28)

As with other discourses, skill in CCD can be parlayed into an advantage. Gouldner added:

> The new discourse (CCD) . . . bears the seeds of a new domination. . . . The New Class begins by monopolizing truth and by making itself its guardian. . . . The New Class sets itself above others, holding its speech is better than theirs . . . the New Class silently inaugurates a new hierarchy of the knowing, the knowledgeable, the reflexive and insightful. Those who talk well, it is held, excel those who talk poorly or not at all. (1979: 85)

Deetz and Mumby (1990), in contrasting the work of Habermas and Foucault, made a similar point – any emancipatory discourse risks replacing one mode of domination with another. In short, all discourses, CCD included, are potential tools of control.

Following this line of thought, we see the potential for a paradoxical outcome from CSS. Critical social scientists may not only provide some of the raw materials for a new elite, but in fact, because they 'talk well' and shape the ascendant discourse, may themselves become an elite of sorts. This possibility is, of course, not unique to CSS. It is merely another expression of the classical dilemma faced by those who seek to help emancipate others. How does one help emancipate others without controlling them? How do aspiring emancipators avoid placing their interests above others? How do would-be emancipators avoid becoming so distant from those they seek to help that they devalue them and develop diverging and conflicting interests?

In a sense, these issues go beyond our exploration of a CSS for managers. Yet they are related, because they emerged from our treatment of CSS for elite groups as problematic. CSS may not only serve current elites in their battles with others; it could itself, paradoxically, help spawn a new elite.

Conclusions

Our exploration of the value of CSS to managers leads us to a mixed set of conclusions.[7] On one hand, we have seen that managers are receptive to CSS in ways that are consistent with emancipatory interests. CSS can play an emancipatory role for managers in much the same way that it can any group of human beings, by increasing their awareness of capital accumulation pathologies, reifications, and latent sources of social control. In addition to this general enlightenment function, it can help the relatively oppressed segments of managers free themselves from domination.

On the other hand, the effort to apply CSS from the perspective of an elite, rather than from that of oppressed groups (as is typically done), revealed the potential of CSS to produce perverse effects. CSS can help elites dominate more completely and be more effective in intra- and inter-elite struggles. More perversely, we have suggested that CSS could become a discourse that leads to the evolution of a new elite. Is there any way out?

In some ways, we are pessimistic. Are critical social scientists sufficiently different from other human beings to avoid the perils of the past? Is CSS different from any other approach devised by human beings to improve the human condition? Possibly, but we have outlined a number of features of CSS that appear likely to enable elites to use CSS in ways that further oppress rather than emancipate. Still, critical social scientists might be able to alleviate some of the perverse outcomes we envision.

One of the most valued lessons to be learned from the critical tradition is the importance of self-reflexiveness in scholarship. While we are often as guilty of a lack of reflexiveness as most people, we believe it is important for critical social scientists to examine their own discourse, the interests it serves for them, and the consequences that the social construction of critical knowledge has for theory and society. If the perverse outcomes we have discussed are recognized, students of CSS might be able to introduce structures into their own enterprise that stimulate reflexivity. Such endeavours are highly consistent with the tenets of CSS, such as those advanced by the spirit of 'ideal speech'. How might we go about approaching this ideal within our own intellectual community?

Deetz and Mumby (1990) suggested one answer – perpetual critique. Clearly the spirit behind our thoughts is consistent with this view. However, we are still searching for the best ways to foster perpetual critique when it is inconsistent with our interests.

Another step concerns relationships among students of CSS and between them and other groups – an effort to make discourse open to all. Given competing interests, we are not prepared to rely on any one group to carry the critique or champion political action for another. Rather, we believe that the oppressed must champion their own causes.[8] Students of CSS can contribute by working towards processes that enable the inarticulate to speak with greater clarity and forcefulness. There are problems in doing this, of course, but if CSS is to be effective in emancipation, we suspect it needs to become more available to working people.

Publishing CSS studies using formats that are more engaging and language that is more accessible than that found in academic books and journal articles might facilitate this. Literary formats, such as poems, short stories and novels, may deliver critical insights to a wider audience. Jermier (1985) experimented with the short story format, attempting to illustrate CSS descriptions of the contemporary alienated worker. This type of writing could be practised by critical social scientists and published in popular magazines and newspapers where more working men and women would encounter it. On this theme, scholarly journals that report on everyday life using everyday language (e.g. the *Journal of Contemporary Ethnography*) could become important outlets for critical research. To some degree, the Frost et al. (1986) compendium can be useful in this regard. The key to reaching more readers is using language closer to the world of the subjects.

The current practice of CSS is inconsistent with this aim. Frankfurt School literature in particular, but CSS in general, is not used by the vast majority of management science researchers. Part of the problem lies in the critical nature of the content, about which nothing can or should be done. However, unnecessarily technical and stilted prose (which characterizes our work as well) presents a more formidable barrier.

In our efforts to explore the value of CSS for an elite group such as managers we have emphasized the troublesome entailments of these ideas. Still, we believe CSS has much to offer the emancipatory project. Even Gouldner wrote: 'the New Class is elitist and self-seeking and uses its special knowledge to advance its own interests and power . . . to control its own work situation. Yet, the New Class may also be the best card that history has presently given us to play' (1979: 7). We agree, but suggest that the contribution of CSS to human emancipation can be advanced most rapidly if it finds ways to address the perverse uses that elites may put it to.

Notes

We gratefully acknowledge the help of Mats Alvesson and Hugh Willmott in refining our argument. Of course, we take responsibility for its current content.

1 These efforts have been limited to a few sessions with members of an executive institute, courses offered to part-time students in master's programmes in human resources management and general management, some executive and full-time MBA classes, and casual interactions with executives in informal contexts.

2 Other dehumanizing categories used to classify human beings (e.g. race, ethnicity) have negative consequences similar to gender. We recognize these but our work so far has not systematically dealt with them.

3 Of course, other sources of stratification such as race are also important. But as

noted earlier, we do not deal with them here, because we have not dealt with them systematically in our efforts to expose managers to CSS.

4 It should be noted that some have said that Critical Theory may be less vulnerable to such misuse because its advocates have deliberately made it difficult to access. In the terms we discussed, however, such inaccessibility may make it *especially* subject to elite uses since elites are most likely to have the resources enabling access.

5 In a sense, we may be overly concerned here. Since modern elites show evidence of doing some of these things already, it is clear that one can get to the same points without formal knowledge of CSS. Still, CSS seems especially prone to appropriation given the characteristics we have described and its focus on how advantage and exploitation are obscured and reproduced.

6 Of course, in addition to helping elites in their struggles with other elites, these ideas could also be applied to intra-elite struggles and to further control more fully oppressed groups.

7 There is always the possibility that while CSS will excite a number of academics, its effects outside the university will be negligible. There is also the chance that it might influence elites to champion more emancipatory ways of controlling.

8 We recognize, following Clegg (1989), the problems that people may have in knowing their own interests. Simply allowing them access to the discourse does not mean that their 'true interests' will necessarily emerge. For present purposes, however, we assume that it will increase the chances.

References

Alvesson, M. and Willmott, H. (1988) 'Critical theory and the sciences of management', paper presented at the Conference 'The Frankfurt School: How relevant is it today?', Erasmus University, Rotterdam.

Astley, W. G. (1984) 'Toward an appreciation of collective strategy', *Academy of Management Review*, 9: 526–35.

Barnard, C. I. (1938) *The Functions of the Executive*. Cambridge, MA: Harvard University Press.

Boulding, K. E. (1981) *Evolutionary Economics*. Beverly Hills: Sage.

Bronner, S. E. and Kellner, D. M. (eds) (1989) *Critical Theory and Society*. London: Routledge.

Clancy, J. J. (1989) *The Invisible Powers*. Lexington, MA: Lexington Books.

Clegg, S. (1989) *Frameworks of Power*. London: Sage.

Collinson, D. L. and Knights, D. (1986) 'Men only: theories and practices of job segregation in insurance', in D. Knights and H. Willmott (eds), *Gender and the Labour Process*. Aldershot: Gower. pp. 140–78.

Culbert, S. A. and McDonough, J. J. (1985) *Radical Management: Power, Politics and the Pursuit of Trust*. New York: Free Press.

Deetz, S. and Mumby, D. K. (1990) 'Power, discourse, and the workplace: reclaiming the critical tradition', *Communication Yearbook*, 13: 18–47.

Fay, B. (1987) *Critical Social Science*. Ithaca, NY: Cornell University Press.

Forester, J. (1983) 'Critical theory and organizational analysis', in G. Morgan (ed.), *Beyond Method: Strategies for Social Research*. Beverly Hills: Sage. pp. 234–46.

Frost, P. J., Mitchell, V. F. and Nord, W. R. (1986) *Organizational Reality: Reports from the Firing Line*, 3rd edn. Glenview, IL: Scott, Foresman.

Gottfried, H. and Fasenfest, D. (1984) 'Gender and class formation: female clerical workers', *Review of Radical Political Economics*, 16: 89–103.

Gouldner, A. W. (1976) *The Dialectic of Ideology and Technology.* New York: Seabury Press.

Gouldner, A. W. (1979) *The Future of Intellectuals and the Rise of the New Class.* New York: Seabury Press.

Gouldner, A. W. (1980) *The Two Marxisms. Contradictions and Anomalies in the Development of Theory.* New York: Seabury Press.

Habermas, J. (1984) *The Theory of Communicative Action, Vol. I: Reason and the Rationalization of Society,* trans. T. McCarthy. Boston, MA: Beacon Press.

Horkheimer, M. and Adorno, T. W. (1972) *Dialectic of Enlightenment* (1944). New York: Seabury Press.

Jacoby, S. M. (1985) *Employing Bureaucracy: Managers, Unions, and the Transformation of Work in American Industry, 1900–1945.* New York: Columbia University Press.

Jermier, J. M. (1981) 'Infusion of critical social theory into organizational analysis', in D. Dunkerley and G. Salaman (eds), *The International Yearbook of Organization Studies, 1981.* London: Routledge & Kegan Paul. pp. 195–211.

Jermier, J. M. (1983) 'Labor process control in modern organizations: subtle effects of structure', *Journal of Business Research,* 11: 317–32.

Jermier, J. M. (1985) '"When the sleeper wakes": a short story extending themes in radical organizational theory', *Journal of Management,* 11: 67–80.

Jermier, J. M. (1988) 'Sabotage at work: the rational view', *Research in the Sociology of Organizations,* 6: 101–34.

Jermier, J. M. (1991) 'Critical epistemology and the study of organizational culture: reflections on W. F. Whyte's *Street Corner Society*', in P. Frost et al. (eds), *Reframing Organizational Culture.* Newbury Park: Sage.

LaNuez, D. and Jermier, J. M. (1992) 'Sabotage by managers and technocrats', in J. M. Jermier and W. R. Nord (eds), *Resistance and Power in Organizations.* London: Macmillan.

Laurent, A. (1978) 'Managerial subordinacy: a neglected aspect of organizational hierarchies', *Academy of Management Review,* 3: 220–30.

Melin, H. (1989) 'Managers and social classes', in S. R. Clegg (ed.), *Organization Theory and Class Analysis: New Approaches and New Issues.* Berlin: Walter de Gruyter. pp. 211–32.

Morgan, G. (1986) *Images of Organization.* Beverly Hills: Sage.

Nord, W. R. (1974) 'The failure of current applied behavior science: a Marxian perspective', *Journal of Applied Behavioral Science,* 10: 557–78.

Nord, W. R. (1977) 'A Marxist critique of humanistic psychology', *Journal of Humanistic Psychology,* 17: 75–83.

Nord, W. R. (1978) 'Dreams of humanization and realities of power', *Academy of Management Review,* 3: 674–8.

Nord, W. R. and Stablein, R. (1985) 'Practical and emancipatory interests in organizational symbolism: a review and evaluation', *Journal of Management,* 11: 13–28.

Rodgers, D. T. (1974) *The Work Ethic in Industrial America 1850–1920.* Chicago: University of Chicago Press.

Schiemann, W. A. and Morgan, B. S. (1983) *Managing Human Resources: Employee Discontent and Declining Productivity.* Princeton, NJ: Opinion Research Corporation.

Tar, Z. (1977) *The Frankfurt School.* New York: Wiley.

Vande Berg, L. R. and Trujillo, N. (1989) *Organizational Life on Television.* Norwood, NJ: Ablex.

Wardell, M. (1990) 'Labour and labour process', in D. Knights and H. Willmott (eds), *Labour Process Theory*. London: Macmillan. pp. 153–76.

Watson, T. J. (1977) *The Personnel Managers. A Study in the Sociology of Work and Employment*. London: Routledge & Kegan Paul.

Wright, E. O. (1985) *Classes*. London: Verso.

Index

Printed in the United Kingdom
by Lightning Source UK Ltd.
104307UKS00001B/205-213